North America's Environment

A Thirty–Year State of the Environment and Policy Retrospective

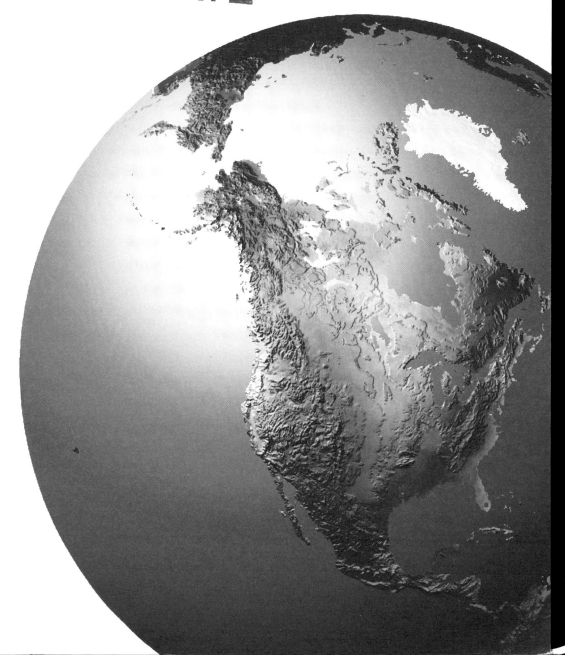

United Nations Environment Programme
PO Box 30552, Nairobi, Kenya
Tel: +254 2 621234
Fax: +254 2 623943/44
E-mail: geo@unep.org
Web: **www.unep.org**
   www.unep.net

United Nations Environment Programme
Regional Office for North America
1707 H Street, NW, Suite 300, Washington, D.C. 20006 USA
Tel: 1-202-785-0465
Fax: 1-202-785-2096
E-mail: info@rona.unep.org
Web: **www.rona.unep.org**
   www.unep.org

United Nations Environment Programme
Division of Early Warning and Assessment–North America
47914 252nd Street, EROS Data Center, Sioux Falls, SD 57198-0001 USA
Tel: 1-605-594-6117
Fax: 1-605-594-6119
E-mail: info@na.unep.net
Web: **www.na.unep.net**
   www.unep.org

A Regional Product of the Global Environment Outlook 3 Report Process

North America's Environment

*A Thirty–Year State of the Environment
and Policy Retrospective*

UNEP

in cooperation with

CEC   IISD   WRI

Acknowledgments

UNEP acknowledges the contributions made by the many individuals and institutions to the preparation and publication of *North America's Environment: A Thirty–Year State of the Environment and Policy Retrospective*. A full list of names is included on page 200. Special thanks are extended to:

Commission for Environmental Cooperation of the
North American Agreement on Environmental Cooperation
(CEC of NAAEC)
393 rue St-Jacques Ouest
Montréal, Québec H2Y1N9 Canada

International Institute for Sustainable Development (IISD)
161 Portage Avenue East, 6th Floor
Winnipeg, Manitoba R3B0YA Canada

World Resources Institute (WRI)
10 G Street NE, Suite 800
Washington, DC 20002 USA

Production Team

Production and Support Team
Ashbindu Singh
Jane Barr
László Pintér
Robin White
H. Gyde Lund
Kim Giese
Paul Sands
Trevor Bounford
Jane A. Peterson, Editor

GRID Sioux Falls Support Team
Mark Ernste
Nazmul Hossain
Shingo Ikeda
Jane Smith

UNEP Regional Office for North America Support Team
Brennan Van Dyke
Keith Robinson
John Peter Oosterhoff
Durga Ray
Sandrine Ourigou

UNEP Nairobi Support Team
Dan Claasen
Marion Cheatle
Munyaradzi Chenje
Volodymyr Demkine
Norberto Fernandez
Tessa Goverse
Anna Stabrawa

Contents

List of Figures

List of Boxes

Tables

Foreword

It has been 30 years since the United Nations Conference on the Human Environment in Stockholm, when the world community was alerted to the unprecedented scale of environmental transformation effected by human activity and set on a course to protect and improve the human environment. UNEP's third Global Environment Outlook (GEO-3) examines environmental trends since the 1972 Stockholm conference and analyzes the social, economic, political and cultural drivers of change and the spectrum of policy measures adopted. GEO-3 is also published 10 years after the 1992 Earth Summit in Rio de Janiero, when the world's nations committed themselves to a path towards sustainable development. In time for its successor, the 2002 World Summit on Sustainable Development in Johannesburg, GEO-3 sets an action-oriented environmental agenda for the future. This publication, a corollary to GEO-3, examines the state of North America's environment and provides a more detailed description and analysis of its priority environmental issues and how the region addressed them during that time, as well as the critical and emerging trends it still faces.

It is encouraging to see the notable progress Canada and the United States have made in addressing a number of the most evident and serious environmental problems in the past 30 years. Improvements to North America's environment were made possible by the institution of environmental governance and environmental laws and policies at all levels, as well as the growth in cooperation between the two countries to protect shared resources and ecosystems. As this report shows, however, it is ever more apparent that although North America generally has and accords the necessary material and human resources to address local pollution problems and straightfoward global ones, affluence stimulates consumption and energy use. Choices related to consumer lifestyles have limited the region's further advancement on the environmental front, particu-

larly in resource efficiency, waste reduction and the control of greenhouse gas emissions.

Although many environmental policies underscored in this report provide blueprints for other regions, with globalization there is the danger that inefficient and wasteful consumption patterns will also

spread. Unsustainable patterns of consumption and production in North America are a major cause of global environmental deterioration and there is an urgent need for the region, along with the other developed countries, to accept more responsibility for environmental change.

On the eve of the World Summit on Sustainable Development, it has become evident that protecting the environment and human security is a more challenging task than it may have seemed 30 years ago, or even 10 years ago. There is an ever more urgent need for us to recognize that human security depends on the abundance and health of environmental assets, goods and services. Significant changes will be needed – in decision-making at all levels and in day-to-day behavior by producers and consumers – for us to ensure their benefits are delivered in a sustainable and equitable way for current and future generations.

Klaus Töpfer

United Nations Under-Secretary General and Executive Director, United Nations Environment Programme

Preface

One of UNEP's fundamental mandates is to conduct accurate assessment and up-to-date reporting on the state of the world's environment. The Global Environment Outlook (GEO) biennial report series contributes to the fulfillment of this role. GEO–1, published in 1997, provided a regionally focused, qualitative appraisal of key environmental issues and trends and relevant socio-economic driving forces in all the world's regions. GEO–2, published in 2000 presented a coordinated and comprehensive State of the Environment (SOE) overview at regional and global levels. It analyzed how underlying pressures (such as social developments) affect the land, atmosphere, fresh and marine waters, biological resources, and forests, and provided a separate presentation of environmental policy.

This report, *North America's Environment: A Thirty–Year State of the Environment and Policy Retrospective,* expands on the North American regional contribution to the SOE chapter of GEO-3, published in May 2002. GEO-3 takes an integrated approach to SOE reporting and emphasizes the linkages between policy and the environment, past trends and possible future directions, and thematic areas. It also highlights the links among sectors (environmental, economic, social, cultural, etc). Its ultimate purpose is to connect environmental outcomes to activities, policies, and decisions. By providing a policy retrospective on progress made towards sustainable development since the 1972 Stockholm Conference on the Human Environment, GEO-3 will influence conclusions drawn at the World Summit on Sustainable Development in Johannesburg in 2002.

The SOE component of GEO-3, and of this more detailed appraisal of North America, assesses the environment over the past 30 years by documenting how it has changed and how that change has impacted key human and environmental systems in the region. The policy aspect of this analysis seeks to explain how various policies have affected the environment in the past 30 years, to describe what is being done to lessen human impact on the environment and repair damage, and to evaluate the effectiveness of these policy measures.

Focus, Approach and Content

Focusing on UNEP's North American region, comprised of Canada and the United States, this report provides an integrated analysis of the state of resource assets and 30-year trends in nine major themes: atmosphere, biodiversity, coastal and marine areas, disasters, freshwater, forests, human health and the environment, land, and urban areas. Rather than offering a comprehensive description and analysis of the state of North America's environment in all its aspects, the report zeroes in on two priority issues for each of the nine themes. Following the approach taken in GEO-3, the specific issues identified under each theme build on those highlighted in GEO-2000 and include critical issues, emerging trends, hot spots, and once critical issues that illustrate successful policy responses. The thematic structure and discrete chapters belie the crosscutting nature of environmental issues; many of the topics overlap and are dependent upon and influence the character of the others. For this reason, attempts have been made at every opportunity to underscore the linkages between them. Because conclusions were drawn from the assessment of priority issues, they do not reflect all issues related to the condition of North America's environment since 1972.

The basis of this analysis is the Pressure/State/Impact/Response (PSIR) framework. This reporting approach is a useful way of conceptualizing the cycle of changes in environmental conditions and exploring the linkages between humans and their environment. The PSIR approach seeks to provide information and data about:

- the natural and anthropogenic pressures on the environment, which range from drivers and agents of change such as socio-economic, political, and cultural conditions to direct indicators such as weather hazards, polluting emissions, and resource extraction;

- the state of resource assets and the condition of, and trends in, environmental media;

- the impacts of environmental change on ecosystems and functions, human health and well-being, and on the economy; and

- the responses by governments and civil society attempting to mitigate or redress environmental problems and their consequences.

Presented in an integrated narrative, this information shows how environmental issues have been addressed in Canada and the United States over the 30-year period in an iterative cycle of pressures, impacts, and responses. Boxes provide definitions, highlight subregional issues, and serve to illustrate the text through examples. A series of boxes throughout the report also underscores the cooperative efforts by Canada and the United States to address transboundary issues and environmental problems of mutual concern.

Information and data are drawn from reliable published sources, such as the global datasets produced by the World Resources Institute (WRI), the Organization for Economic Cooperation and Development (OECD), and the Food and Agriculture Organization (FAO); national SOE reports and indicator bulletins, such as those produced by Environment Canada (EC), the US Environmental Protection Agency (EPA), and other environmental and natural resource departments; analyses by authoritative non-governmental organizations such as the Worldwatch Institute; and some supplementary unpublished material, including academic literature. Despite the similarities between Canada and the United States regarding definitions, approaches, and time series used in environmental reporting, differences remain that in some instances have led to data reconciliation difficulties and data gaps. In addition, given the significantly larger population and economy of the United States, the issues highlighted in some themes tend to focus more on conditions there than in Canada.

Key Conclusions

There have been signs of progress.
Over the past 30 years, North America has had notable success with a number of environmental problems. It has:

- protected the ozone layer: non-essential CFC consumption was reduced to nearly zero by 1996;

- controlled emissions that cause acid rain: SO_2 emissions in the US declined 31 percent between 1981 and 2000, and 24 percent between 1991 and 2000;

- set aside parks and other protected areas: today, between 11 and 13 percent of the region's land area is protected;

- slowed wetland losses: between 1988 and 1993, over 850,000 ha of wetland and associated upland habitat were protected in Canada alone;

- stemmed emissions from point sources: aggregate emissions of six principal pollutants in the US have been cut 29 percent;

- reduced pollution in the Great Lakes: since 1972, there has been an overall reduction of 71 percent in the use, generation, and release of seven priority toxic chemicals into the Great Lakes;

- stabilized desertification: expansion of plant cover on rangelands and other conservation approaches led to substantial reductions in wind and water erosion.

But improvements have slowed.
In many instances, gains made in arresting environmental pollution and degradation have recently been eroded by choices related to consumption increases and population growth:

- total energy use in North America grew by 31 percent between 1972 and 1997;

- progress in fuel efficiency has been offset by increases in the number of automobiles and the total number of kilometers traveled, and by a trend since 1984 toward heavier and less fuel-efficient passenger vehicles;

- a consumer lifestyle based on the desire for mobility, convenience, and product disposability has undercut the further advancement of resource efficiency and waste reduction.

North America's global impact is disproportionately large.
North America's success in improving local environments where people can live with clean water and air and enjoy green spaces has come at the expense of global natural resources and climate:

- with about 5 percent of the world's population, North America accounted for 25.8 percent of global emissions of carbon dioxide (CO_2) in 1998;

- per capita annual gasoline consumption for motor vehicles was nine times the world average;

- in 1997, the US transport sector accounted for more than one-third of total world transportation energy use; and

- by 1996, North America's ecological footprint was four times greater than the world average, its forest footprint 4.4 times larger. Its CO_2 footprint was almost five times the world average.

Effective reforms are possible.
We live with the decisions of the past. Today's decisions—and more importantly, our actions—will affect the future of our children and grandchildren for good or bad through their impact on our global environment. North America needs to accept more responsibility for environmental change:

- it needs substantial and concrete changes in its automobile use, more fuel-efficient technologies, and changes in municipal planning and urban development strategies that curb sprawl, including investment in public transport;

- people need to start connecting climate to individual behavior; and

- decision-makers need the political will to introduce improvements.

Executive Summary

Atmosphere

Over the past 30 years, North America has achieved notable gains in protecting stratospheric ozone and controlling emissions that cause acid rain. Both countries managed to shrink their non-essential chlorofluorocarbon (CFC) consumption to nearly zero by 1996. Regional levels of most

US Carbon Dioxide Emissions from Transportation, 1984–1998

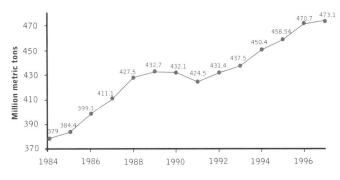

traditional air pollutants were gradually pushed down as well, with especially dramatic declines in sulphate emissions.

Ground-level Ozone and Smog: Relatively new concerns have arisen over ground-level ozone (O_3), fine particulate matter ($PM_{2.5}$), and nitrogen oxide (NO_x) emissions. Ground-level ozone causes more than US $500 million annually in agricultural and commercial forest yield losses in the United States alone. In 1997, some 47.9 million citizens lived in counties with O_3 above existing health standards. Scientific evidence that O_3 and $PM_{2.5}$ can trigger or exacerbate respiratory illnesses prompted recent regulatory changes in health standards in both nations. They also stepped up cooperative efforts to address production and transboundary movement of O_3 and NO_x.

Climate Change and Passenger Transport: With about 5 percent of the world's population, North America accounted for 25.8 percent of global emissions of carbon dioxide (CO_2) in 1998. Transport in Canada and the United States generates between 25 and 40 percent respectively of total North American CO_2 emissions. In the United States, emissions from the transportation sector increased rapidly between 1984 and 1998 (see Figure 1). Automobile use is a significant factor in North America's greenhouse gas emissions and thus in its contribution to global climate change. Light-duty motor vehicles accounted for 15 and 17 percent of total CO_2 emissions in Canada and the United States respectively. Although average automobile fuel efficiency doubled between 1975 and 1989, progress has been offset by increases in the number of automobiles, the total number of kilometers traveled, and a trend since 1984 toward light-duty trucks and sport-utility vehicles (SUVs).

Biodiversity

North America is home to many different types of ecoregions, and the United States contains a broader array than any other nation. About half of the two countries' most diverse ecoregions are now severely degraded.

Wetlands: Wetlands cover about 264 million hectares (ha), with about 24 percent of the world's wetland area lying in Canada. About a third of the region's threatened and endangered species depend on wetlands. Although wetlands continue to be destroyed by development, losses have slowed considerably since the 1980s, thanks in large part to bilateral cooperation in conserving wetland habitat for waterfowl: between 1986 and 1997, there was an 80 percent reduction in US wetland losses from the previous decade and between 1988

and 1993, 850,000 ha of Canada's wetlands were fully protected under the North American Waterfowl Management Plan.

Bioinvasion: In recent years, the introduction of exotic species has increased, imperiling nearly half of the US species listed as threatened or endangered. In Canada, alien

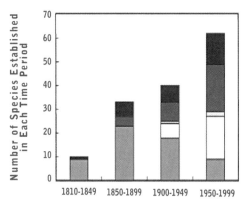

Number of Exotic Species Established in the Great Lakes

☐ Plants ☐ Algae ☐ Disease Pathogens & Parasites ■ Invertebrates ■ Fishes

species have been involved in causing risk to about 25 percent of endangered species. In 1998, about a quarter of the annual US agricultural GNP was lost to damage from and control of invasive species. The influx of new species into the Great Lakes continues (see Figure 2) and is considered to be the most serious threat to the integrity of the ecosystem.

Coastal and Marine Areas

The region's fisheries have declined precipitously since the mid-1980s (see Figure 3). Twenty-one of the 43 groundfish stocks in Canada's North Atlantic are in decline and nearly one-third of US federally managed

Figure 2
Number of exotic species established in the Great Lakes.

Source: H. John Heinz III Center, 2001.

fishery species are overfished. Initially used to enhance natural stocks, aquaculture has become a large-scale industry; since 1980, US aquaculture has grown fourfold. However, aquaculture has its own environmental impacts.

Total Fish Catch, All Fishing Areas, 1972–1999

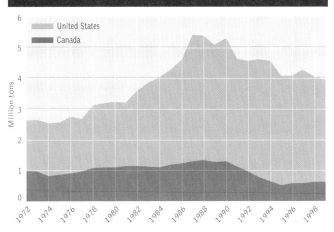

Figure 3
Total fish catch, all fishing areas, 1972-1999.

Source: Fishstat 2001

Pacific Northwest Salmon Fishery: Historically abundant in many Pacific coastal and interior waters, salmon runs have been shrinking since the late 19th century. And despite restricted harvests and other measures during the 1980s, these declines have persisted. A total of 26 distinct groups are now listed by the United States as either threatened or endangered. Although there is a natural variability of abundance levels for Pacific salmon, uncertainty exists about the exact magnitude of recent declines. As fishing, climatic change, and habitat conditions have been changing simultaneously over recent decades, their relative importance has shifted as well. Harvest restrictions, recent bilateral cooperation, and new ecosystem approaches have helped to improve the ocean survival of some important salmon stocks, but their future is uncertain.

Nutrient Loading: North America has had notable success in stemming nutrient emissions from point sources; today, it is non-point sources that give major cause for concern. Nutrient additions to marine and coastal ecosystems jumped dramatically over the past several decades due to large increases in population density, fossil fuel use, sewage inputs, animal production, and fertilizer use. Over the past 30 years, fertilizer use rose by almost 30 percent. Today, 65 percent of US coastal rivers and bays are moderately to severely degraded by nutrient pollution. Nutrients from human activity are likely a contributing factor in the recent dramatic increase in the number, intensity, frequency, and spatial extent of harmful algal blooms, which have caused harm to humans, fish, and marine birds and mammals, along with sectors of the economy that depend on healthy marine ecosystems.

Freshwater

Endowed with abundant water resources, North America holds about 13 percent of the world's renewable freshwater (excluding glaciers and ice caps). And North Americans use more water per person per year than any other people. Agriculture accounts for the largest proportion of total water consumed. While gross-point source water pollution has been successfully reduced in North America since the

1970s, non-point sources, such as agricultural runoff and urban storm drainage, have increased.

Groundwater: Contaminants from non-point sources are present in groundwater throughout large regions of North America, presenting risks to human health. Agriculture, with its widespread use of commercial fertilizer and unsustainable manure management, is the dominant factor impairing groundwater quality. Underground storage tanks and septic tank systems are also leading sources of groundwater contamination. In general, groundwater extraction slowed after the 1980s, but use of stored groundwater still accounted for about 10 percent of all freshwater withdrawal in the United States in the mid-1990s. Despite recent conservation measures and reductions in withdrawals since the 1980s, extraction exceeds the rate of renewal in the Ogallala Aquifer, which underlies one of the world's major agricultural regions in the midwestern Plains states.

The Great Lakes: The Great Lakes Basin contains the world's largest freshwater systems as well as North America's biggest urban-industrial complex. It has 18 percent of the world's fresh surface water and provides drinking water for 27 percent of Canadians and 11 percent of US citizens. By the early 1970s, a mix of industrial, agricultural, and municipal effluents had created serious pollution. The 1972 signing of the Great Lakes Water Quality Agreement (GLWQA) (see Box 1)

> **Box 1: Bilateral Cooperation: The Great Lakes Water Quality Agreement (GLWQA)**
>
> The 1972 Great Lakes Water Quality Agreement committed the two countries to controlling and cleaning up pollution in the Great Lakes from industrial and municipal wastewaters. Amendments required developing Remedial Action Plans (RAPs) to clean up 43 Areas of Concern and renewals and expansions to the Agreement have since introduced the ecosystem approach and measures to address persistent toxic chemicals, airborne pollutants, pollution from land based activities, and the problems of contaminated sediment and groundwater.

launched a concerted bilateral effort to restore the Basin's water quality. Since 1972, there has been an overall reduction of 71 percent in the use, generation, and release of seven priority toxic chemicals and a significant reduction in the number and magnitude of chemical spills. This success in addressing the serious problems in the Great Lakes offers a notable example of cooperation among nations and local users. Nevertheless, challenges remain in the form of impacts from urban and suburban growth, persistent toxic chemicals, atmospheric deposition of toxins such as Persistent Organic Pollutants (POPs), invasion by exotic species, and the threats associated with climate change.

Land

North America has about 11 percent of the world's agricultural croplands, and about 46 percent of all US land is under agricultural production. The region produces ample amounts of food, fiber, and other products both for its own needs and for export around the world.

Land Degradation: Agricultural expansion, intensification, and industrialization have also contributed to land degradation. Government conservation programs (see Box 2) and conservation farming practices spurred a decline in soil erosion of about one-third in the United States between 1987 and 1997, while in Canada, the share of cultivated land at high-to-severe risk of wind erosion declined from 15 percent to 6 percent between 1981 and 1996. Desertification has

---

Box 2: Conservation Programs

Both countries adopted strategies that took fragile lands out of agricultural production to protect them from erosion. In all, about 13 percent of US cropland was idled under federal programs between 1982 and 1997 compared to 11 percent of cropland between 1950 and 1970. About 555,000 ha of marginal prairie agricultural land was removed from annual cultivation under Canada's Permanent Cover Program.

---

generally been stabilized over the past 30 years with expansion of plant cover on rangelands and control of erosion and water logging. Historically, government agricultural policy in North America focused on short-term economic and production goals, but since the 1990s, sustainability has become an important consideration.

Pesticides: North America leads the world in the manufacture and use of pesticides, accounting for 36 percent of their consumption. Over

the past 30 years, the area treated with chemical pesticides has rapidly expanded, increasing in Canada, for example by 3.5 times between 1970 and 1995. Evidence of their damaging impacts on wildlife led to the banning in the 1970s of some Persistent Organic Pollutant (POP) pesticides and the significant decline in their concentrations in biota since the 1990s. But because they bioaccumulate, last so long and can travel great distances in air and water currents, POPs are still found in the environment and in food supplies where they pose significant health threats, especially to indigenous peoples in the north. Pesticide regulation became more stringent during the 1990s. The introduction of Integrated Pest Management (IPM) programs and new 'soft' pesticides (such as oils, soaps and plant extracts) were among the factors that led to a marked decline in insecticide use since the late 1970s. Yet problems remain with the characteristics of some new pesticides, the rise of pesticide resistance, the increased intensity of use in some regions over the last decade, and scientific uncertainties over genetically modified organisms.

Forests

Forests cover about 26 percent of North America's land area and represent 12 percent of the world's forests. Canada has about 30 percent of the world's boreal forest, the largest North American forest ecosystem. Estimates for the late-1990s show that North America grows 255.5 million m^3 more timber annually than is harvested (see Figure 4).

Forest Health: In some areas, forests are becoming increasingly fragmented, biologically impoverished, and weakened or stressed. Factors implicated in the trend include a significant warming trend and increased lightning, tree age, fire-fighting policy, harvesting, air pollution, and bioinvasions. As a result, many forest stands have become less resistant to catastrophic outbreaks of insects, diseases, and fires, which reduce habitat diversity and utilizable timber and add CO_2 to the atmosphere. For example, the area annually disturbed by fire and insects in the boreal forests of central and northwestern Canada doubled over the past 20 to 30 years compared to the previous 50-year period. Since 1992, policies have changed the definition of sustainable forestry from the promotion of a sustained yield of fiber to a new emphasis on maintaining wildlife habitat, protecting soils, retaining natural landscape characteristics and natural disturbances such as wildfires.

Old-Growth Forests in the Pacific Northwest: Most of the region's remaining old-growth forests lie in the Pacific Northwest, which probably contains about half the world's remaining un-logged coastal temperate rainforest. A growing worldwide demand for timber and higher prices in the 1970s drove the rapid harvesting of old growth, which provoked much-publicized debates focused on the spotted owl in the United States and on sensitive remaining rainforest areas such as Clayoquot Sound in Canada.

Pressure from nongovernmental organizations (NGOs) led to increased protection for old-growth forests. By about 2000, almost four million ha, or 15 percent, of British Columbia's (BC) old growth forests

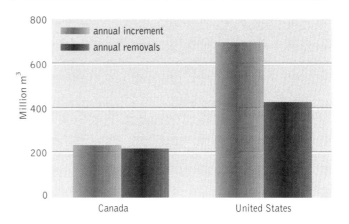

Annual Timber Increment and Annual Removals on Available Forest Land

were fully protected. Over the past 30 years, the timber industry and the governments responsible for old-growth forests have gradually been influenced by the combined power of scientific knowledge of forest ecosystems, NGO action, public awareness, and market pressures. As a result, forest policies have changed to reflect broader concerns for biodiversity and more inclusive forest management.

Figure 4
Annual timber increment and annual removals on available forest land, late 1990s

Source: UN-ECE and FAO 2000

Disasters

Although there have been no major environmental catastrophes such as the Exxon Valdez oil spill in the last few years, the incidence of smaller disasters has increased, threatening human and environmental health and safety. North America is also subject to a range of naturally occurring events which impact on human lives. A mix of factors, including global climate change, population growth, urbanization, and affluence, have stepped up the frequency and severity of some types of natural hazards, such as floods, resulting in steep economic losses.

Floods and Climate Change: In the United States, the average amount of moisture in the atmosphere rose by 5 percent per decade between 1973 and 1993, mostly due to heavier precipitation events, which resulted in floods and storms. More people and their settlements have been exposed to floods because of population increase and concentration in flood-prone areas. Flood policies in both countries that focused primarily on building protective structures (levees, reservoirs, and floodways) were modified in recent years, representing a shift from a strategy of resisting natural hazards to one of building resilience into ecosystems and flood-prone communities. Climate change models forecast an increase in the magnitude, frequency, and cost of extreme hydrological events in some regions of North America.

Figure 5
Total area burned, 1970-2000.

Source: CCFM 2000, CIFFC n.d., NIFC 2000

Forest Fires: Forest fires are a natural part of North America's landscape and play an important role in maintaining and regenerating some types of forest ecosystems. Since the 1970s, the annual area burned by forest fires has expanded (see Figure 5), particularly in the western United States, due to a number of factors: fuel buildup from past effective fire protection programs; changed forest structure and make-up; changes in fire policy related to prescribed burning; and increased public access to and use of the forests. Higher temperatures and lower rainfall associated with climate change have also been implicated.

The challenge of managing wildfire in North America has been exacerbated in recent decades by population increases in the urban-wildland interface: the population growth rate in the US West now ranges from 2.5 to 13 percent per year, compared to the national annual average of about 1 percent.

Human Health and the Environment

Early policy decisions in North America banned some very hazardous substances from the region, but success has not been sound. Today, knowledge of the more subtle human health effects of environmental pollution is beginning to come to light. For example, there is now evidence that more than 2 percent of all US deaths annually can be attributed to air pollution.

Total Area Burned, 1970-2000

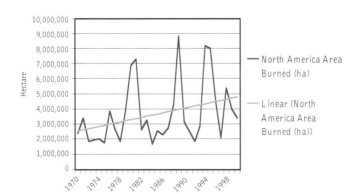

Children's Health and Environmental Contamination: Because of behavioral, physiological and development characteristics, children are more susceptible than adults to the harmful health effects of most pollutants. One in every 200 US children suffers developmental or neurological deficits as a result of exposure to known toxic substances. Air pollution, both outdoor and indoor, is among the most significant triggers for asthma symptoms. And childhood asthma is on the rise, affecting over 5.5 million children in North America and accounting for more than 60 percent of all their hospital visits. There is also mounting evidence that childhood and fetal exposure to trace amounts of pesticides creates adverse health effects. In recent years, recognition of children's environmental health issues has increased dramatically, and consequently some stricter regulations that consider their special vulnerabilities have been introduced.

Emergence/Resurgence of Vector-Borne Diseases: By 1972, public health policies and the effective use of pesticides had significantly reduced the threat of vector-borne infectious diseases. In the last 20 years, however, new vector-borne diseases have emerged and some old ones are resurging in the region. Climate change and human-induced land use change appear to disrupt predator-prey relationships, increasing the numbers of disease-carrying pests and human contact with them. For example, there is a relationship

between the expansion of suburbs and reforestation in the eastern United States, the abundance of deer and deer ticks, and a rise in the numbers of reported tick bites and infections of Lyme disease, a

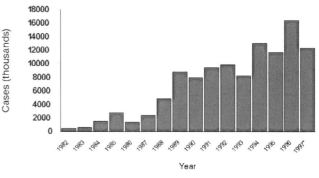

Reported Cases of Lyme disease in the United States, 1982–1997

* Provisional Data

bacterial tick-borne infection and the leading vector-borne infectious illness in the United States (see Figure 6). A high degree of mobility and increasing trade have intensified the risk of exotic diseases being introduced into new areas. Warmer weather, too, may have contributed to the recent occurrence of West Nile Virus in North America and the resurgence of Hantavirus pulmonary syndrome in 1993.

Urban Areas

In the past 30 years, North America's urban population grew from 72 to 77.2 percent. North American urban populations consume high levels of energy and other resources and dispose of large amounts of waste. Canadian and US citizens are some of the highest per

Figure 6
Reported cases of Lyme Disease in the United States, 1982-1997.

Source: Gubler 1998a

capita producers of solid municipal waste in the world, generating, respectively, an annual average of 630 and 720 kg per person in the mid-1990s.

Sprawl: By the 1970s, North America's postwar exodus from city centers had created a settlement pattern characterized by low-density suburbs surrounding city cores, commonly referred to as 'sprawl'.

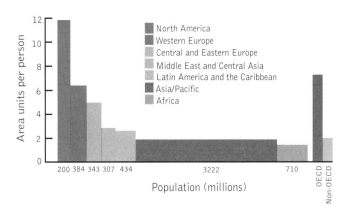

Comparison of Ecological Footprints by World Region

Figure 7 Comparison of ecological footprints by world region, 1996.

Source: WWF 2000

Although relatively more controlled in Canada, sprawl in North America was made possible by policies and incentives that encouraged dispersed settlement, leading to declining available public transit, increased car use, and longer commuting distances. Between 1981 and 1991, the number of car km traveled by Canadian and US citizens grew by 23 and 33.7 percent respectively, while the distances traveled by public transport declined. Sprawl has brought about the conversion of agricultural and wilderness lands to urban uses,

problems with urban runoff, traffic congestion, air pollution and related human health impacts. Abetted by civil society groups, state and local governments and, more recently, national governments are increasingly developing 'smart growth' and sustainable city plans to address sprawl.

The Ecological Footprint: North America's urban and suburban pattern of growth is one of the principal forces driving the global increase in energy demand. North America's cities are major consumers of the world's natural resources and producers of its wastes. Wealthy cities and the wealthier groups within cities tend to appropriate from other regions more materials, food, and energy as well as waste assimilation capacity. In 1996, North America's total impact on the Earth's resources and ecosystem services, or its 'ecological footprint', was about four times larger than the world average (see Figure 7).

One of the most significant aspects of the disproportionate size of North America's ecological footprint is its large and growing energy use and related carbon dioxide (CO_2) emissions from fossil fuels. Total energy use rose by 31 percent between 1972 and 1997. An estimated 40 percent of total North American CO_2 emissions come from 50 metropolitan areas. In 1996, North America's CO_2 footprint was almost five times the world average.

Socio-economic Dynamics and the Environment

1

Socio-economic Dynamics and the Environment

The last three decades of the 20th century brought increasing affluence and power to North America. North Americans not only live long lives in increasingly diverse societies, their production of material wealth and consumption of goods rank among the highest in the world. North American capital, technology, goods, and ideals are fueling globalization, a defining trend of the new millennium that carries both unprecedented risks and extraordinary opportunities.

Human Development

As a region, human development in North America has generally improved over the last 25 years, and the region probably enjoys the highest level of human development in the world. With Canada ranked third and the United States sixth on the Human Development Index (HDI) in 2001, the region has an average HDI value of 0.935, compared to 0.928 for the high-income OECD countries (UNDP 2001).

Despite the overall promising picture of human development, poverty is not unknown in North America. In general, poverty rates over the last decade in the United States have been declining, while in Canada they have been rising. Although debates about the definition, measurement, and thus extent of poverty continue, data clearly show that some social groups are more vulnerable than others. Poverty is more likely to affect aboriginal people, visible minorities, and single parents (Ross, Scott, and Smith 2000; Dalaker 2001).

Demographics

In contrast with other countries in the industrialized world, particularly those in Europe, population growth continues, and growth rates have stayed constant at about 1.0 percent over the last three decades (UN 2000). Although birth rates are low, there is continuous immigration, mostly from Latin America, the Caribbean and Asia-Pacific. As a result of immigration and higher birth rates among immigrants, the population is becoming more diverse (Blank 2001). Despite net growth, the region's share of global population has declined slightly, from 6.3 percent in 1970 to 5.2 percent in 2000, or a total of 314 million (UN 2000).

In addition to becoming more diverse, the population is also growing older. The number of people aged 60 and over accounted for 14 percent of the population in 1970 and 16 percent by 2000. It is projected that by 2025 this portion will increase to 25 percent (UN 1998). The gradual 'graying' of the population stems from declining birth rates and increasing life expectancy as well as the ageing of the post World War II generation. The resulting higher number of the elderly in turn has implications for social security systems and for global financial flows also as the growing number of retirees stop saving and instead start drawing down their accumulated assets (World Bank 2000a).

Urbanization in North America over the past 30 years has been characterized more by the spatial distribution of development than by the rate of urban growth. The urban growth rate has remained steady at less than 2 percent per year since 1972, with the share of the urban population increasing from 72 percent in 1972 to 77 percent in 2000. During this time, suburbs expanded and low-density, car dependent settlements surrounding city cores became the dominant settlement pattern. Sprawl was fueled by incentives for home ownership, low gas prices, convenient highway networks, and economic prosperity (UNDP, UNEP, World

Bank, and WRI 2000). At the turn of the 21st century, some were beginning to recognize these trends as socially, economically, and environmentally unhealthy. Commuter traffic congestion siphoned off time and money, quality of life in city centers declined, and sprawl devoured agricultural land, to name but a few problems.

Economic Development

Since 1972, North America has experienced greater regional integration, a higher scale of economic activity, and a gradual shift in economic structure toward the service sector. North American companies have become truly transnational and invested heavily abroad in emerging economies, significantly influencing development patterns elsewhere. Despite periodic drawbacks, North America has strengthened its role as

GDP per capita, with service sector share: North America, 1972-1997

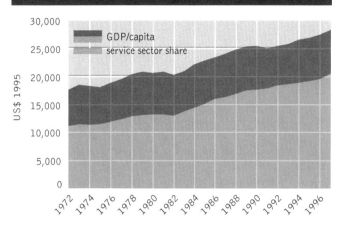

Figure 8
GDP per capita with service sector share: North America, 1972-1997.

Source: World Bank 2000

an engine of the global economy over the past 30 years. Concerns about the vulnerability of the energy sector largely vanished as economic restructuring and the growth of the service sector followed the 1973 and 1979 oil crises (OECD 2000). With the conclusion of a free trade agreement and the emergence of information technology and biotechnology, many regional economies soared through most of the 1990s until the first collapse shook the stock markets in 2000. Taking advantage of the new geopolitical situation, North American companies expanded abroad and became agents of global change (Blank 2001).

It is estimated that the 285 million people (including 135 million workers) of the United States produced about US $10,000 billion in GDP in 2001; the 31 million people (including 15 million workers) of Canada about US $670 billion in GDP (US Department of Commerce 2002; US Census Bureau 2001; US Department of Labor 2002; Statistics Canada 2002). GDP per capita grew

strongly in North America over the past three decades, with the service sector share of the economy growing from 63 to 72 percent during the period 1972–1997 (see Figure 8). On a per capita basis, GDP has grown from US $17,167 in 1970 (at constant 1995 US $) to US $28,376 in 1998 (World Bank 2000b), and private consumption per capita has similarly grown from US $10,667 in 1970 to US $18,167 in 1997. The growth in GDP, however, contrasts with the stagnation indicated by alternative measures of progress, such as the Genuine Progress Index (GPI), available for the United States and currently under development for Canada (GPI Atlantic 2002).

North America became not only a key global engine for producing economic output, but also a leader in consumption. Although representing only around 5 percent of the global population, the United States and Canada consume nearly 25 percent of energy based on total final consumption figures (IEA 2002). Through economic subsidies and taxation measures that keep labor expensive and materials cheap, key national policies continue to drive consumption and its impacts on the North American and global environment toward unsustainability.

There was evidence of a slight decoupling of energy use and economic growth, yet per capita energy use remained consistently higher than in any other of the world's regions (Mathews and Hammond 1999). Some North American constituencies were also among the first to introduce economic instruments designed to curtail pollution. A wide range of jurisdictions on the federal, state/provincial, and local levels introduced measures ranging from taxation of ozone-depleting substances through user fees on waste disposal, to tax incentives to promote fuel conservation (IISD 1995). Urban use of private vehicles continues to increase, whereas use of public transportation has generally remained constant (see Figures 51 and 52 in the urban areas section).

Science and Technology

Over the last three decades, the region continued to lead the world in scientific and technological innovation, as illustrated by the fact that 43 percent of global investment in research and development in 1999 came from North America (SciDev.Net 1999). A rising proportion of the investment comes from the private sector, which now represents 67 percent in the United States and 45 percent in Canada. Venture capital continued to be a particularly important source of funding for new technology-based firms, particularly in the information and communication and biotechnology sectors. Spending on higher education is among the highest in the world, with values over US $18,000/student/year in the United States and over US $14,000/student/year in Canada in 1998. The region also attracts the largest number of foreign-born scientists (OECD 2001).

According to 1995 data, with 34.8 percent of all patents filed, the United States is a global leader in worldwide patent applications, and along with Canada also leads in terms of scientific papers published per capita. North America has led worldwide in the diffusion of information and communication technologies, key assets for a knowledge-based economy. Access to computers and the Internet are among the highest in the world, and access rates, including those through high-speed connection, continue to grow. Multi-factor productivity, or the efficiency of the use of capital and labor in the production process, grew rapidly in both countries during the second half of the 1990s (OECD 2001).

Governance

As the world moves toward global integration, political, fiscal, and administrative power is increasingly devolving to states and provinces in North America. This has led to 'flatter' corporate structure and decentralized decision-making. At the same time, nongovernmental organizations (NGOs) have emerged as important new social actors, many with little formal authority structure.

But growing interconnectedness has also exposed the region to new risks associated with events halfway across the world. The lethal attacks on New York and Washington DC in September 2001 demonstrated not only interconnectedness, but also exposure, vulnerability, and a need to understand the driving forces of conflict. The protection of American economic interests and investments has become integrated into the concept of national security (IIP

2001). Protests over liberalized trade in Seattle in 1999 and Quebec City in 2001 were evidence of marginal but growing public anxiety about globalization and strengthening support for environmental values and labor rights. At the same time, a trend toward greater corporate accountability and transparency has potentially important implications for regulation and for civil society's engagement in influencing the private sector.

The last 30 years also brought an increasingly conscious struggle to balance continued economic growth with environmental and social objectives. Concern about the state of the natural environment has come to the forefront during this time as environmentalism has become a legitimate social movement. Prodded by the grassroots in the 1970s, governments quickly enacted environmental laws and policies. North America was an early adopter of environmental legislation, the idea of public participation, and at least in the case of Canada, the concept of sustainable development (Barr 1993). Impressive gains were made in controlling many conventional pollutants and in continuing a trend in setting aside protected areas. Environmental concern was further roused during the mid-1980s by a new awareness of the global nature of problems such as deforestation, the greenhouse effect, acid rain and ozone deple-

tion; membership in environmental NGOs (ENGOS) soared. By the 1990s, 'common sense' approaches were advocated as concerns over deficit reduction inspired budget cuts to environmental departments and greater reliance on market incentives and voluntary programs (Dowie 1995; Vig and Kraft 1997). After the UN Conference on the Environment and Development in 1992, both countries became committed to sustainable development as reflected in stated federal goals in Canada and the efforts by many US states and localities in moving forward on Agenda 21 guidelines. More recently, however, it has become apparent that real or assumed socioeconomic interests might force the environment down the list of political priorities (OECD 2000).

Because of its economic and military power, as well as its political and cultural influence, North America is a critical piece in the global puzzle of sustainable human development. As technologically advanced and open societies, Canada and the United States may hold the key to solving many environmental and sustainability problems. At the same time, they contribute more than their fair share to increasing risks, such as climate change. Having provided much of the fuel for globalization, the region now needs to fully engage in not only economic, but also social and environmental development.

References

Barr, Jane (1995). *The Origins and Emergence of Quebec's Environmental Movement: 1970-1985.* Montreal, McGill University (Master's Thesis)

Blank, R. M. (2001). An Overview of Trends in Social and Economic Well-being, by Race. In *America Becoming: Racial Trends and their Consequence,* edited by N. J. Smelser, W. J. Wilson and F. Mitchell. Washington DC, National Academy Press, http://search.nap.edu/books/030906838X/html/. Accessed 15 March 2002

Dalaker, Joseph (2001). *Poverty in the United States.* Washington, DC, US Census Bureau, US Department of Commerce http://www.census.gov/prod/2001pubs/p60-214.pdf. Accessed 15 March 2002

Dowie, Mark (1995). *Losing Ground: American Environmentalism at the Close of the Twentieth Century.* Cambridge, MA, The MIT Press

EC (1998). *Canadian Passenger Transportation, National Environmental Indicator Series, SOE Bulletin No. 98-5.* Ottawa, Environment Canada, State of the Environment Reporting Program http://www.ec.gc.ca/ind/English/Transpo/default.cfm. Accessed 28 May 2002

IEA (2001). *Key World Energy Statistics.* Paris, International Energy Agency http://www.iea.org/statist/keyworld/keystats.htm. Accessed 15 March 2002

IIP (2001). *The Americas.* US Department of State, International Information Programs http://usinfo.state.gov/regional/ar/. Accessed 15 March 2002

IISD (1995). *Government Budgets: Green Budget Reform Case Studies.* Winnipeg, International Institute for Sustainable Development http://iisd.org/greenbud/makingb.htm. Accessed 15 March 2002

Mathews, Emily, and Allen Hammond (1999). *Critical Consumption Trends and Implications: Degrading Earth's Ecosystems.* Washington DC, World Resources Institute

OECD (2000). *Policy Brief: Economic Survey of Canada, 2000.* Paris, Organization for Economic Co-Operation and Development

OECD (2001). *OECD Science, Technology and Industry Scoreboard 2001: Toward a Knowledge Based Economy.* Paris, Organization for Economic Co-Operation and Development http://www1.oecd.org/publications/e-book/92-2001-04-1-2987/index.htm. Accessed 15 March 2002

Ross, David P., Katherine Scott, and Peter Smith (2000). *The Canadian Factbook on Poverty.* Ottawa, Ontario, Canadian Council on Social Development http://www.ccsd.ca/pubs/2000/fbpov00/hl.htm. Accessed 15 March 2002

SciDev.Net (1999). *Global Investment in Research and Development.* SciDev.Net http://www.scidev.net/gateways/images/eng.jp. Accessed 15 March 2002

Statistics Canada (2002). *Canadian Statistics.* Ottawa, Ontario, Statistics Canada http://www.statcan.ca/english/Pgdb/. Accessed 15 March 2002

UN (1998). *World Population Prospects: The 1998 Revision.* Vol. II: Sex and Age, United Nations Population Division, Sales No. E.XIII.8

UNDP, UNEP, World Bank, and WRI (2000). *World Resources 2000-2001: People and Ecosystems, the Fraying Web of Life.* Washington DC, World Resources Institute

UN (2000). *World Population Prospects: The 2000 Revision,* United Nations Population Division

UNDP (2001). *Human Development Report 2001: Human Development Indicators,* United Nations Development Programme http://www.undp.org/hdr2001/indicator/cty_f_CAN.html. Accessed 29 May 2002

US Census Bureau (2001). *Population Estimates. Table US-2001EST-01 – Time Series of National Population Estimates: April 1, 2000 to July 1, 2001.* Washington DC, Population Division, US Census Bureau http://eire.census.gov/popest/data/national/populartables/table01.php. Accessed 15 March 2002

US Department of Commerce (2002). *National Income and Product Account Tables.* Washington DC, Bureau of Economic Analysis, US Department of Commerce http://www.bea.doc.gov/bea/dn/nipaweb/TableViewFixed.asp?SelectedTable=3&FirstYear=2000&LastYear=2001&Freq=Qtr. Accessed 15 March 2002

US Department of Labor (2001). *Labor Force Statistics from the Current Population Survey.* Washington DC, Bureau of Labor Statistics, US Department of Labor http://data.bls.gov/cps/home.htm

Vig, Norman J., and Michael E. Kraft. (1997). Environmental Policy from the 1970s to the 1990s: An Overview. In *Environmental Policy in the 1990s: Reform or Reaction,* edited by N. J. Vig and M. E. Kraft. Washington DC, Congressional Quarterly

Wendell Cox Consultancy (2000b). *The Public Purpose.* In *Urban Transport Fact Book.* The Public Purpose, Urban Transport Fact Book http://www.publicpurpose.com/ut-usptshare45.htm. Accessed 8 February 2002

World Bank (2000a). *World Development Report 1999/2000: Entering the 21st Century.* Washington DC, Oxford University Press

World Bank (2000b). *World Development Indicators 2000.* Washington DC, The International Bank for Reconstruction and Development/The World Bank

World Bank (2000c). *Entering the 21st Century: World Development Report 1999/2000.* New York, Oxford University Press

Atmosphere

2

Atmosphere

Figure 9
US emissions of major air pollutants, 1970-1999.

Source: EPA 2001a

North America has a high level of industrial and transport activity and energy consumption, which have important effects on air quality. Against notable improvements in protecting stratospheric ozone and controlling emissions that cause acid rain, new concerns have arisen about smog, while the effective control of greenhouse gases remains a significant challenge.

North America's northern regions have been subject to serious stratospheric ozone deficits, but with the 1987 Montreal Protocol on Substances that Deplete the Ozone Layer, both countries committed to phasing out Ozone Depleting Substances (ODS). Canada reduced the use of these substances faster

than the protocol required. Responsible for less than 1.0 percent of global production, it reduced production from a high of 27.8 kilotons in 1987 to 1.0 kilotons in 1996. As the formerly largest producer of CFCs, the United States amended the Clean Air Act to require ending their production and promoted cost-efficient means to phase them out, including stiff taxation. Both countries were able to reduce their non-essential CFC consumption to nearly zero by 1996 (OECD 1996; Statistics Canada 2000; EPA 2000a; EC 2001).

Due to Clean Air Acts in Canada and the United States in 1969 and 1970, respectively, as well as actions taken under the Canada–US Air Quality Agreement (see Box 3), regional levels of most traditional air pollutants were gradually reduced over the last 30 years, as reflected in US trends (see Figure 9).

Acid rain control programs in both countries and transboundary cooperation (see Box 3) contributed to a dramatic decline in sulphate emissions after 1995 with US SO_2 emissions reductions of 31 percent from 1981 to 2000 and 24 percent

US Emissions of Major Air Pollutants, 1970-1999

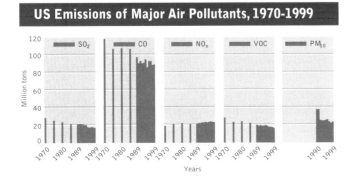

from 1991 to 2000 (EPA 2001a). As a result, acidic sulphates entering lakes and streams in eastern North America also declined over the past 25 years. On the other hand, NO_x emissions have not improved in either country since 1980. And recent evidence suggests that the ways in which acid rain affects the environment are much more complex than was first thought and damage may be more fundamental and long-lasting than was believed; many sensitive areas are still receiving acid deposition that exceeds their neutralizing capacity, and a recent report states that for sensitive soils and waters in the northeastern United States to recover completely would require cutting another 80 percent of SO_2 emissions from power plants (Munton 1998; Driscoll, Lawrence, and others 2001).

A number of North American cities have successfully reduced emissions of some of the most evident and harmful pollutants that

Box 3: Binational Agreement and Co-operation

The Agreement between the Government of Canada and the Government of the United States of America on Air Quality (commonly called the Canada–US Air Quality Agreement) was signed in 1991 to control transboundary air pollution between the two countries. The Agreement provides for assessment, notification, and mitigation of air pollution problems. It commits the parties to specific targets and timetables to reduce SO_2 and NO_x emissions and includes related provisions on visibility, prevention of significant deterioration, and compliance monitoring. Since 1994, the two nations also cooperate by identifying possible new sources and modifications to existing sources of transboundary air pollution within and over 100 km of the border and sustain successful, ongoing consultations on sources of concern (EC 2000a). The two countries have surpassed current reduction requirements, and in December 2000, they signed the Ozone Annex to the Agreement to reduce border NO_x emissions and transboundary flows from fossil fuel power production (EC 2000b).

Both countries also extended their domestic air pollution programs and expanded their commitments to cooperatively address transboundary air issues through the 1997 Joint Plan of Action for Addressing Transboundary Air Pollution on ground-level ozone and PM, and in 1998, they issued a Joint Plan Report, which was followed by cooperative analyses initiatives and a joint work plan for transboundary inhalable particles. AIRNOW, the US Environmental Protection Agency's (EPA) real-time air quality program, expanded into Canada's Atlantic provinces and Quebec in 2000 in a cooperative venture involving New England states, eastern Canadian provinces, the Northeast States for Coordinated Air Use Management (NESCAUM) and Environment Canada (EC 2000a). In addition, both countries signed the 1999 Protocol to the 1979 Convention on Long-Range Transboundary Air Pollution to Abate Acidification, Eutrophication, and Ground-Level Ozone.

Together with Mexico, the Commission for Environmental Cooperation of North America (CEC) also facilitates cooperation in addressing air pollution problems between Canada and the United States. Among its initiatives are projects to coordinate air quality management, develop technical and strategic tools to improve air quality, and address air quality problems associated with North American trade and transportation corridors (CEC 2001a).

affect local air quality, but generally success has been mixed. For example, the number of 'unhealthy days' in Los Angeles decreased by 57 percent between 1989 and 1998, but rose by 10 percent on average in the

rest of the nation's cities. At the same time, in 1990, 274 areas were designated 'non-attainment' for at least one air quality standard, whereas by 1999 the number had dropped to 121. The situation in Canada is equally mixed. Whereas national concentrations of NO_2, SO_2, and suspended particulate matter have improved, the situation in individual cities is not as clear. The number of days of 'good' air quality decreased in Canada's two most populous cities—by 20 percent in Toronto, and by 8 percent in Montreal—yet increased by 9 percent in Vancouver (CEC 2000).

New concerns have arisen over ground level ozone and fine particulate matter, whose emissions have not decreased as markedly as other common pollutants. Smog, a mixture of many air pollutants including ozone, has become a high-priority issue in North America as

levels continue to rise and the health effects of ozone exposure become clearer. High levels of fine particulates and ground-level ozone are also associated with the growth in the number of motor vehicles and the distances they are driven (CEC 2000). North America's dependence on automobiles and the resulting increase in emissions from the transportation sector also have global impacts. The transport sector contributes the greatest proportion of CO_2 to the atmosphere and North America's CO_2 emissions are among the highest in the world. Thus, the region's passenger transport and its contribution to global climate change is a priority issue for both North America and the world.

Ground Level Ozone and Smog

Ground-level ozone is a common, pervasive, and harmful air pollutant with a complex photochemistry (see Box 4) and it is now the most pervasive air pollution problem in North America. Research in the last decade has demonstrated that ozone (O_3) is responsible for far greater impacts on human health than previously thought. Even average concentrations of O_3 can exacerbate asthma and other respiratory conditions and allergies and inhibit or interfere with the immune system, especially in young children (see the health and environment section), the elderly and outdoor sport enthusiasts (OMA 2000; EPA 2001a). Recent studies suggest there are no safe levels of human exposure (EC 2001a). Research in both countries

Box 4: Ground Level Ozone and Smog

Ground-level ozone (tropospheric O_3) results from the reactions of precursors – nitrogen oxides (NO_x) and volatile organic compounds (VOCs) – in the presence of sunlight. It forms on warm, sunny days where NO_x and VOCs are present, especially in cities and industrial areas and regions prone to stagnant air masses. Seasonal concentrations are strongly influenced by weather, but ambient O_3 concentrations also depend on the state of control measures, population growth, levels of human activity, and topography (ELP 1992; EPA 1998). Fossil fuel combustion by power plants, industries, and motor vehicles is the major source of NO_x with the transportation sector alone responsible for 60 percent of NO_x emissions in Canada and 53 percent in the United States (Hancey 1999; EPA 2000b).

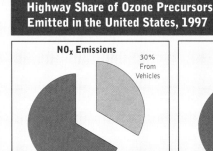
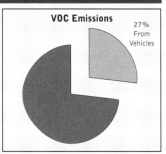

Highway Share of Ozone Precursors Emitted in the United States, 1997

NOₓ Emissions — 30% From Vehicles

VOC Emissions — 27% From Vehicles

Figure 10 *Source: EPA 2001b*

Motor vehicles are responsible for a large share of ground-level ozone precursors (see Figure 10).

Smog, the hazy and unhealthy pall that can be seen floating above large cities, is often confused with ground-level ozone. Smog is a mixture of many air pollutants, including O_3 and particulate matter. The latter are fine airborne particles derived from natural sources such as windblown agricultural soil, and from human activities, including combustion, that contribute sulphates, nitrates, soot, and other particles and particle precursors to the air (Hancey 1999; EC 2000c). Travel contributes more fine ($PM_{2.5}$) than large particles, accounting for about 4 percent of $PM_{2.5}$ emissions in the United States (EPA 1999a). Levels of smog-causing pollutants in the air closely resemble those emitted by human activity (EC 2001c).

repeatedly documents a strong correlation between hospitalization and worker absenteeism, and episodic high O_3 levels (CEC 1997a). Ozone also affects vegetation and it has been estimated that it causes more than US $500 million in annual reductions of agricultural and commercial forest yields in the United States (EPA 2001a).

Canada and the United States issue advisories in smog-prone communities. Periods of high O_3 concentrations are termed episodes when the concentration exceeds guidelines or standards. Canada's

National Ambient Air Quality Objectives (NAAQO) were established in 1970 and the US National Ambient Air Quality Standards (NAAQS) in 1971. Between 1984 and 1991, Canada's existing ozone guideline of 0.082 parts per million (ppm) over a one-hour period was exceeded at least once in all major cities, and the number of days deemed 'fair' and 'poor' as measured on the Index of the Quality of Air increased between 1995 and 1998 because of higher ground-level ozone and fine particulate levels (EC 2000c; EC 2001a).

Transport of Tropospheric Ozone in Eastern North America

Transport vectors on highest 20% of ozone days in Northeast

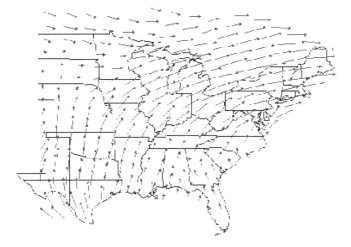

Transport vectors on lowest 20% of ozone days in Northeast

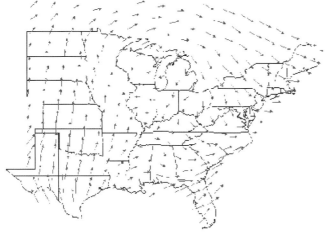

Wind and weather tie air quality in Canada and the United States together through transport from "upwind" source regions to "downwind" receptor regions. The wind diagram below that was created during the U.S. Ozone Transport Assessment Group discussions illustrates vividly the dynamic at play with respect to transport of air pollution - in this case, ozone in the eastern half of North America (EC 1998a).

Figure 11
Transport of tropospheric ozone in eastern North America

Source: EC 1998a

Ground-level ozone concentrations in the United States (as measured in one-hour concentrations) dropped 30 percent between 1978 and 1997, and yet some 47.9 million citizens still lived in counties with O_3 above the existing 1997 standards (EPA 1999a; EPA 2001a). Ground-level ozone continues to be a problem in many regions throughout North America, including but not restricted to New England, the Lake

Michigan area, the Ohio River Valley, southeastern Texas, parts of California, the Washington-Baltimore area, North Carolina, along Canada's Windsor-Quebec City corridor, and to a lesser degree, in its Lower Fraser Valley and South Atlantic provinces (EPA 1997a; EPA 1997b; EC 2000c).

Until recently, high-ground-level ozone episodes were generally viewed as local issues (CEC 1997). Control measures in the 1970s focused primarily on reducing VOCs and, in some cases, NO_x emissions from factories and vehicles in regions that were most affected. In many cases, however, controls failed to reduce O_3 concentrations enough to meet national health standards (EPA 1997a).

It is now evident that O_3 molecules can travel relatively long distances from emission sources and its precursors can stay aloft in the atmosphere and travel even further. Depending on meteorological conditions, the typical transport range can be 240 to 800 kilometers (CEC 1997). An estimated 30 to 90 percent of eastern Canada's ozone comes from the United States. The province of Ontario, the region in Canada that suffers from the worst ground-level ozone problem, is a source of NO_x downwind into northeastern United States (EC 2000c) (see Figure 11). Research suggests that NO_x and VOC emissions from midwestern US states create ozone in the Ohio Valley, which, in turn, flows into Canada as well as other parts of the United States (CEC 1997). For example, emissions from Ohio and other Midwestern US states contribute more than 50 percent of O_3, particulate, and acid aerosol levels found in southwestern Ontario (EC 2000c). For this reason, the two countries recognize the importance of working together to stem emissions production and transport.

Ozone or its precursors arriving from elsewhere can create dangerous conditions even where local emissions are only moderate. Rural areas

the role and significance of NO_x in regional ozone formation and transport led to more aggressive NO_x emission controls. Numerous studies have shown that fossil fuel power plants are the largest individual sources of NO_x, and significant amounts of ozone are formed and transported in the plumes of power plants (Miller 1999). In addition, while VOCs decreased in the United States over the last 30

Box 5: Haze in US National Parks

Over the last 10 years, the average ozone levels in 29 US national parks rose by over 4 percent (EPA 2001a). Some parks in the United States, such as the Great Smoky Mountains National Park in Tennessee, Acadia National Park in Maine, and Shenandoah in Virginia, have had to issue health warnings because of smog and have experienced decreased visibility (Miller 1993; Cushman Jr. 2000). In Acadia, some smog episodes have been worse than those in the cities of Boston or Philadelphia. On some days in the Great Smokies, the most visited national park, visibility can be reduced to about 24 km and the park had to issue more than 100 unhealthy air alerts between 1999 and 2001 (Seelye 2001). An amendment to the Clean Air Act in 1997 called for rules to improve visibility in parks by 15 percent per decade over the following 60 years so as to achieve pristine air quality by 2064. The rules apply to power plants built between 1962 and 1977 that emit more than 227 ton of pollutants every year. These are found all over the country and their airborne pollution can travel as far as 1,609 km. In April 1999, the EPA initiated a new regional haze program to address visibility impairment in national parks and wilderness areas caused by a number of sources over broad regions (EPA 2001a).

and protected parks (see Box 5) are subject to high ozone levels and smog not only due to local emissions from rural power plants but also from the inflow of ozone and its precursors from distant sources carried by winds (Miller 1999).

The recent recognition of a number of parameters related to ozone and smog formation has inspired shifts in control strategies to address persistent air pollution problems. First, the understanding of

years with efficient controls, NO_x emissions have continued to increase: between 1970 and 2000, VOC emissions fell 43 percent while NO_x emissions rose 20 percent (EPA 2000a) (see Figure 9).

In the United States, the EPA issued a rule in 1998 requiring 19 eastern states and the District of Columbia to develop plans to reduce harmful NO_x by 1.4 million tons beginning in the summer of 2003 (Connole 2000). The two countries now cooperate to reduce transboundary emissions under the Canada–US Air Quality Agreement and other bilateral and international initiatives (see Box 3).

A second new measure related to controlling smog grew out of the recognition that exposure to ground level ozone at concentrations below 0.08 ppm resulted in significant and often severe health effects on North American populations. This discovery prompted changes in both US and Canadian ozone health standards: in 1997 the United States lowered the standard from 0.12 ppm for one-hour concentrations to 0.08 ppm for eight-hour concentrations (EPA 1997c), and in June 2000, Canada set a target of 0.065 ppm over eight hours to be met by 2010 (CCME 2000).

A third new control measure relates to the health effects of fine airborne particles called Particulate Matter (PM), which with O_3 contributes to smog formation (see Box 4). 'Coarse' particles range from 2.5 to 10 micrometers in diameter (PM_{10}). Fine particles, largely formed in the atmosphere from gaseous precursors, are less than 2.5 micrometers in diameter ($PM_{2.5}$). Their small size allows them to penetrate the lungs where they can handicap lung function and cause respiratory symptoms (EPA 1999b). Some people sensitive to ozone are most affected by these airborne particles as well, which have also been linked to aggravated heart conditions (EC 2000a). Although levels of total suspended particulates (TSP) have decreased by 40 percent since 1980,

recent research reveals that it is the finer airborne particles at concentrations well below those allowed by earlier PM standards that cause the more serious health concerns such as early death and hospital admissions (OMA 2000).

Consequently, North American standards for particulate matter were recently adjusted. In 1997, the United States promulgated new standards for $PM_{2.5}$, with implementation beginning after 2002 (EPA 1997c; Kaiser 2000). In June 2000, Canadian federal and provincial governments agreed to new Canada wide standards for $PM_{2.5}$ and ozone, with reductions to be achieved by 2010. In 2001, Canada added PM_{10} and four other smog-causing substances (VOCs) to the List of Toxic Substances under the Canadian Environmental Protection Act (EC 2001b).

It remains to be seen how soon new air quality standards can improve air quality and reduce human exposure to ozone and smog. Concerns about future emissions are mounting over the potential for a growing economy to increase factory and power plant production, and the degree to which electricity demand will be met by traditional sources of generation, such as coal, rather than being met through energy efficiency and alternative, less polluting fuels and processes. The electricity sector in the region is in the midst of unprecedented change and the two countries are cooperating to examine some of the regional environmental dimensions arising out of its transformation (see Box 6). A recent

Box 6: Bilateral Cooperation

Competitive electricity markets have been introduced, or remain under consideration, in Canada, Mexico and the United States. Affordable and reliable electricity provides a foundation of economic stability upon which prosperity depends. Presently, concerns exist over the prospect of electricity shortages and their effect on economic development in affected regions. At the same time, electricity—its generation, distribution and usage—has significant impacts on human health and the environment. The Commission for Environmental Cooperation of North America's (CEC) working paper, *Environmental Challenges and Opportunities of the Evolving North American Electricity Market*, examines some of the regional environmental dimensions arising out of the transformation of the electricity market, including the key features, trends and variables shaping events in this dynamic sector. A new level of cooperation in meeting North America's electricity needs opens up possibilities for identifying ways in which affordable and reliable electricity can be provided while at the same time protecting human health and the environment in the region (CEC 2001b).

statement by Canada's Commissioner of the Environment and Sustainable Development applies to both countries: To address the smog problem requires strong leadership and the need to change the way we produce and use energy (Government of Canada 2000a).

Climate Change and Passenger Transport

Since 1972, North America's climate has warmed considerably, reflecting a global trend. About half of the average rise in surface temperature during the past century—over 0.6 degrees Celsius—occurred since the late 1970s, as illustrated by the US trend (see Figure 12). Like other regions in the world's higher latitudes, North America has warmed more than equatorial regions, with temperature increases greatest in the northernmost parts, such as Alaska and Canada's Mackenzie River Basin. The latter warmed at three times the global rate (Cohen 1998; Gawthrop 1999; USGCRP 2000). Spring snow-cover depth in western Canada has decreased by as much as one cm per

year over the past 30 years and disappeared about one day earlier per year – a trend that has serious implications for water supply, among other effects (EC 2000; APSC 2001). Ice extent and area in the Arctic regions decreased by 4.5 percent from 1978 to 1987 and by 5.6 percent from 1987 to 1994 (Gawthrop 1999).

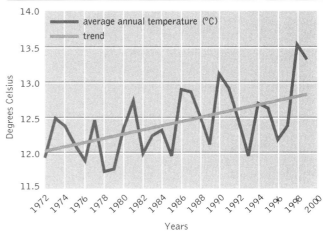

Trend in Average US Annual Temperature, 1972-1999

These climatic changes are due, in part, to the natural phenomena known as El Niño and La Niña. These periodic oscillations in the tropical Pacific's surface tempera-

Figure 12
Trend in average US annual temperature, 1972-1999.

Source: DOC, NOAA and NCDC 2000

Per Capita Trends in CO_2 Emissions from Fossil Fuels, Cement Manufacture, and Gas Flaring in North America, 1950-1998

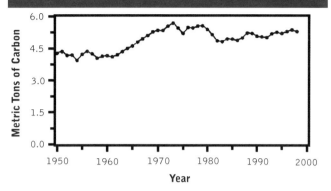

Figure 13

Per capita trends in CO_2 emissions from forssil fuels, cement manufracture, and gas flaring in North America, 1950-1998.

Source: Marland, Bowden, and Anders 200l

ture modify North America's climate. Human activities that emit carbon and other gases, however, have contributed to climate change, as concluded by the Intergovernmental Panel on Climate Change's (IPCC) Second Assessment Report, supported by other studies and subsequently by the IPCC's third report in 2001 (Mann 2000; Crowley 2000; IPCC 2001). The IPCC predicts that unless changes are made, rising greenhouse gases will lead to an

US Carbon Dioxide Emissions from Transportation, 1984-1998

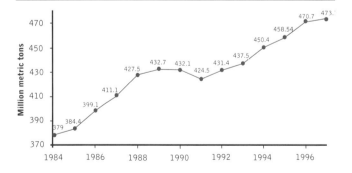

Figure 14

US Carbon Dioxide emissions from transportation, 1984-1998.

Source: EPA 2001b

increase in worldwide mean temperatures of between 1.4 and 5.8 degrees C by 2100, a rate thought to be without precedent in the last 10,000 years (Sandalow and Bowles 2001).

North America is responsible for more of this human-influenced change than any of the world's regions and the United States is the world's leading carbon emitter in absolute, per capita, and growth values (OECD 1996). In 1998, with about 5 percent of the world's population, the two countries accounted for 25.8 percent of global emissions of carbon dioxide (Marland, Bowden, and others 2001), the most abundant of the greenhouse gases (CO_2 accounts for more than 80 percent of North America's greenhouse gas emissions) (EIA 2001). Per capita emissions (see Figure 13) have been consistently high and well above those for any other region (Marland, Bowden, and Anders 2001).

Most CO_2 emissions come from burning fossil fuels for energy. North America has one of the world's most energy-intensive economies, in part because of its climate and because of its large land area and low population density, which help to encourage motorized travel (OECD 1995; OECD 1996). Indeed, the transportation sector is the largest source of CO_2 emissions: for example, it produced 25 percent of Canada's total emissions in 1999 and 32 percent of US emissions from fossil fuels in 1997 (EC 2002a; EPA 2001a). United States transportation also has a strong impact on worldwide CO_2 emissions. In 1997, it accounted for more than one-third of total world transportation energy use and about 5 percent of CO_2 emitted worldwide as a result of human activity (NRC

1997; O'Meara Sheehan 2001). Carbon dioxide emissions from US transportation increased significantly over the past two decades (see Figure 14), and over the next 20 years, the transport sector is predicted to be the fastest-growing contributor of carbon emissions

(EPA 2001a). If current Canadian trends continue, greenhouse gas emissions from transportation are expected to exceed 1990 levels by 33.8 percent by 2010 and by 54 percent by 2020, further challenging commitments made under the Kyoto Protocol (see Box 7) (NR Can 1999).

Box 7: The Kyoto Protocol

North America joined the international community to address climate change by signing the 1992 UN Framework Convention on Climate Change (UNFCCC), in which the two countries agreed to voluntarily reduce greenhouse gas emissions to1990 levels by 2000. In response, the US 1993 Climate Change Action Plan and Canada's 1995 National Action Program on Climate Change introduced strategies for emission reductions. At the same time, voluntary programs, such as Canada's Climate Change Voluntary Challenge and Registry and the US Credit for Voluntary Early Action were set up to encourage private sector reductions (CRS 2000; Government of Canada 2000b). These efforts failed to significantly curb CO_2 emissions in the 1990s.

Targets were surpassed by the time the two countries renewed their commitment with the 1997 legally binding Kyoto Protocol, when Canada agreed to reduce greenhouse gas emissions to 6 percent and the United States to 7 percent below 1990 levels between 2008 and 2012. Already by 1998, Canada's greenhouse gas emissions had risen by nearly 14 percent over 1990 levels and total US emissions had increased by 11 percent (EPA 2000b; Sustainability Reporting Program 2000). Strong economic growth during the 1990s and generally low oil prices are among the reasons for lack of progress in curbing emissions. Non-carbon-emitting renewable energy production from hydroelectricity, wind, solar, biomass, and geothermal is increasing but still contributes only a small fraction of North America's energy needs, supplying about 7 percent of total US domestic gross energy demand in 2000 (EIA 2001).

In the spring of 2001, the United States announced that implementing the Kyoto treaty would be too harmful to the economy and that it would pursue other ways of addressing the climate change issue. At the July 2001 UNFCCC Conference in Bonn, a compromise was struck allowing carbon-absorbing forests to be counted against emissions such that Canada may obtain more than 20 percent of its target with such credits. Finally, in early 2002 the United States announced its plan to cut greenhouse gases relative to economic output, setting out the goal to reduce greenhouse gas intensity—emissions per unit of economic activity—by 18 percent by the year 2012, using clean energy tax incentives and voluntary measures, while Canada re-asserted its intention to ratify the treaty (EIA 2001; UNFCCC 2001; EC 2002b; US Department of State 2002).

Bilateral Cooperation

In August 2001, Eastern Canadian premiers and New England governors resolved to reduce greenhouse gas (GHG) emissions in the first bilateral agreement to address climate change. The agreement commits the regions to reduce GHG emissions by at least 10 percent below 1990 levels by the year 2020, calling on the states and provinces to monitor their emissions levels, develop plans to reduce them, use more efficient fuel sources and vehicles, reduce energy consumption, and promote mass transit (Auld 2001).

Reliance on private automobiles for transport is a significant factor in North America's greenhouse gas emissions. Light-duty motor vehicles (cars and other vehicles of less than 3,856 kg) are responsible for about 17 percent of total US CO_2 emissions and about 15 percent of all of Canada's CO_2 emissions (Keoleian 2000; Schingh, Brunet, and Gosselin 2000).

Nevertheless, over the past 30 years, North America has made considerable strides in transport efficiency. Two sharp price shocks in the oil market in the 1970s helped to raise awareness that fossil petroleum is not a renewable resource and to spur changes. Energy-saving standards for vehicle bodies, engines, and fuel efficiency in new passenger cars pioneered by the United States were introduced in the 1970s and strengthened in the 1980s (OECD 1996; CEQ 1997). From 1973 to 1996 the average fuel efficiency of new passenger cars entering the US fleet increased from 6 km per liter (kmpl) to 12.1 kmpl (CEQ 1997).

Amendments strengthened fuel efficiency standards and introduced additional and enhanced programs for inspection and maintenance (OECD 1996). The 1975 Corporate Average Fuel Economy (CAFE) standards, created by the Energy Policy and Conservation Act (EPCA) to control oil consumption, helped to improve the average fuel efficiency of light-duty vehicles by 60 percent by 1992. It has been estimated that CAFE improvements

have saved about 2.5 million barrels of oil per day (Ayres 2001; Prouty 2000).

In 1994, Canada set up the Canadian Task Force on Cleaner Vehicles and Fuels to work toward stricter fuel and emission controls and greater reconciliation with US standards (EC and Transport Canada 1997) and Natural Resources Canada's Transportation Energy Technologies Program supported the development of competitive, energy-efficient and environmentally responsible technologies for alternative transportation fuels (EC 1998b). Canada set up a voluntary Corporate Average Fuel Consumption (CAFC) program in 1980 that was eventually harmonized with the US CAFE standards, which are currently at 8.6 L/100 km for the new passenger car fleet and 11.4 L/100 km for the new light-duty truck fleet. Modest changes to US auto fuel efficiency standards were passed in 2001 and the two countries are now working bilaterally to harmonize policies promoting greater road transportation energy efficiency and alternative fuels (EC and Transport Canada 1997; NRTEE 1998; Schingh, Brunet, and Gosselin 2000).

Because of the 1975 US CAFE standards, average automobile fuel efficiency doubled between 1975 and 1989 (CIBE 2000). However, after this period, improvements steadily declined; the automakers' average fuel economy dropped from 11 kmpl in 1988 to 10.1 kmpl in 1999 (CIBE 2000; FOE 2001). Progress made in car fuel efficiency and emission controls has been partially offset by increases in the number of automobiles and in the total number of kilometers traveled, the continued use of older or poorly maintained vehicles, and a trend since 1984 toward light-duty trucks and Sport Utility Vehicles (SUVs) (see Box 8) (CEQ 1997; EC 1998b).

For example, between 1990 and 1995, there was a 15 percent increase in automobile travel in Canada, a decrease in urban transit ridership, and a 6 percent increase in total fossil fuel use (EC 1998c). Vehicle Miles Traveled (VMT) in the United States rose 110 percent between 1974 and 1999, and 35 percent between 1989 and 1999 (Hu and Young 1999). In the last decade, VMT exceeded the US rates of population, employment, and

Box 8: Sport Utility Vehicles

Much of the decline in fuel economy since the late 1980s has resulted from the increasing market share of light trucks and Sport Utility Vehicles (SUVs) (EPA 2001c). Most SUVs are used for everyday driving and even though North American family sizes have been decreasing, there has been a marked trend toward this type of larger passenger vehicle (FOE 2001). The SUV market share increased dramatically over a short period of time, jumping from less than 2 percent in 1975 to nearly 22 percent of the overall market in the United States in 2001 and from less than 1 percent to 10 percent in Canada between 1981 and 1988 (EPA 2001c; Schingh, Brunet, and Gosselin 2000).

Standards for air pollution and fuel economy are lower for vehicles whose weight exceeds 3,856 kg than they are for cars because initially, light trucks were made for farm and commercial use and so were exempt from the more stringent regulations (Lalonde 2001; Prouty 2000). But under the law, SUVs are also characterized as light trucks, and as such only have to achieve 8.8 kmpl while new cars need to attain 11.7 kmpl (CIBE 2000). The US National Highway Traffic Safety Administration announced in January 2002 that it would not raise the average fuel efficiency requirements for light trucks, minivans, and sport utility vehicles for the 2004 model year (Ohnsman 2002) whereas Canada has imposed stricter emissions standards beginning that year (EC 2002c).

Cars produce an average of four tons of carbon dioxide per year, while light-duty trucks emit an average of 5.4 tons. Forty-five percent of the rise in greenhouse gas emissions from the automotive sector between 1990 and 1999 was due to rapid growth in sales of minivans, SUVs, and pickup trucks (Lalonde 2001).

In addition to their contribution to CO_2, SUVs have a significant impact on air quality. US federal law allows SUVs to emit 30 percent more carbon monoxide and hydrocarbons and 75 percent more nitrogen oxides than passenger cars. Hydrocarbons and nitrogen oxides are precursors to ground level ozone, which can trigger asthma and cause lung damage (see Box 4) (FOE 2001).

Numerous carmakers are now developing fuel cell vehicles, including SUVs. In these systems, electricity is created through the reaction between hydrogen and oxygen and only water vapor is released, while fuel cells using natural gas or gasoline emit some measure of pollutants. Fuel cell vehicles will not be ready for the commercial market for another 9 years (Greenwire 2001a; Greenwire 2001b).

Box 9: Potential Impacts of Climate Change

Nationally, both countries recognize the threats of climate change to their domestic economies, resources, and ecosystem functions. The US Global Change Research Program reports that although the agricultural sector will likely adapt well to climate change, other potential effects include a rise in sea level that could cause losses to the country's coastal wetlands, more coastal erosion, the likely disappearance of unique Alaskan landscapes, water shortages that could exacerbate conflicts throughout the western states, and more frequent heat waves (USGCRP 2000). In Canada, the possible consequences include more severe weather events such as droughts, winter storms, and tornadoes; flooding in coastal regions; increased threats to forests and farmland from pests, diseases, and fires; and damage to water sources (Government of Canada 1999). North America bears a disproportionate responsibility for the global impacts of climate change, which include severe threats to the world's heavily populated low-lying areas and global weather patterns that could impose heavy tolls on the lives of millions of people throughout the globe.

---

economic growth (EPA 2001a). Driving these trends were increases in population numbers, disposable income, number of households, number of people commuting to work, urban sprawl, and number of vehicles per household (Miller and Moffet 1993, CEQ 1997). In 1994, nearly 60 percent of US households owned two or more cars and 19 percent owned three or more (De Souza 1999). Cheap parking and other hidden subsidies, such as funds for highway development and low fuel prices, continue to encourage car dependency and feed into a 'vicious cycle' promoting urban sprawl and declining transit use (see urban section) (Miller and Moffat 1993; EC1998b).

Negotiations leading to and since Kyoto expanded public and private sector awareness of global warming and its potential impacts (see Box 9). Driven by this threat as well as by air pollution legislation, competitive research into alternative vehicles and fuels has intensified (Motavalli and Bogo 2000).

Given its large share of the planet's CO_2 emissions, and since they are so abundant and directly proportional to fuel use, the region will need a substantial change in its automobile use, more fuel-efficient technologies, and changes in municipal planning and urban development strategies, including investment in public transport (EC 1998b). Overcoming investments already made in present-day energy and transportation infrastructure and moving toward new technologies while avoiding major disruptions remains a significant challenge (Sandalow and Bowles 2001).

References

APSC (2001). Study Shows Early Signals of Climate Change in Earth's Cold Regions. *Space Daily.* Asia Pacific Space Centre http://www.spacedaily.com/news/climate-01k.html. Accessed 17 February 2002

Auld, Alison (2001). Pollution Agreement 'Historic'. *The Globe and Mail,* 28 August, A7

Ayres, Robert U. (2001). The Energy We Overlook. *World Watch* 14 (6): 30-9

Bruce, James P., Ian Burton, and I. D. Mark Egener (1999). *Disaster Mitigation and Preparedness in a Changing Climate: A Synthesis Paper Prepared for Emergency Preparedness Canada, Environment Canada, and the Insurance Bureau of Canada.* Ottawa, Minister of Public Works and Government Services http://www.epc-pcc.gc.ca/research/down/DisMit_e.pdf. Accessed 16 February 2002

CCME (2000). *Canada-Wide Standards for Particulate Matter (PM) and Ozone.* Canadian Council of Ministers of the Environment http://www.ccme.ca/pdfs/backgrounders_060600/PMOzone_Standard_E.pdf. Accessed 17 February 2002

CEC (1997). *Long-Range Transport of Ground Level Ozone and its Precursors: Assessment of Methods to Quantify Transboundary Transport within the Northeastern United States and Eastern Canada.* Montreal, Commission for Environmental Cooperation of North America

CEC (2000). *Booming Economies, Silencing Environments, and the Paths to Our Future: Background Note by the Commission for Environmental Cooperation on Critical and Emerging Environmental Trends.* Montreal, Commission for Environmental Cooperation of North America http://www.cec.org/pubs_docs/documents/index.cfm?varlan=english&ID=66. Accessed 16 February 2002

CEC (2001a). *Pollutants and Health.* Montreal, Commission for Environmental Cooperation of North America http://www.cec.org/programs_projects/pollutants_health/index.cfm?varlan=english. Accessed 16 February 2002

CEC (2001b) *Environmental Challenges and Opportunities of the Evolving North American Electricity Market: Working Paper.* Montreal, Commission for Environmental Cooperation of North America http://www.cec.org/pubs_docs/documents/index.cfm?varlan=english&ID=542. Accessed 29 May 2002

CEQ (1997). *Environmental Quality, The World Wide Web: The 1997 Report of the Council on Environmental Quality.* Washington DC, The White House, Council on Environmental Quality

CIBE (2000). SUV's Called Trucks in Order to Bypass Emissions Standards. *Canadian Institute for Business and the Environment* 4 (7)

Cohen, Stewart J. (1998). *Mackenzie Basin Impact Study (MBIS) Final Report.* Environment Canada http://www.msc-smc.ec.gc.ca/airg/mbis/mackenzie.htm#Three. Accessed 16 February 2002

Connole, Patrick (2000). EPA Wins Court Decision for Cleaner Eastern Air. *Reuters,* 26 June

Crowley, Thomas J. (2000). Causes of Climate Change Over the Past 1000 Years. *Science* 289 (5477): 270

CRS (2000). *Global Climate Change Briefing Book.* Congressional Research Service, National Library for the Environment http://www.cnie.org/NLE/CRSreports/BriefingBooks/Climate/. Accessed 16 February 2002

De Souza, Roger-Mark (1999). *Household Transportation Use and Urban Air Pollution: A Comparative Analysis of Thailand, Mexico, and the United States.* Washington, DC, Population Reference Bureau http://www.prb.org/Template.cfm?Section=PRB&template=/ContentManagement/ContentDisplay.cfm&ContentID=2838. Accessed 16 February 2002

Driscoll, Charles T., Gregory B. Lawrence, Arthur J. Bulger, Thomas J. Butler, Christopher S. Cronan, Christopher Eagar, Kathleen F. Lambert, Gene E. Likens, John L. Stoddard, and Kathleen C. Weathers (2001). Acidic Deposition in the Northeastern United States: Sources and Inputs, Ecosystem Effects, and Management Strategies. *BioScience* 51 (3): 180-98

EC, and Transport Canada (1997). *Sustainable Transportation: Prepared in Connection with Canada's Participation at the Meeting of the United Nations Commission on Sustainable Development, April 1997.* Ottawa, Environment Canada and Transport Canada

EC (1998a). *Finding of Significant Contribution and Rulemaking for Certain States in the Ozone Transport Assessment Group Region for Purposes of Reducing Regional Transport of Ozone: Proposed Rule: Supporting Documentation.* Environment Canada, The Green Lane http://www.ec.gc.ca/air/ EPA_Comment/index_e.html. Accessed 21 January 2002

EC (1998b). *Canadian Passenger Transportation, National Environmental Indicator Series, SOE Bulletin No. 98-5.* Ottawa, Environment Canada, State of the Environment Reporting Program http:// www.ec.gc.ca/ind/English/Transpo/default.cfm. Accessed 28 May 2002

EC (1998c). Cars More Efficient, But Canadians Driving More. *Science and the Environment Bulletin,* June. Environment Canada http://www.ec.gc.ca/science/sandejune/PrintVersion/ print4_e.html. Accessed 28 May 2002

EC (2000). Cryosphere and Climate Change. *Science and the Environment Bulletin,* November. Environment Canada http://www.ec.gc.ca/science/sandenov00/article5_e.html. Accessed 17 February 2002

EC (2000a). *Clean Air.* Environment Canada, The Green Lane http://www.ec.gc.ca/air/ introduction_e.cfm. Accessed 21 January 2002

EC (2000b). *Canada-United States Air Quality Agreement 2000: Progress Report.* Environment Canada http://www.ec.gc.ca/special/aqa_2000_e.pdf. Accessed 14 February 2002

EC (2000c). Canada and the United States Reach a Draft Agreement to Reduce Transboundary Smog: Statement by the Hon. David Anderson, Minister of the Environment. *News Releases – Archives.* Environment Canada http://www.ec.gc.ca/press/001013_n_e.htm. Accessed 14 February 2002

EC (2001a). *Tracking Key Environmental Issues.* Ottawa, Environment Canada http:// www.ec.gc.ca/tkei/main_e.cfm. Accessed 28 May 2002

EC (2001b). Government of Canada Takes Further Action for Clean Air. *News Releases.* Environment Canada, The Green Lane http://www.ec.gc.ca/press/2001/010511_n_e.htm. Accessed 14 February 2002

EC (2001c). *Sustainable Transportation: The Canadian Context. Monograph No. 15.* Environment Canada. A Canadian Contribution to the Dialogue at the Ninth Session of the United Nations Commission on Sustainable Development, April 16 to 27, 2001 http://www.ec.gc.ca/agenda21/ 2001/pdfs/transport.pdf. Accessed 14 February 2002

EC (2002a) GHG Trends Information from Environment Canada's Greenhouse Gas Division. *Factsheet 3 - Transportation: 1990-1999.* Environment Canada, The Green Lane http:// www.ec.gc.ca/pdb/ghg/factsheets/fact3_e.cfm#anchor1.1. Accessed 29 May 2002

EC (2002b). Statement by Environment Minister David Anderson Following the Release of the US Proposal on Clean Air and Climate Change. *News Releases.* Environment Canada, The Green Lane http://www.ec.gc.ca/press/2002/020214_n_e.htm. Accessed 20 February 2002

EC (2002c). Proposed On-Road Vehicle and Engine Emission Regulations. *Backgrounder.* Environment Canada, The Green Lane http://www.ec.gc.ca/Press/2002/020404_b_e.htm. Accessed 29 May 2002

EIA (2001). *Emissions of Greenhouse Gases in the United States 2000.* Energy Information Administration, Office of Integrated Analysis and Forecasting, US Department of Energy ftp:// ftp.eia.doe.gov/pub/oiaf/1605/cdrom/pdf/ggrpt/057300.pdf. Accessed 21 January 2002

ELP (1992). *No Room to Breathe: Photochemical Smog and Ground-Level Ozone.* Air Resources Branch, Ministry of Environment, Lands and Parks, Government of British Columbia http:// wlapwww.gov.bc.ca/air/vehicle/nrtbpsag.html. Accessed 21 January 2002

EPA (1997a). *Regional Approaches to Improving Air Quality.* US Environmental Protection Agency, Office of Air Quality Planning and Standards http://www.epa.gov/oar/oaqps/airtrans/ groundoz.html. Accessed 21 January 2002

EPA (1997b). *Ground-Level Ozone (Smog) Information.* US Environmental Protection Agency, Region 1 http://www.epa.gov/region01/eco/ozone/. Accessed 21 January 2002

EPA (1997c). *EPA's Updated Air Quality Standards For Smog (Ozone) And Particulate Matter.* US Environmental Protection Agency, Office of Air and Radiation http://www.epa.gov/ttn/oarpg/naaqsfin/. Accessed 21 January 2002

EPA (1998). *1997 National Air Quality: Status and Trends.* US Environmental Protection Agency, Office of Air & Radiation, Office of Air Quality Planning & Standards http://www.epa.gov/oar/aqtrnd97/brochure/o3.html. Accessed 25 January 2002

EPA (1999a). *Indicators of the Environmental Impacts of Transportation, Updated Second Edition (EPA 230-R-001).* Washington DC, US Environmental Protection Agency

EPA (1999b). *Smog–Who Does it Hurt?* US Environmental Protection Agency, Office of Air & Radiation, Office of Air Quality Planning & Standards http://www.epa.gov/airnow/health/smog1.html. Accessed 21 January 2002

EPA (2000a). *Ozone Protection Regulations.* US Environmental Protection Agency, Global Programs Division http://www.epa.gov/docs/ozone/title6/usregs.html. Accessed 21 January 2002

EPA (2000b). *1998 National Air Quality and Emissions Trends Report.* US Environmental Protection Agency, Office of Air & Radiation, Office of Air Quality Planning & Standards http://www.epa.gov/oar/aqtrnd98/. Accessed 21 January 2002

EPA (2001a). *Latest Findings on National Air Quality: 2000 Status and Trends.* US Environmental Protection Agency, Office of Air Quality Planning and Standards http://www.epa.gov/oar/aqtrnd00/brochure/00brochure.pdf. Accessed 21 January 2002

EPA (2001b). *Our Built and Natural Environments: A Technical Review of the Interactions between Land Use, Transportation, and Environmental Quality.* Washington DC, US Environmental Protection Agency, Development Community and Environment Division http://www.smartgrowth.org/library/built.html. Accessed 21 January 2002

EPA (2001c). *Light-Duty Automotive Technology and Fuel Economy Trends 1975 Through 2001: Executive Summary.* US Environmental Protection Agency, Advanced Technology Division, Office of Transportation and Air Quality http://www.epa.gov/otaq/cert/mpg/fetrends/s01001.pdf. Accessed 21 January 2002

FOE (2001). *The SUV Info Link: Environmental Double Standards for Sport Utility Vehicles.* Friends of the Earth http://www.suv.org/environ.html. Accessed 21 January 2002

Gawthrop, Daniel (1999). *Vanishing Halo: Saving the Boreal Forest.* Vancouver/Toronto, Greystone Books

Government of Canada (1999). *Our Climate is Changing.* Global Climate Change http://www.climatechange.gc.ca/info/. Accessed 21 January 2002

Government of Canada (2000a). Chapter 4, Smog: Our Health at Risk. In *Report of the Commissioner of the Environment and Sustainable Development to the House of Commons.* Ottawa, Minister of Public Works and Government Services Canada

Government of Canada (2000b). *Climate Change 2000 Backgrounder: Actions to Date on Climate Change.* Natural Resources Canada http://www.nrcan.gc.ca/communications/cc2000/html/actions_to_date.html. Accessed 21 January 2002

Greenwire (2001a). Autos: Toyota Unveils New Fuel Cell Vehicle. *Greenwire* 082301 (12)

Greenwire (2001b). Autos: Ford Introduces Hydrogen Engine on Prototype. *Greenwire* 082201 (16)

Hancey, Caitlin (1999). *Particulate Matter, Ground-Level Ozone, and the Canada-Wide Standards Regulatory Process.* Sierra Club http://www.sierraclub.ca/national/climate/ground-level-ozone.html. Accessed 21 January 2002

Hu, Patricia S, and Jennifer R. Young (1999). *Summary of Travel Trends: 1995 Nationwide Personal Transportation Survey.* US Department of Transportation, Federal Highway Administration http://www-cta.ornl.gov/npts/1995/DOC/trends_report.pdf. Accessed 21 January 2002

IPCC (2001). *Climate Change 2001: The Scientific Basis. Summary for Policymakers. A Report of Working Group I of the Intergovernmental Panel on Climate Change.* Intergovernmental Panel on Climate Change http://www.ipcc.ch/pub/spm22-01.pdf. Accessed 20 February 2002

Kaiser, Jocelyn (2000). Panel Backs EPA and 'Six Cities' Study. *Science* 289 (5480): 711

Keoleian, Gregory (2000). The Automobile and Environmental Sustainability? In *State of the Great Lakes 1999 Annual Report, Office of the Great Lakes,* Office of the Great Lakes, Michigan Department of Environmental Quality

Lalonde, Michelle (2001). Vehicles, Environment Linked. *The Gazette*, 16 June, A1, A14

Mann, Michael E. (2000). Lessons for a New Millennium. *Science* 289 (5477): 253-4

Marland, G, T. A. Boden, and R. J. Andres (2001). Global, Regional, and National CO2 Emissions. In *Trends: A Compendium of Data on Global Climate Change.* Oak Ridge, Tenn., Carbon Dioxide Information Analysis Center, Oak Ridge National Laboratory, US Department of Energy

Mejia, Gerardo M., Jim McTaggart, Bruce Hicks, and Carlos Santos-Burgoa (1997). Ozone and Particulate Matter in the Atmosphere. In *Meeting the Challenges of Continental Pollutant Pathways: Volume II: Case Studies, Draft Interim Report submitted March 27 to the Secretariat of the Commission for Environmental Cooperation.* Montreal, Commission for Environmental Cooperation of North America

Miller, Paul J. (1993). Cutting Through the Smog: The 1990 Clean Air Act Amendments and a New Direction Towards Reducing Ozone Pollution. *Stanford Environmental Law Journal* 12:124-63

Miller, Peter, and John Moffet (1993). *The Price of Mobility: Uncovering the Hidden Costs of Transportation,* Natural Resources Defense Council

Miller, Paul J. (1999). Lifting the Veil of Smog: Why a Regional Ozone Strategy is Needed in the Eastern United States. *EM* April 1999:19-23

Montavalli, Jim, and Jennifer Bogo (2000). Vehicles: The Race to Build a Cleaner Car. *E. Magazine* 29 (August)

Munton, Don (1998). Dispelling the Myths of the Acid Rain Story. *Environment* 40 (6):27-33

NRC (1997). Vehicle Emissions. *National Research Council* XLVII (3): 10

NRCan (1999). *Canada's Emissions Outlook: An Update,* National Climate Change Process Analysis and Modeling Group, Natural Resources Canada http://www.nrcan.gc.ca/es/ceo/outlook.pdf. Accessed 29 May 2002.

NRCan (2001). Government of Canada Targets Largest Source of Greenhouse Gas Emissions – Transportation. *Press Release: 2001/44.* Natural Resources Canada http://www.nrcan.gc.ca/css/imb/hqlib/200144e.htm. Accessed 1 February 2002

NRTEE (1998). *Backgrounder: Greenhouse Gas Emissions from Urban Transportation.* Ottawa, National Round Table on the Environment and the Economy

O'Meara Sheehan, Molly (2001). Making Better Transportation Choices. In *State of the World 2001,* edited by L. Starke. New York, W.W. Norton and Company

OECD (1995). *Environmental Performance Reviews: Canada.* Paris, Organization for Economic Co-operation and Development

OECD (1996). *Environmental Performance Reviews: United States.* Paris, Organization for Economic Co-operation and Development

OECD (1998). *Environmental Indicators: Towards Sustainable Development.* Paris, Organization for Economic Co-operation and Development

Ohnsman, Alan (2002). US to Let Fuel Rules for Trucks Stand. *The Philadelphia Inquirer* http://inq.philly.com/content/inquirer/2002/01/19/business/SUV19.htm. Accessed 23 January 2002

OMA (2000). *The Illness Costs of Air Pollution: OMA Ground Level Ozone Position Paper.* Ontario Medical Association Web Link http://www.oma.org/phealth/smogmain.htm. Accessed 21 January 2002

Prouty, Christopher (2000). *How Successful has the CAFE Standard been in Curtailing Carbon Dioxide Emitted from Automobiles?* Colby College http://www.colby.edu/personal/t/thtieten/air-carbon.html. Accessed 21 January 2002.

Sandalow, David B., and Ian A. Bowles (2001). Fundamentals of Treaty-Making on Climate Change. *Science* 292 (5523): 1839-40

Schingh, Marie, Érik Brunet, and Patrick Gosselin (2000). *Canadian New Light-Duty Vehicles: Trends in Fuel Consumption and Characteristics (1988-1998).* Transportation Energy Use Division, Office of Energy Efficiency, Natural Resources Canada http://oee.nrcan.gc.ca/english/programs/Doc5e.cfm#03. Accessed 13 February 2002

Seelye, Katharine Q. (2001). EPA to Issue Air Rules to Protect Park Vistas. *The New York Times* 22 June

Statistics Canada (2000). *Human Activity and the Environment 2000.* Ottawa, Minister of Industry

US Department of State (2002). *Bush Announces Climate Change, Clean Air Initiatives.* US Department of State, International Information Programs http://usinfo.state.gov/topical/global/climate/02021403.htm. Accessed 21 February 2002

USGCRP (2000). *Climate Change Impacts on the United States. The Potential Consequences of Climate Variability and Change.* US Global Change Research Program, National Assessment Synthesis Team http://www.usgcrp.gov/usgcrp/Library/nationalassessment/overview.htm. Accessed 17 February 2002

Biodiversity

3

Biodiversity

Biodiversity refers to the variety of ecosystems, species, and genes. As part of the North American continent, Canada and the United States contain a large number of different ecosystem types, with biodiversity increasing along a north-south gradient (CEC 1997). The United States has a broader array of ecosystems than any other nation (Stein, Kunter, and Adams 2000).

The World Wildlife Fund (WWF) reports that about half of North America's most diverse ecoregions are now severely degraded (Ricketts, Taylor, and others 1997). Ecosystem degradation and loss leads to the decline in plant and animal diversity. Figure 15 depicts one interpretation of the most ecologically significant and most threatened regions on the North American continent (Hoth 2001). Produced under the auspices of the Commission for Environmental Cooperation of North America, it includes Mexico as part of the NAFTA (North American Free Trade Agreement) region, and shows the obvious transboundary nature of ecosys-

Figure 15

North America's most ecologically important and threatened regions.

Source: CEC 2001a

North America's Most Ecologically Important and Threatened Regions

Regions

1. Arctic Tundra/Archipelago
2. Arctic Coastal Tundra/North Slope
3. Baja to Bering: Gulf of California Coastal/Marine Systems
4. Yukon/Yellowstone/Sierra Madre Corridor
5. Shortgrass Prairie/Chihuahuan Desert Corridor
6. Northern Forests/Softwood Shield
7. Great Lakes/St. Lawrence Lowlands
8. Greater Gulf of Maine/Coastal/Marine System (Newfoundland to New England)
9. Chesapeake Bay
10. Southern Appalachians
11. Rio Bravo/Laguna Madre Corridor
12. Transverse Neo-volcanic Belt
13. Maya Reef and Southern Florida Coastal/Marine Systems
14. "Selva Maya" Tropical Dry and Humid Forests

Areas of Ecological Threat

Areas of Ecological Importance

Most Ecologically Important and Threatened Regions

tems. The prairie is thought to be North America's most endangered ecosystem. For example, some 55-prairie grassland wildlife species are now listed under the US Endangered Species Act (see Box 10, next page) as either threatened or endangered (Bachand 2001).

According to Canada's endangered species list, as of May 2001, a total of 380 species were at risk of imminent or eventual extinction (endangered, threatened, or of special concern) while in the United States, 1,231 species were listed as endangered or threatened under the US Endangered Species Act (ESA) (see Box 10, next page) (COSEWIC 2001; Alonso, Dallmeier, and others 2001). Species that depend on freshwater habitat appear to be most at risk. Almost one-third of the world's freshwater mussel species live

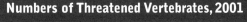

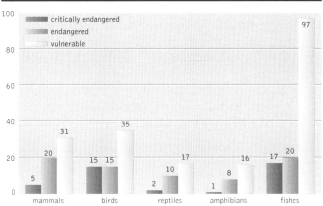

extinction in North America as a whole (see Figure 16).

To safeguard biological diversity, North America has increasingly set aside protected areas. According to The World Conservation Union (IUCN) categories, 11 percent of North America's land area was protected in Classes I–V in 2001 (see Table 1) (UNDP, UNEP, World Bank,

Figure 16
Numbers of threatened vertebrates, 2001.

Source: UNEP-WCMC 2001a

Table 1: Protected Area by IUCN Categories I-V

	Number	Area (000 ha)	Percent of Land Area	No. of Areas at least:		Marine-Protected Areas (IUCN Categories I-VI) Number Area**			Biosphere Reserves		World Heritage Sites		Wetlands of International Importance	
				100,000	1m	Total	Littoral	Marine	Number	Area**	Sites	Area**	Number	Area**
Canada	3,083	90,702	9.1	102	20	139	102	76	8	1,512	8*	10,664	36	13,051
United States	3,063	123,120	13.1	153	26	386	255	187	44	20,838	12*	9,741	17	1,178
North America	6,146	213,822	11.1	255	46	525	357	263	52	22,350	18	20,405	53	14,229

Note: *Includes sites shared by two or more neighboring countries, **Area (000 ha)
Source: UNDP, UNEP, World Bank, and WRI 2000

in the United States, for example, but 70 percent of these are at risk. Particularly high concentrations of imperiled species are found in Hawaii, California, the southern Appalachians, and Florida (Stein 2001). Some 309 vertebrate species are considered threatened with

and WRI 2000). By 2002, 13.9 percent was protected in Classes 1–VI, covering 267.4 million ha (UNEP–WCMC 2001b). IUCN categories are defined at http://www.unep-wcmc.org/protected_areas/categories/index.html.

Box 10: The US Endangered Species Act

The Endangered Species Act (ESA) of 1973 provides for the conservation of both vertebrate and invertebrate species listed as either 'endangered' or 'threatened' according to assessments of the risk of their extinction throughout all or a significant portion of their range, as well as the conservation of the ecosystems on which they depend. An individual or organization may petition to have a species considered for listing as endangered or threatened under the Act. Once a species is listed, powerful legal tools are available to protect both it and its habitat (Buck, Corn, and others 2001; NOAA 2001). A recovery plan is prepared, which includes designating critical habitat necessary for the continued survival of the species (NOAA 2001; O'Loughlin 2001).

The ESA is considered by some to be the most comprehensive of US Environmental laws, but it has also been one of the most controversial (O'Loughlin 2001). Since threatened species often flag broader issues of resource scarcity and altered ecosystems, in recent years the ESA has been the subject of debate about allocating scarce or diminishing lands or resources in the face of pressures on species' habitats from growing human populations and economies. Salmon and spotted owls in the Pacific Northwest, both highlighted elsewhere in this report, are examples of resource debates in which ESA-listed species were part of larger economic issues (Buck, Corn, and others 2001). Debate also centers on the listing process and how to determine priorities (Stein 2001).

Eleven species have been removed from the list since 1973, and less than 10 percent of listed species have exhibited improvement in status in that time (O'Loughlin 2001). Litigation and budgetary constraints have made the listing process cumbersome and slow in recent years. During 2000, most of the budget dedicated to listing newly endangered species was used in fighting litigation. But in August 2001, an agreement in principle was announced between the Fish and Wildlife Service and a coalition of ENGOs that begins to address litigation and budget concerns so as to increase protection for dozens of rare species and their habitat (Buck, Corn, and others 2001). The ENGOs agreed to allow more time to designate habitat for eight protected species in compliance with court orders, in return for which the government would accelerate the process for listing 29 of the more than 200 species still under consideration (Schrope 2001).

Canada has signed and ratified the Convention on Biological Diversity (CBD) and continues to work toward introducing a federal Species at Risk Act (SARA), while the United States is not yet party to the CBD, but has a strong Endangered Species Act (ESA). The latter has been used effectively by NGOs to protect substantial areas of habitat for threatened species (see the forestry section in this report and Box 10).

As in other parts of the world, habitat destruction and degradation is the most pervasive threat to biodiversity (Wilcove, Rothstein, and others 2000). For many species, human disturbance of habitat can lead to their demise. But disturbance of some habitat and its conversion to human uses can also favor some species. Canada geese, for example, have adapted to golf courses and urban parks and their numbers have increased significantly over the past

two decades. In such cases, species abundance does not equate with biodiversity, as some adaptable species compete with and often supplant native ones (Martin 2001).

North American wetlands have high biological productivity, providing critical habitats for many species and essential ecological services such as absorbing floodwaters and protecting water quality by filtering pollutants (see Box 11) (Schmid 2000). Wetland protection is therefore a priority issue for biodiversity conservation in North America.

Bioinvasion, now thought to be the second-gravest threat to global biodiversity, is another priority issue for North America. Introduced non-native species can pose threats to domestic species through predation, competition, parasitism, and hybridization. Increased globalization and trade has heightened the risk of invasive species entering and changing the region's ecosystems and the biodiversity they harbor.

Wetlands

Wetlands in North America are generally understood to be marshes, swamps, bogs, and similar transition zones between dry land and deep

Box 11: Wetland Services

Like rain forests and coral reefs, wetlands are among the most biologically productive natural ecosystems in the world, providing habitat and the organisms that form the base of the food web to a wide variety of fish, plants, and wildlife, including many rare and endangered species. Wetlands also provide many other services and benefits: they filter and cleanse the water that passes through them; by absorbing water from snow melt, which recharges the water table for times of drought, wetlands reduce the risks of flooding, shoreline erosion, and sedimentation; and they are important areas for recreation, education, and research (Pembina Institute n.d.; EPA 2001).

The microbes, plants, and wildlife in wetlands also form part of global water, nitrogen, and sulphur cycles. Furthermore, wetlands may moderate global climate conditions by storing carbon within their plant communities and soil instead of releasing it to the atmosphere as carbon dioxide (EPA 2001).

water (EPA 1997; EC 1999). The different ecological conditions found from the Arctic to the tropics create a great diversity of wetland types (Cox and Cintron 1997). Wetlands provide food and habitat for about one-third of bird species in the United States and although the percentage is unknown for Canada, more than 200 bird species, including 45 species of waterfowl, rely in wetlands in Canada. They are also home to some 5,000 plant species and 190 species of amphibians in the United States and 50 species of mammals and 155 species of birds (CEQ 1997; NRC 2000). Thirty-nine percent of North America's plant species depend on wetlands (Revenga, Brunner, and others 2000). Furthermore, about a third of

Table 2: Wetlands in North America			
	Wetland Area (1000 ha)	Percent of National Land Area	Percent of North American Wetlands
Canada	153,000	16	58
United States	111,104	12	42
North America	264,104	–	–

(Sources: *Dahl 1990; Rubec and Thibault 1998; Rubec 2000; Wilen 1999*)

North America's threatened and endangered species depend on wetlands (CEQ 1997; NRC 2000).

North America contains a large percentage of the world's wetlands, with Canada holding about 24 percent, accounting for about 16 percent of its landscape (NRC 2000; Rubec 2000). Wetlands make up more than five percent of the total US area and cover about 111 million ha. Of this amount, almost 69 million ha are found in Alaska, while 42.2 million hectares of wetlands are found in almost a third of the 2,123 watersheds located in the conterminous 48 states (Dahl 1990; USDA 2000a). An estimated 80 percent (33.1 million ha) are located on non-federal rural land (Brady and Flather 1994). Wetlands cover about 264 million ha of North America's land area (see Table 2 and Figure 17).

Prior to the 1970s, North America's wetlands were perceived as wastelands, nuisance areas, and the breeding grounds of pests. Government programs encouraged wetland drainage and filling to allow conversion to agriculture, settlements, and industrial sites (EPA 1997). As a result, North America, excluding Alaska and Canada's northern regions, lost over half of its original wetland habitat (EC 1999; Bryer, Maybury, and others 2000). Agricultural expansion was responsible for between 85 and 87 percent of the losses (NCSU 1998; NRC 2000).

Since the 1980s, wetland losses in North America have slowed considerably. Recognition of their ecological services (see Box 11), changes in agricultural policies, particularly good hydrological conditions, and cooperative efforts among the North American countries to conserve wetlands for waterfowl were factors in these achievements (NAWMP 1998).

In the mid-1980s, wetlands in the lower 48 states covered an area the size of California, which represents a third of Canada's wetland area (EPA 1997). Between 1974 and 1983, net wetland conversion dropped to about 117,359 ha per year and in the 10 years between 1982 and 1992, it further dropped to 28,328–36,422 ha per year (USDA 2000a). A net of 266,820 ha of wetlands was still lost in the United Sates between 1986 and 1997, although this represents an 80 percent reduction from the previous decade. During this period,

Figure 17
Map of North America's wetlands.

Source: USDA 1997

Map of North America's Wetlands

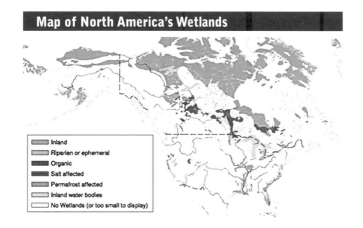

- Inland
- Riparian or ephemeral
- Organic
- Salt affected
- Permafrost affected
- Inland water bodies
- No Wetlands (or too small to display)

a wide mix of land use change accounted for losses, with urban development responsible for 30 percent, agriculture for 26 percent, silviculture for 23 percent and rural development for 21 percent (American Rivers 2000).

To make up for wetland losses, both countries endorsed goals of 'no net loss' and instituted mitigation policies that provided incentives to create marshes or to replace those built over. In 1980, the US revised the 1972 Clean Water Act to include a mitigation policy, and in 1997, Canada launched its Wetland Mitigation and Compensation Project (Kaiser 2001; WCC 2001). These efforts have had mixed results, while cooperative efforts to conserve wetland habitat for waterfowl have had notable success (see Box 12. next page).

Since 1985, federal and provincial/state governments adopted wetland conservation and management policies. Over 70 percent of Canada's wetland resources are now covered by federal and provincial wetland policies and about 15 states regulate inland wetlands (NRC 2000; Schmid 2000). US federal subsidies that allowed wetlands to be converted to agriculture ceased in 1985 through the wetland conservation provisions of the Food Security Act, and a new Wetland Plan was issued in 1993 to make wetland regulation more fair, flexible, and effective (EPA 1999; USDA 2000a; Schmid 2000). The Wetlands Reserve Program, set up under the Farm Bill in 1996, is a voluntary program offering

landowners the opportunity and government support to protect, restore, and enhance wetlands on their property. By 1999, fully 313,257 ha had been enrolled (TPL 1999, NRCS 2001).

At the global level, the Ramsar Convention on Wetlands of International Importance was signed in 1971, providing a farsighted framework for national and international action to conserve wetlands and use

their resources wisely (The Ramsar Convention 2000; Smart 1997). It is the only international convention addressing wetlands and both countries are Contracting Parties (Cox and Cintron 1997). The Convention establishes a List of Wetlands of International Importance. These sites, of which there are 53 in North America, act like migratory bird sanctuaries (Canada: 36, US: 117) (The Ramsar Convention 2000).

Although past US government authority over wetlands has been fragmented and inconsistent, plans for the restoration of the Florida

Box 12: Bilateral Cooperation, Wetlands and Waterfowl

For at least part of the year, North America's migratory waterfowl use coastal and inland wetlands as feeding, breeding, resting, and nesting grounds, benefiting from the diversity of food organisms (Bacon 1997). Discrete wetlands are used as 'stepping stones' for migratory waterfowl, with the loss of a vital link in the chain threatening the very survival of some species (Davidson 1999). With the extensive wetland loss over the years from the mid-1950s to the mid-1970s, waterfowl species were deprived of crucial habitat, and by the mid-1980s there had been alarming decreases in the populations of some key species compared to 1970s levels (EC 1998a).

Waterfowl have always been the most economically important migratory species of bird in North America. Nature tourism and hunter-related activities have brought substantial economic returns:

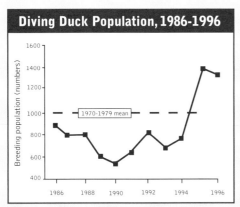

Figure 18 *Source: AAFC 2000*

annually, more than US $20 billion in economic activity is generated by the more than 60 million people who watch migratory birds and the 3.2 million who hunt waterfowl (NAWMP 1998). Because of waterfowl's importance to hunters, their declines drew notable attention to the issue of wetland loss. Ducks Unlimited, a private organization originally established to preserve waterfowl for hunters, initiated a cooperative program among their branches in Canada, the United States, and Mexico in the 1990s that helped to restore, protect, or enhance over 3.8 million ha of wetlands (DU 2000).

Canada and the United States signed the North American Waterfowl Management Plan (NAWMP) in 1986, joined by Mexico in 1994. NAWMP is an innovative joint venture partnership among several levels of government, NGOs, the private sector, and landowners. The aim was to restore waterfowl populations to the 1970s benchmark levels (a breeding population of 62 million ducks, and winter populations of 6 million geese and 152,000 swans) through habitat protection, restoration, and enhancement (EC 1998a). During the 1988–1993 period, over 850,000 ha of wetland and associated upland habitat were protected through NAWAMP in Canada alone (NRC 2000). The Plan's vision was expanded in 1998 in a move away from restoring habitat for one particular group of animals to include biologically based planning to support other wetland species and ecological processes; integrated management of conservation, economic, and social programs; and collaborative efforts to find sustainable uses of landscapes (NAWMP 1998). As of April 1995, over a million ha of wetland habitat have been restored or enhanced and nearly 810,000 ha have been protected in the three countries (Cox and Cintron 1997).

As a result of these and other conservation efforts, there has been a marked rebound in most populations of duck, geese, and swans. Figure 18 shows the rapid recovery of diving duck populations after 1993. The rebuilding of migratory waterfowl populations since the 1980s is considered by some to be one of the most successful aquatic ecosystem conservation efforts in North America and a model of international conservation (Agardy, Hanson, and others 1999; Davidson 1999).

Everglades is testimony to the potential success of combined efforts among many levels of government, business, and ENGOs (see Box 13) (Schmid 2000; UNDP, UNEP, World Bank, and WRI 2000).

As yet, the Canadian government does not track or report on the status of its wetland resources (Rubec 2000). On the other hand, in 1992, Canada was the first nation to adopt a Federal Policy on Wetland Conservation, outlining guiding principles and seven key strategies to implement them. It commits the federal government to

---

Box 13: Restoration of the Florida Everglades

The Everglades is the central part of a 23,000 km² watershed covering the lower third of Florida (see Figure 19). With both fresh and salt water, it harbors a large variety of ecosystems, including rivers and lakes, sawgrass marshes, prairies, tropical hardwood forests, mangrove swamps, pine rocklands,

Map of the Florida Everglades

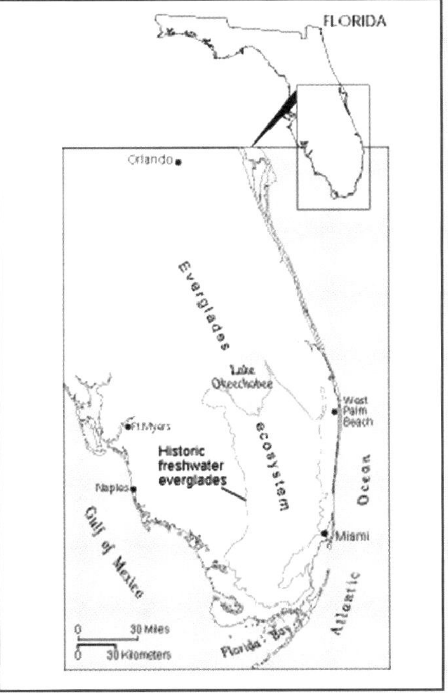

Figure 19 *Source: USGS 2001a*

and offshore coral reefs (NRDC 2000). Viewed as 'swampland' and an impediment to urban and agricultural development in the early part of last century, large tracts were drained and water supplies reconfigured. Protected from flooding by levees and canals, the process accelerated over the past 30 years, and South Florida became home to 6 million people along the Miami–Palm Beach corridor and an important sugarcane, fruit- and vegetable-producing region (UNDP, UNEP, World Bank, and WRI 2000).

Originally stretching over 11,650 km², nearly half of the Everglades' wetlands have succumbed to development and to ecosystem destruction from exotic species and polluted runoff from sugarcane fields and other agricultural activity. This has led to less freshwater flowing to the coast, disrupted salinity levels, and altered the ecosystem's natural capacity to store and release water. The health of the Everglades deteriorated most rapidly in the past two decades with seagrass dieoffs, the invasion of non-native species, nutrient contamination, large algal blooms in Florida Bay, and declines in fishing harvests and in some

bird populations. The region's wading bird population, for example, has declined by 90 percent over the past two decades (NRDC 2000; UNDP, UNEP, World Bank, and WRI 2000).

Regional efforts to address the problems began in the early 1980s, but it took until 1998 for all parties—the sugar industry, environmentalists, real estate developers, and American Indian tribes—to come together to support a comprehensive plan to restore and preserve south Florida's natural ecosystem while enhancing water supplies and maintaining flood protection. Developed by the Army Corps of Engineers, it is the world's most ambitious and extensive wetlands restoration effort, costing the federal government US $7.8 billion and taking over 20 years to complete (Alvarez 2000; Army Corps of Engineers 2000; UNDP, UNEP, World Bank, and WRI 2000).

'no net loss of wetland functions' on federal lands, a policy that is being complemented by conservation strategies in the provinces. Wetlands ecosystems make up about 17 percent of Canada's national parks and all together, about 10 percent are excluded from development (EC 1998b; Rubec and Thibeault 1998).

North America's abatement in wetland loss is a considerable achievement, but the fact remains that wetlands are still being lost to development. Changing conditions such as population growth, expan-

Bioinvasion

Bioinvasion (see Box 14) is now thought to be the second-gravest threat to global biodiversity, next to habitat destruction and degradation (CEC 2000a).

Since the 1970s, the largest increases in invasive aliens have been in insect pests and aquatic organisms found in ballast water. Seven and a half million litres of ballast water arrive in the United States every hour. Pacific coastal areas, the eastern part of the Great Lakes, parts of the Northeast, Florida, and Hawaii

---

Box 14: Bioinvasion

Bioinvasion refers to the influx of alien invasive species, or species occurring outside their natural ranges, through direct or indirect assistance by humans. Alien species are considered to be invasive when they become established in natural or semi-natural ecosystems or habitat, are agents of change, and threaten native biological diversity. Alien invasive species include bacteria, viruses, fungi, insects, mollusks, plants, fish, mammals, and birds (IUCN 2001).

Species that become invasive may be introduced either intentionally or unintentionally through pathways (or vectors) that include transportation (by water, land, and air; in the goods themselves; in dunnage, packing materials or containers; and in or on ships, planes, trains, trucks or cars). Agriculture, horticulture and plant nursery stock, the aquaculture industry, the live food fish industry, baitfish, and the aquarium pet trades are major sources (Carlton 2001). Where there are no natural predators, invasive species can come to dominate ecosystems, and can alter the composition and structure of food webs, nutrient cycling, fire cycles, and hydrology and energy budgets, threatening agricultural productivity and other industries dependent on living resources (Westbrooks and Gregg 2000; Alonso, Dallmeier, and others 2001).

---

sion of agricultural production, and economic growth, as well as changes in hydrological conditions linked to climate change may affect wetland habitat and the biodiversity it shelters (NAWMP 1998). Conservation efforts will need to remain flexible and be updated regularly to continue to sustain wetland habitats.

are entry points for high numbers of species. In San Francisco Bay, for example, a new introduction was established every 15 weeks between 1961 and 1995 (Carlton 2001). Competition or predation by non-native species imperils nearly half of the species listed as threatened or endangered under the US Endangered Species Act (Wilcove,

Rothstein, and others 1998). In Canada, alien species have been involved in causing risk to about 25 percent of endangered, 31 percent of threatened, and 16 percent of species of special concern (Lee 2001).

There is no scientific consensus on the characteristics that make a species a successful invader, but repeated and widespread introduction is likely to boost the ability of a species to take hold (Enserink 1999). Opportunities for invasives to establish themselves have also been enhanced due to increases in land disturbance from farming; highway and utility rights-of-way; clearing land for settlements and recreation areas such as golf courses; and constructing ponds, reservoirs, and lakes. Human population growth has increased recreational and commercial activity and the demand for food and fiber, which also opens the way to invasive species (Westbrooks 1998). And increased trade has accelerated the rate of exotic introductions.

The zebra mussel (*Dreissena polymorpha*), a mollusk the size of a thumbnail, has been one of North America's most problematic invasives. It probably first arrived in North America in the ballast water of cargo ships from the Black Sea in the late 1980s. In the past decade, it has spread through all major North American river systems and in 2002, it will have cost some US $5 billion in damage to shipping and power plants alone (PCAST 1998; Westbrooks and Gregg 2000). The

sea lamprey, another species that invaded the Great Lakes, is responsible for the collapse of lake trout and other native Great Lakes fisheries. North America spends about US

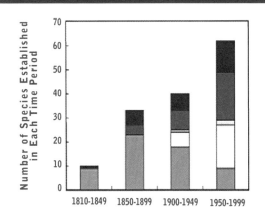

Exotic Species Established in the Great Lakes

Plants ☐ Algae ☐ Disease Pathogens & Parasites ■ Invertebrates ■ Fishes

$13 million a year trying to control it (Alonso, Dallmeier, and others 2001). Despite requirements that ships exchange ballast water at sea, the influx of new species into the Great Lakes continues (see Figure 20) and is considered to be the most serious threat to the integrity of the Great Lakes ecosystem (GLFC 2000).

A few more examples serve to illustrate the various kinds of bioinvasions and the damage they can cause. The wood-boring Asian longhorned beetle (*Anaplophora giabripennis*), which probably arrived in North America in packing crates from China, was found consuming hardwood trees in New York City in 1996 and in Chicago in 1998. Left alone, the spread of infestation would have costly repercussions (Westbrooks and

Figure 20
Number of exotic species established in the Great Lakes.

Source: H. John Heinz III Center, 2001.

Purple loosestrife, (*Lythrum salicaria)*, which was introduced from Europe in the mid-1800s as a garden ornamental, has been spreading in North America at a rate of 115,000 ha a year, invading wetland habitats where it takes over from native plants and deprives waterfowl and other species of food sources. It is now migrating onto agricultural lands. After unsuccessful attempts to eradicate it by burning, mowing, and flooding, biological control programs, which use natural enemies to control pests, have been introduced. Since 1992, a coordinated program brought in four species of European insects that should significantly reduce its abundance in wetland habitat (Haber 1996; DU Canada 1998; Pimentel, Bach, and others 1999). When non-indigenous aquatic weeds such as purple loosestrife, Eurasian water milfoil, and hydrilla replace native species, they establish dense colonies that can impair navigation, water-based recreation, and flood control; degrade water quality and wildlife habitat; hasten the filling of lakes and reservoirs; and depress property values (Haber 1996; ANS Task Force 2000).

Gregg 2000). A wide variety of exotic tree pests arrive on untreated wooden pallets, crating, bracing, and other solid wood packing materials. Quarantines are established to avoid transporting infested trees and branches and to prevent the further spread of insect pests. Nearly all of the quarantine-significant tree pests found by US port inspectors are associated with such packing materials. Early detection of infestations and rapid treatment are crucial to their successful eradication (USDA 1999; USDA 2000b).

The booming exotic reptile trade is another vehicle for exotic introductions. African ticks have been known to arrive this way and are

carriers of heartwater, a disease highly lethal to cattle, deer, sheep, and goats (Simberloff and Schmitz 1999). The US Department of Agriculture warns that with increased trade and movement of animals in a globalized market, heartwater may present a significant threat to the US livestock industry (APHIS 1997).

Invasive aquatic species are particularly threatening to wetland and freshwater ecosystems (see Box 15). Some can also pose serious health risks, as in the case of human cholera bacteria found in ballast tanks and in oyster and finfish samples in Mobile, Alabama in 1991 (ANS Task Force 2000). Others undermine important wetland habitats, as did the Nutria, a beaver-like animal introduced from South America (see Box 16). Alien aquatic species are expected to contribute to the extinction of native freshwater species in North America at a rate of 4 percent over the next century (Ricciardi and Rasmussen 1999).

The high economic costs of damage caused by bioinvasions in North America—to agriculture and other industries, human health and the costs of control—is causing increasing concern. It has been estimated that by 1998, about a quarter of the annual US agricultural GNP was lost to damage from, and control of, invasive species (PCAST 1998).

Responses to the challenge of invasive species include legislation, policies, plans, and programs that focus on preventing the invasion of new species and the eradication or control of established invasives. Biological control, which involves importing a predator organism to feed on the invasive species, is increasingly being used to control invasives. It is usually more specific to the target than pesticides or herbicides. Because of its potential risk to native species and ecosystem harmless, a policy that was proposed by the US Fish and Wildlife Service in 1970 but opposed by many pet stores and nurseries (Kaiser 1999). Today, concerns are that such a policy could alienate trading partners (Licking 1999).

Over the years, isolated alarms led to a patchwork of federal and state laws and agencies to regulate intro-

---

Box 16: The Nutria

The nutria (*Myocastor coypus*) is a large semi-aquatic rodent native to South America. It was introduced into many areas of the world, including North America, primarily to be farmed for its fur. It was first brought to the state of Louisiana between the late 1800s and early 1900s, and released when the price of pelts fell and farms failed. Intentionally introduced into other southeastern states to control undesirable vegetation, or released accidentally, it has established widespread and localized populations in many states (Le Blanc n.d.; Westbrooks and Gregg 2000). Prolific breeders, Maryland's nutria population increased from 150 in 1968 to about 50,000 today (MPT 2001).

The nutria feeds only on plants, digging into wetland soils to eat the soft parts, which kills the vegetation, contributes to erosion, and results in loss of coastal land and wetlands (USGS 2001b). These animals have devastated wetland habitat for rare native species such as the bald eagle and eliminated crab and oyster nurseries. Furthermore, their digging has allowed salt water to invade swamps and wetlands, damaging vegetation and aggravating coastal erosion (Westbrooks and Gregg 2000). Although their pelts are economically valuable—the harvest between 1977 and 1984 was worth $7.3 million—their burrowing activity causes economic losses by undermining flood control structures, fish farming levees, buildings, boat docks, and roads. They graze on sugarcane, rice, and other food crops and destroy gardens and golf courses (Le Blanc n.d.). To provide more incentives for trappers to harvest more nutria, Louisiana has attempted to increase the demand for nutria pelts and to allow its meat to be processed for food (USGS 2001b).

---

functions, new rules were introduced under Canada's 2000 Plant Protection Act calling for environmental assessments before the release of predatory insects (Knight 2001).

Prevention is the best and cheapest approach to the problem of bioinvasions. Current policies ban the import of organisms that are known to be harmful. Some ecologists would prefer that all plants and animals be denied entry until proven ductions (Simberloff 1996). The 1990 US National Invasive Species Act was reauthorized and expanded in 1996 to initiate a voluntary open-ocean exchange program for ballast water with mandatory reporting requirements, but its effectiveness is unproven to date (Carlson 2001). With the recognition that threats posed by bioinvasions are broad and pervasive, an executive order in February 1999 created a high-level

Box 17: Bilateral and International Cooperation

The emerging InterAmerican Biodiversity Information Network (IABIN) is prototyping an invasive species information exchange, and under the auspices of the Commission for Environmental Cooperation of North America (CEC), it works with the North American Biodiversity Information Network (NABIN) to establish a framework to share data on invasive species spread, management, taxonomy, and impacts (CEC 2000b).

The CEC has also initiated a project called Closing the Pathways of Aquatic Invasive Species across North America to protect marine and aquatic ecosystems in Canada, Mexico, and the United States from the effects of aquatic invasive species. It is developing a coordinated, multinational prevention and control campaign to help eliminate the pathways through which invasive species are introduced to the region's coastal and fresh waters. The project will also examine pathways between major drainage basins (CEC 2001).

In another cooperative effort to stem bioinvasions, the North American Plant Protection Organization (NAPPO), a regional body of the International Plant Protection Convention, coordinates the efforts among Canada, the United States, and Mexico to protect their plant resources from the entry, establishment, and spread of regulated plant pests, while facilitating intra/interregional trade (NAPPO 2002). Canada and the United States also cooperate in International Joint Commission efforts related to aquatic invasive species in the Great Lakes.

US Council to devise a management plan to combat alien invasives (Kaiser 1999).

Both countries have developed monitoring plans and information systems to help control exotic introductions (Haber 1996; Kaiser 1999). For example, Canada has begun an Invasive Plants of Canada (IPCAN) monitoring project (Haber 1996) and the US Government's Invasive Species Council has developed an online information system (NAL 2000).

In recent years, bioinvasions have increased with the growth in volume of international trade and flow of people (Wilcove, Rothstein, and others 1998). Since January 1999, more than 50 alien pests, which could cause significant damage to forest, agricultural, and horticultural crops, have been intercepted at Canadian ports of entry (CFIA 2000). As the North American countries trade more with each other as well as countries with climates and habitats similar to those on this continent, new invasions are expected. At the same time, the growing commerce within North America strengthens the likelihood that one country's established invaders will spread to the others (Westbrooks and Gregg 2000). Canada and the United States increasingly work together and in international cooperative efforts to help to stem the tide of bioinvasions (see Box 17).

Global climate change is likely to increase the risks associated with invasive species. Warmer conditions may open up ecosystems that were once inhospitable to intruders, longer growing seasons may allow more plants to set seed, and rising CO_2 levels could boost the speed with which some invasive plants grow (Holmes 1998). The ability of exotic annual grasses to invade the deserts of western North America may be enhanced, for example, which could not only reduce biodiversity and alter ecosystem function, but also accelerate the fire cycle (Smith, Huxman, and others 2000).

The threats posed by the introduction of exotic species in the wake of globalization illustrates that increased cooperation is required to adequately conserve the diversity of shared biological resources. Wider application of lessons learned as well as new strategies and more public understanding of why biodiversity is important are needed, and North American and global cooperation is essential to stem the tide of bioinvasions and the damage they cause.

References

AAFC (2000). *The Health of Our Water: Toward Sustainable Agriculture in Canada.* Agriculture and Agri-Food Canada, Research Branch http://res2.agr.ca/research-recherche/science/Healthy_Water/e07d.html. Accessed 4 February 2002

Agardy, Tundi Spring, Arthur J. Hanson, Gil Salcido, and Ramón Pérez (1999). *Securing the Continent's Biological Wealth: Towards Effective Biodiversity Conservation in North America, Working Draft of a Status Report for Stakeholder Input.* Montreal, Commission for Environmental Cooperation of North America

Alonso, A., F. Dallmeier, E. Granek, and P. Raven (2001). *Biodiversity: Connecting with the Tapestry of Life.* Washington, D.C., Smithsonian Institution/Monitoring and Assessment of Biodiversity Program and President's Committee of Advisors on Science and Technology

Alvarez, Lizette (2000). *Everglades: Congress Puts Finishing Touches on Massive Restoration Bill.* New York Times News Service http://www.naplesnews.com/00/11/naples/d541553a.htm. Accessed 28 January 2002

American Rivers (2000). *Losing Wetlands.* American Rivers: Restore, Protect, Enjoy http://www.amrivers.org/flood/losingwetlands.htm. Accessed 28 January 2002

ANS Task Force (2000). *What are Aquatic Nuisance Species and Their Impacts.* Aquatic Nuisance Species Task Force of the US Fish and Wildlife Service http://www.anstaskforce.gov/ansimpact.htm. Accessed 28 January 2002

APHIS (1997). *Heartwater.* US Department of Agriculture, Animal and Plant Health Inspection Services, Veterinary Services http://www.aphis.usda.gov/oa/pubs/fsheartw.html. Accessed 29 January 2002

Army Corps of Engineers (2000). *Corps Facts: Florida Everglades.* US Army Corps of Engineers, Office of the Chief of Engineers http://www.hq.usace.army.mil/cepa/pubs/Everglades.htm. Accessed 28 January 2002

Bachand, Richard R. (2001). *The American Prairie: Going, Going, Gone? A Status Report on the American Prairie.* National Wildlife Federation http://www.nwf.org/grasslands/pdfs/americanprairie.pdf. Accessed 24 January 2002

Bacon, Peter R. (1997). Chapter One: Wetlands and Biodiversity. In *Wetlands, Biodiversity and the Ramsar Convention: the Role of the Convention on Wetlands in the Conservation and Wise Use of Biodiversity*, edited by A. J. Hails. Gland, Switzerland, Ramsar Convention Bureau, http://www.ramsar.org/lib_bio_1.htm. Accessed 29 January 2002

Brady, Stephen J., and Curtis H. Flather (1994). Changes in Wetland on Non-Federal Rural Land of the Conterminous of the United States from 1982 to 1987. *Environmental Management* 18 (5):693-705

Bryer, Mark T., Kathleen Maybury, Jonathan S. Adams, and Dennis H. Grossman (2000). More Than the Sum of the Parts: Diversity and Status of Ecological Systems. In *Precious Heritage: The Status of Biodiversity in the United States*, edited by B. A. Stein, L. S. Kutner and J. S. Adams. New York, Oxford University Press

Buck, Eugene H., M. Lynne Corn, and Pamela Baldwin (2001). *IB10072: Endangered Species: Difficult Choices.* CRS Issue Brief for Congress, National Council for Science and the Environment http://cnie.org/NLE/CRSreports/Biodiversity/biodv-1.cfm#_1_1. Accessed 23 January 2002

Carlton, James T. (2001). *Introduced Species in US Coastal Waters: Environmental Impacts and Management Priorities.* Prepared for the Pew Oceans Commission http://www.pewoceans.org/reports/introduced_species.pdf. Accessed 28 January 2002

CEC (1997). *Ecological Regions of North America: Toward a Common Perspective.* Montreal, Commission for Environmental Cooperation of North America

CEC (2000a). *Booming Economies, Silencing Economies, and the Paths to Our Future: Background Note by the Commission for Environmental Cooperation on Critical and Emerging Environmental Trends.* Montreal, Commission for Environmental Cooperation of North America http://www.cec.org/pubs_docs/documents/index.cfm?varlan=english&ID=66. Accessed 16 February 2002

CEC (2000b). *North American Biodiversity Information Network: Project Summary.* Montreal, Commission for Environmental Cooperation of North America http://www.cec.org/programs_projects/conserv_biodiv/improve_nab/index.cfm?varlan=english. Accessed 28 January 2002

CEC (2001). *North America's Most Ecologically Important and Threatened Regions.* Montreal, Commission for Environmental Cooperation of North America http://www.cec.org/programs_projects/conserv_biodiv/priority_regions/index.cfm?varlan=english. Accessed 16 February 2002

CEQ (1997). *Environmental Quality, The World Wide Web: The 1997 Report of the Council on Environmental Quality.* Washington DC, The White House, Council on Environmental Quality

COSEWIC (2001). *Canadian Species at Risk, May 2001.* Committee on the Status of Endangered Wildlife in Canada http://www.cosewic.gc.ca/cosewic/pdf/English/Cosewic_List.pdf. Accessed 28 January 2002

Cox, Kenneth W., and Gilberto Cintrón (1997). Chapter Seven: The North American Region, An Overview of North American Wetlands. In *Wetlands, Biodiversity and the Ramsar Convention: the Role of the Convention on Wetlands in the Conservation and Wise Use of Biodiversity,* edited by A. J. Hails. Gland, Switzerland, Ramsar Convention Bureau, http://www.ramsar.org/lib_bio_1.htm. Accessed 28 January 2002

DU (2000). *Ducks Unlimited: World Leader in Wetlands Conservation.* Ducks Unlimited http://www.ducks.org/. Accessed 28 January 2002

DU Canada (1998). *Biocontrol Insects Feast on Purple Loosestrife.* Manitoba Purple Loosestrife Project, Purple Loosestrife InfoCentre, Ducks Unlimited Canada http://www.ducks.ca/purple/biocontrol/. Accessed 23 January 2002

EC (1998a). *The North American Waterfowl Management Plan: Background Information.* Environment Canada http://www.qc.ec.gc.ca/faune/sauvagine/html/nawmp.html. Accessed 28 January 2002

EC (1998b). *Canada and Freshwater: Monograph No. 6.* Ottawa, Environment Canada, Minister of Public Works and Government Services Canada

EC (1999). *Freshwater Facts.* Environment Canada http://www.on.ec.gc.ca/glimr/classroom/millennium/wetlands/wetland-facts-e.html. Accessed 29 January 2002

Enserink, Martin (1999). Biological Invaders Sweep In. *Science* 285 (5435):1834-6

EPA (1997). *The Wetlands Program.* US Environmental Protection Agency, Office of Water http://www.epa.gov/OWOW/wetlands/about.html. Accessed 28 January 2002

EPA (1999). *Values and Functions of Wetlands.* http://www.epa.gov/owow/wetlands/facts/fact2.html US Environmental Protection Agency's Office of Wetlands, Oceans, Watersheds. Accessed 23 January 2002

EPA (1999). *The Administration Wetlands Plan: An Update.* http://www.epa.gov/OWOW/wetlands/facts/fact7.html United States Environmental Protection Agency, Office of Wetlands, Oceans, and Watersheds

EPA (2001). *America's Wetlands, Our Vital Link Between Land and Water.* US Environmental Protection Agency, Office of Water http://www.epa.gov/OWOW/wetlands/vital/toc.html. Accessed 23 January 2002

GLFC (2000). *Letters to Lloyd Axworthy, Minister of Foreign Affairs, Canada and Madeline Albright, Secretary of State, United States* Dr. Burton Ayles, Chairman Great Lakes Fishery Commission, 11 April

H. John Heinz III Center (2001). *Designing a Report on the State of the Nation's Ecosystem: Selected Measurements for Croplands, Forests, and Coasts and Oceans.* The H. John Heinz III Center for Science, Economics and the Environment http://www.us-ecosystems.org/index.html. Accessed 28 January 2002

Haber, Erich (1996). *Invasive Exotic Plants of Canada: Fact Sheet No. 1.* National Botanical Services http://infoweb.magi.com/~ehaber/fact1.html. Accessed 15 March 2002

Holmes, Bob (1998). The Coming Plagues – Non-native Species on the Move Due to Global Warming. *New Scientist* 18 April

Hoth, Jürgen (2001). CEC Setting Biodiversity Priorities. *Trio,* Fall. Commission for Environmental Cooperation of North America http://www.cec.org/trio/stories/index.cfm?varlan=english&ed=2&id=18. Accessed 16 February 2002

IUCN (2001). *IUCN Guidelines for the Prevention of Biodiversity Loss Caused By Invasive Alien Species. Approved by the 51st Meeting of the IUCN Council, February.* Gland, Switzerland, IUCN Species Survival Commission

Kaiser, Jocelyn (1999). Stemming the Tide of Invading Species. *Science* 285 (5435):1836-41

Kaiser, Jocelyn (2001). Recreated Wetlands No Match for Original. *Science* 293 (5527):25

Knight, Jonathan (2001). Alien Versus Predator. *Nature* 412 (6843):115-6

Le Blanc, Dwight J. (n.d.). *Nutria: Damage Prevention and Control Methods.* Jefferson Parish, State of Louisiana http://www.jeffparish.net/pages/index.cfm?DocID=1213. Accessed 23 January 2002

Lee, G. (2001). *Alien Invasive Species: Threat to Canadian Biodiversity.* Ottawa, Natural Resources Canada, Canadian Forest Service, Forthcoming

Licking, Ellen (1999). They're Here, and They're Taking Over. *Business Week* 24 May:68-70

Martin, Glen (2001). Tipping the Scale in Wildlife Habitats: Human Development Causes Disruption that Favor Some Species. *San Francisco Chronicle, 3 September,* http://www.sfgate.com/cgi-bin/article.cgi?f=/chronicle/archive/2001/09/03/MN226317.DTL. Accessed 23 January 2002

MPT (2001). *Maryland Looks at New Ways to Control Nutria and Protect Marshes and Wetlands.* Maryland Public Television: Planet Maryland http://www.mpt.org/newsworks/archives/planetmd/010523.shtml. Accessed 23 January 2002

NAPPO (2002). *NAPPO Home Page.* The North American Plant Protection Organization http://www.nappo.org/menu_e.shtml. Accessed 29 January 2002

NAWMP (1998). *1998 Update to the North American Waterfowl Management Plan: Expanding the Vision.* http://www.nawmp.ca/pdf/update-e.pdf, US Department of the Interior, Fish and Wildlife Service, SEMARNAP, Mexico, Environment Canada

NAWMP (2000). *North American Waterfowl Management Plan* http://www.nawmp.ca/. Accessed 28 January 2002

NCSU (1998). *Information on Wetlands.* North Carolina State University http://h2osparc.wq.ncsu.edu/info/wetlands/. Accessed 28 January 2002

NOAA (2001). *Endangered Species Act of 1973.* NOAA, National Marine Fisheries Service, Office of Protected Resources http://www.nmfs.noaa.gov/prot_res/laws/ESA/ESA_Home.html. Accessed 23 January 2002

NRC (2000). *The National Atlas of Canada: Wetlands.* Natural Resources Canada http://atlas.gc.ca/english/facts/wetlands/1. Accessed 28 January 2002

NRCS (2001). *Wetlands Reserve Program.* US Department of Agriculture, Natural Resources Conservation Service http://www.nhq.nrcs.usda.gov/PROGRAMS/wrp/. Accessed 23 January 2002

NRDC (2000). *Everglades In Brief: FAQs.* Natural Resources Defense Council http://www.nrdc.org/water/everglades/qever.asp. Accessed 25 September 2001

O'Loughlin, Stan (2001). *The Endangered Species Act After Almost 30 Years.* Colby College Personal Pages http://www.colby.edu/personal/t/thtieten/en-sp-act.html. Accessed 23 January 2002

PCAST (1998). *Teaming with Life: Investing in Science to Understand and Use America's Living Capital,* President's Committee of Advisers on Science and Technology Panel on Biodiversity and Ecosystems

Pembina Institute (n.d.). Wetlands: The State of Alberta's Wetlands. *GPI Background Report* http://www.pembina.org/green/gpi/. Accessed 26 September 2001.

Pimentel, David, Lori Bach, Rodolfo Zuniga, and Doug Morrison (1999). *Environmental and Economic Costs Associated with Non-Indigenous Species in the United States.* Cornell News Service http://www.news.cornell.edu/releases/Jan99/species_costs.html. Accessed 28 January 2002

Revenga, Carmen, Jake Brunner, Norbert Henninger, Ken Kassem, and Richard Payne (2000). *Pilot Analysis of Global Ecosystems: Freshwater Systems.* Washington DC, World Resources Institute

Ricciardi, A., and J. B. Rasmussen (1999). Extinction Rates of North American Freshwater Fauna. *Conservation Biology* 13 (5):1220-22

Ricketts, Taylor H., Eric Dinerstein, David M. Olson, Colby J. Loucks, William Eichbaum, Kevin Kavanagh, Prashant Hedao, Patrick T. Hurley, Karen M. Carney, Robin Abell, and Steven Walters (1997). *A Conservation Assessment of the Terrestrial Ecoregions of North America, Volume I – The United States and Canada.* Washington DC, World Wildlife Fund

Rubec, Clayton, and Jacques J. Thibault (1998). Managing Canadian Peatlands – Status of the Resource and Restoration Approaches. Paper read at the International Symposium on Peatland Restoration and Reclamation, July 14-18, at Duluth, Minnesota

Rubec, Clayton (2000). Canadian Wetland Inventory: Hard Issues and Realities. Paper read at the Wetland Inventory Workshop, Natural Resources Canada, January 24-25, at Ottawa, Ontario

Schmid, James A. (2000). Wetlands as Conserved Landscapes in the United States. In *Cultural Encounters with the Environment: Enduring and Evolving Geographic Themes,* edited by A. Murphy, B. Johnson, D. L. and the assistance of Viola Haarmann. Boston, Rowman & Littlefield

Schrope, Mark (2001). Listing Resumes for Species at Risk. *Nature* 413 (6851):7

Simberloff, Daniel, and Don D. Schmitz (1999). An Invasive Species Threat Intensifies, US Steps Up Fight. *Issues in Science and Technology* 15 (3):25

Smart, Michael (1997). Chapter Two: The Ramsar Convention, Its Role in Conservation and Wise Use of Wetland Biodiversity. In *Wetlands, Biodiversity and the Ramsar Convention: the Role of the Convention on Wetlands in the Conservation and Wise Use of Biodiversity,* edited by A. J. Hails. Gland, Switzerland, Ramsar Convention Bureau, http://www.ramsar.org/lib_bio_1.htm. Accessed 29 January 2002

Smith, Stanley D., Travis Huxman, E., Stephen F. Zitzer, Therese N. Charlet, David C. Housman, James S. Coleman, Lynn K. Fenstermaker, Jefrey R. Seemann, and Robert S. Nowak (2000). Elevated CO_2 Increases Productivity and Invasive Species Success in an Arid Ecosystem. *Nature* 408 (6808):7981

Stein, Bruce A., Lynn S. Kutner, and Jonathan S. Adams eds. (2000). *Precious Heritage: The Status of Biodiversity in the United States.* Oxford University Press, The Nature Conservancy and the Association for Biodiversity Information, http://www.oup-usa.org/sc/0195125193/summary.pdf. Accessed 24 January

Stein, Bruce A. (2001). A Fragile Cornucopia: Assessing the Status of US Biodiversity. *Environment* 43 (7):11-22

The Ramsar Convention (2000). *The Ramsar Convention on Wetlands* http://www.ramsar.org/. Accessed 28 January 2002

TPL (1999). *Wetlands Reserve Program.* The Trust for Public Lands http://www.tpl.org/tier3_cdl.cfm?content_item_id=982&folder_id=191. Accessed 29 January 2002

UNEP–WCMC (2001a). *GEO-3 Endangered Animals Snapshot.* United Nations Environment Proramme–World Conservation Monitoring Centre http://valhalla.unep-wcmc.org/isdb/GEO3.cfm. Accessed 1 June 2002

UNEP–WCMC (2001b). *GEO-3 Protected Areas Snapshot.*United Nations Environment Proramme–World Conservation Monitoring Centre http://valhalla.unep-wcmc.org/wdbpa/GEO3.cfm. Accessed 1 June 2002

USDA (1997). World Soil Resources Map Index. *Global Distribution of Wetlands.* US Department of Agriculture, Natural Resources Conservation Service. http://www.nrcs.usda.gov/technical/worldsoils/mapindx/wetlands.html. Accessed 30 May 2002

USDA (1999). *Asian Longhorned Beetle (Anoplophora glabripennis): A New Introduction.* US Department of Agriculture, Forest Service, Animal and Plant Health Inspection Service http://www.forestworld.com/forestry/outreach/pestalerts/asian_lhb/asian_lhb.html. Accessed 24 January 2002

USDA (2000a). *Agricultural Resources and Environmental Indicators, 2000.* US Department of Agriculture, Economic Research Service, Resource Economics Division http://www.ers.usda.gov/briefing/arei/newarei/. Accessed 4 February 2002

USDA (2000b). *Pest Risk Assessment for Importation of Solid Wood Packing Materials into the United States.* US Department of Agriculture, Animal and Plant Health Inspection Service and Forest Service http://www.aphis.usda.gov/ppq/pra/swpm/intro.pdf. Accessed 24 January 2002

USGS (2001a). *Florida Everglades (Excerpt from USGS Circular 1182).* US Department of the Interior, US Geological Survey, Center for Coastal Geology, South Florida Information Access http://sofia.usgs.gov/publications/circular/1182/. Accessed 24 January 2002

USGS (2001b). *Nutria, Eating Louisiana's Coast.* US Geological Survey, National Wetlands Research Center http://www.nwrc.usgs.gov/factshts/nutria.pdf. Accessed 24 January 2002

WCC (2001). *Wetland Mitigation in Canada: A Framework for Application.* Issues Paper No. 2000-1. North American Wetlands Conservation Council (Canada) http://www.cws-scf.ec.gc.ca/habitat/publications/mitigation_e.pdf. Accessed 28 January 2002

Westbrooks, R. (1998). *Invasive Plants, Changing the Landscape of America: Fact Book.* Washington DC, Federal Interagency Committee for the Management of Noxious and Exotic Weeds (FICMNEW)

Westbrooks, Randy, and William Gregg (2000). Super Invaders Spreading Fast. *Trio* Winter 2000-2001. Commission for Environmental Cooperation of North America http://www.cec.org/trio/stories/index.cfm?varlan=english&ed=2&id=9. Accessed 28 January 2002

Wilcove, David S., David Rothstein, Jason Dubow, Ali Phillips, and Elizabeth Losos (1998). Quantifying Threats to Imperiled Species in the United States. *Bioscience* 48 (8): 607-15

Wilcove, David S., David Rothstein, Jason Dubow, Ali Phillips, and Elizabeth Losos (2000). Leading Threats to Biodiversity. In *Precious Heritage: The Status of Biodiversity in the United States,* edited by B. A. Stein, L. S. Kutner and J. S. Adams. New York, Oxford University Press

WRI, UNEP, UNDP and World Bank, (1998). *World Resources 1998-99: A Guide to the Global Environment: Environmental Change and Human Health.* New York, USA and Oxford, UK, Oxford University Press

WSR (1997). *Global Distribution of Wetlands.* World Soil Resources, Office of the US Department of Agriculture, Natural Resources Conservation Service, Soil Survey Division http://www.nhq.nrcs.usda.gov/WSR/mapindx/wetlands.htm. Accessed 29 January 2002

Coastal and
Marine Areas

4

Coastal and Marine Areas

The continental shelf, a region of shallow water extending beyond the coastline and giving way to deep ocean, is the dominant physical feature of North America's marine zone. The shelf is typically high in nutrients, giving rise to a large production of algae and, in turn, a highly productive fish habitat (Botkin and Keller 1995). The width of the continental shelf varies considerably. Much of the Pacific coast has a narrow shelf, whereas in sections of the east it is extensive, providing for much of the commercial harvest of groundfish in North America. Canada's shelf region, one of the world's largest, covers 3.7 million km^2, mostly under a 200 m depth (EC 1996).

Canada's coastline is the longest in the world. Twenty-three percent of the population lives near the coast while about 55 percent of the US population lives in coastal areas that cover less than 17 percent of the total land mass (DFO 2001a; EPA 2001). The US coastal population is growing at four times the national average with some of the highest levels of urban growth taking place in small coastal cities, a trend that is expected to continue (CEC 2000). By the year 2010, coastal population in the United States will increase by almost 60 percent (Culliton, Blackwell and others n.d.).

Coastal ecosystems are the richest storehouses of marine biodiversity, and the physical conversion of these fragile areas to urban uses; their pollution from air, water, and land-based activities; and the exploitation of marine resources have degraded them and threaten the services they provide. Especially endangered are North America's most productive coastal ecosystems such as tidal flats, saltwater marshes, seagrass beds, mangrove swamps, estuaries, and other wetlands (see the biodiversity section) (CEC 2000).

One issue of high priority for North America's coastal and marine ecosystems is the precipitous decline in its fisheries since the mid-1980s (see Figure 21). Twenty-one of the 43 groundfish stocks in Canada's North Atlantic are in decline and nearly one-third of US federally managed fishery species are over-fished (CEC 2000). The collapse of the North Atlantic cod fishery inspired a Canadian moratorium on Northern Cod in 1992, which has caused considerable hardship for local and commercial fisheries in the region. In addition, significant salmon stock declines have become apparent on the Pacific and Atlantic coasts. For example, about 1.5 million small and large wild Atlantic salmon returned to spawn each year in North America's eastern rivers thirty years ago compared to fewer than 350,000 in 2000 (ASF 2000). Highlighted below is the decline in this region's Pacific Northwest salmon fishery. The situation is a complex one that involves migratory fish that cross national boundaries and a debate about the various roles of human impact and natural disturbance in the fish declines.

Initially used to enhance natural stocks, aquaculture has become a large-scale industry in North America, with commercial production expanding and new species being developed for fish farming. Since 1980, there has been a four-fold increase in US aquaculture, for example (see Figure 22) (Hanfman 1993). Harvests of farmed fish in North America grew from 375,000 tons to 548,000 tons between 1985 and 1995. Large-scale fish farming,

Annual Fish Catch, 1972-1998

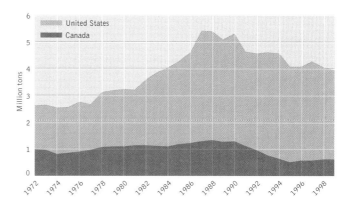

however, can be unsustainable due to nutrients from wastes entering local waters and disease spreading, among other environmental impacts (CEC 2000).

An issue of increasing gravity to coastal and marine ecosystems is the overabundance of nitrogen from land-based activities. This priority

Figure 21
Annual fish catch, 1972-1998.

Source: Fishstat 2001

Aquaculture Production in North America, 1984-1998

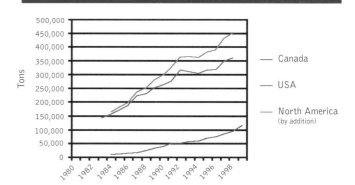

issue is explored in greater depth in the following pages, showing the severity of the problem, especially in US coastal waters, where 60 percent of coastal rivers and bays are moderately to severely degraded by nutrient pollution. A related concern is that of harmful algal blooms,

Figure 22
Aquaculture production in North America, 1984-1998.

Source: Hanfman 1993; Kope 1999; DFO 2000a

Box 18: Pacific Northwest Salmon

The Pacific Northwest is home to five species of salmon: Chinook, coho, sockeye, pink, and chum (or six when Steelhead is classified as a Pacific salmon), most of which hatch in rivers along the west coast then migrate to the sea, making their way northward to mature in colder waters. Several years later, they retrace their ocean journey south to spawn in the freshwater streams of their origin. Each group or stock has unique biological traits, uses its marine habitat (stream, estuary, coast, and ocean) to different extents, and is genetically adapted to its environment (Myers, Kope, and others 1998). British Columbia's approximately 1,000 spawning streams may support as many as 3,000 genetically and ecologically distinct salmon populations (Walters 1995). Salmon, therefore, are significant components of the region's ecosystems. The fish are particularly important to the history, culture, and social fabric of smaller coastal communities and indigenous peoples, whose way of life has been shaped by fishing. Salmon are also extremely significant for the economic role they play along North America's Pacific Northwest, both commercially and for recreational anglers (PSC 2000). In 1989, salmon accounted for 56 percent of the landed value of the fishery industry on Canada's West Coast (Statistics Canada 2000).

which have been spreading over the past 20 years, causing harm to humans, fish, marine birds, and mammals and to sectors of the economy that depend on healthy marine ecosystems.

Pacific Northwest Salmon Fishery

The Pacific Northwest of North America is a region of extensive temperate forests drained by large rivers linking the land and sea. In the mid-1990s, a population of 6.5 million was concentrated in coastal cities and towns and it is still growing. The forests along the marine west coast are among the most productive in North America and forestry is the major resource activity there (see the forest section). The streams, estuaries, and ocean waters support rich fishery resources and the commercial fishery offshore is

another key industry, with salmon being of primary importance (see Box 18) (CEC 1997).

Historically abundant in many Pacific coastal and interior waters, salmon runs and species diversity have been shrinking since the late 19th century (Walters 1995). In the beginning, dam construction (particularly in the United States), rockslides, poor management, and over-fishing were blamed (DFO 1999a). Over the years, fish ladders were built to permit migration, and enhancement activities, including hatcheries, spawning channels, and fish rearing were set up to allow for the survival to adulthood of more young fish (PSC 2000). Still, declines in Pacific salmon harvests accelerated after the 1970s. Newer dams and turbines that had been added along some major US rivers in the late 1970s were now blamed. In response, turbines were modified and additional structural and transport-oriented measures were taken to enable salmon migration (Mann and Plummer 2000).

By the late 1980s, both countries had imposed severe restrictions on harvests of some salmon species. Despite these and other measures, by the early 1990s, salmon values showed significant declines (see Figure 23). By the mid-1990s, the salmon population of the Columbia River had dropped by at least 70 percent, and Washington state severely restricted coho and Chinook. By 1996, there had been a 62 percent decline in total BC landings from 1989 (Statistics Canada 2000) (see Figure 24). A number of salmon species were threatened and in 1992 were added to the US ESA, which prohibits taking endangered salmonids (see Box 10 in the biodiversity section) (Carlisle 1999; TU/TUC 1999). The blame for salmon declines was increasingly debated among all those involved within and between the two countries sharing the fish, including federal fisheries managers, sports fishers, commercial fleets, and indigenous fishers (Glavin 1996).

In 1999, nine populations of salmon and steelhead on the Pacific Northwest coast were added to the ESA, bringing the number of listed subspecies of west coast salmon to 24. The US government stated that the listings were the result of habitat degradation from land and water development projects, over-harvesting, dam construction and opera-

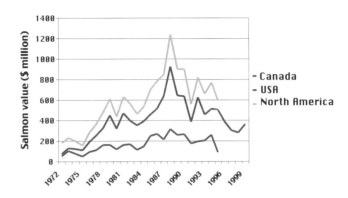

Commercial Pacific Northwest Salmon Values, 1972-Latest Year

tion, and some hatchery practices (Rabalais 1999). In 1998, Canada closed coho fishing to protect stock in the Tompson River and upper Skeena, instituting a coho recovery plan that restructured Canadian fisheries (Carlisle 1999; TU/TUC 1999). At the end of the decade, of the five species of Pacific salmon, two were considered overexploited and the others deemed to be fully

Figure 23
Commercial Pacific Northwest salmon values, 1972-latest year.

Source: DFO 2000b; NMFS 2000

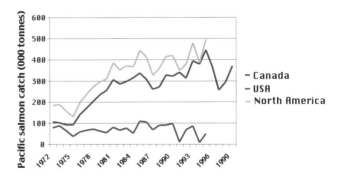

Commercial Pacific Northwest Salmon Catch, 1972-Latest Year

exploited when compared with levels necessary to achieve maximum sustained yield (Kope 1999).

Over-harvesting combined with habitat destruction or degradation

Figure 24
Commercial Pacific Northwest salmon catch, 1972-latest year.

Source: DFO 2000b; NMFS 2000

Box 19: Impacts of Logging on the West Coast Salmon

Salmon depend on freshwater habitat to spawn and so are particularly vulnerable to its degradation. Forest clearing and road building expose stream habitats to more sunlight and heat than is required for salmon health and can lead to erosion and flash flooding that disrupts sediment levels. Naturally fallen trees create spawning ponds and contribute necessary nutrients to the streams, while logging debris can clog them, inhibiting fish migration and reducing dissolved oxygen levels. A 1992 survey of salmon streams on Vancouver Island revealed that logging had partially or permanently damaged over 60 percent of them (YCELP 1995).

from dams, hatcheries, logging (see Box 19), mining, overgrazing, urbanization, agricultural runoff, industrial pollution and water development projects were considered by most to be the key causes, and there is little doubt that the cumulative effects of these activities contributed to declines in harvests of some salmon populations (Walters 1995).

By the end of the 1990s, some scientists considered the role of natural cycles, such as the occurrence of several El Niño events over the last few decades, as increasingly important in the dramatic decline in marine survival of some stocks (NMFS 1998; Statistics Canada 2000). El Niño events trigger the flow of unusually warm seawater along the west coast, affecting species productivity and prey and predator distribution (NMFS 1998). During the last century, the 1997 El Niño was the strongest, and that

of 1983 the second hottest (Welch 1999).

In addition, in the early 1990s, scientific data began to indicate the existence of 20- to 30-year cycles of plentiful and then scarce salmon related to a regime shift called the Pacific Decadal Oscillation (PDO) (Carlisle 1999; Brown 2000). Warm phases in this pattern of Pacific climate variability correlate with enhanced biological productivity in Alaska's coastal ocean and inhibited productivity off the coast of the Pacific Northwest. Cold phases have the opposite characteristics (JISAO 2000). This could explain that while Chinook and coho salmon declined, those species that migrate further offshore have been relatively stable. It is now widely accepted that the regime shifted in the winter of 1976–77 (Kope 1999; Hare and Mantua 2000). Historically, the salmon have withstood such natural regime shifts, but now the combination of habitat loss and the particularly low levels in some salmon populations may have made these fish more vulnerable to extinction from their effects (NMFS 1998).

Complicating the issue are the two international borders that separate British Columbia's waters from Alaska's and those of the Northwest US states (DFO 1999a; TU/TUC 1999). During their life cycle, salmon of US origin travel through Canada's waters and Canadian fish pass through US zones with a resulting history of intercepting fishery practices. Expansion of high-intercepting fisheries during the 1950s and '60s by the two countries discouraged conservation and enhancement and encouraged over-harvesting (DFO 1999a). Negotiations between Canada and the United States to resolve the issue began in the 1960s and culminated with the 1985 Pacific Salmon Treaty (see Box 20). Initially unsuccessful, the treaty was renegotiated and new, fairer, and more protective measures were added in 1999.

Although there is a natural variability of abundance levels for Pacific salmon, uncertainty remains about recent salmon declines. The relative importance of fishing, climatic change, and habitat conditions has been changing over recent decades and varies with each location and population (Walters 1995). The dilemma has prompted a number of

status reviews, renewed fishing agreements, and new management approaches (Alden 1999).

For example, in 1998, Canada initiated the Pacific Fisheries Adjustment and Rebuilding Program to conserve and rebuild Pacific salmon stocks and to revitalize Pacific

Box 20: Bilateral Agreement, The Pacific Salmon Treaty

The 1985 Pacific Salmon Treaty was based on the principles of conservation to prevent over-fishing and allow for optimum production and equity so that each party receives benefits equal to those from salmon production originating in its waters (PSC 2000). However, harvest rates and ceilings were set too high for stocks to rebuild and the United States considered Canada's approach to the equity issue unacceptable, which led to a stalemate. The original fishing arrangements ended in 1992 because of disagreements (TU/TUC 1999).

Between 1992 and 1999, a series of initiatives were taken to reach a new bilateral fishing arrangement. As of 1994, the Treaty lacked effective implementation, which culminated in a total breakdown of negotiations in 1997. One of the initiatives was the appointment of special representatives from the two countries, whose 1998 report refers to the unresolved dispute between them as a case of unregulated self-interest risking the unsustainable harvest of the commons (Strangway and Ruckelhaus 1998).

In 1999, the Pacific Salmon Treaty was renegotiated. A new, comprehensive accord signed on 3 June 1999 finally resolves the long-standing differences over Pacific salmon conservation (NOAA 1999). It is based on sustaining wild stocks, preventing over-fishing by matching harvest levels to actual abundance, sharing the burdens of conservation and the benefits of stock recovery, and establishing a common basis to assess stocks, monitor fish, and evaluate performance. The agreement signals a cooperative, conservation-based approach to the management of Pacific salmon fisheries, and a more equitable sharing of salmon catches between Canada and the United States. It should help to protect weak stocks and stabilize harvest arrangements for 10 to 12 years (DFO 2001b; DFAIT 2002).

salmon fisheries. It also implemented a precautionary approach to salmon management, resulting in significant harvest reductions to protect stocks at risk (DFO 1999b).

Pending decisions on ESA listing of Pacific salmon and steelhead

survival standards, reviewed at five-, eight-and 10-year points, are not met. The standards include habitat restoration, harvesting curtailment, limits to harmful hatchery operations, measures to conserve wild salmon, ways to improve survival

---

Box 21: Impacts of Climate Change on Pacific Salmon and Other Wild Fish Stock

Both countries are concerned about the potential for climate change to affect salmon populations and other wild fish stocks in North America's coastal and ocean waters. Studies by Canadian government scientists that simulated expected changes from a doubling of CO_2 in the atmosphere indicate that the resulting change in climate could virtually eliminate salmon habitat from the Pacific Ocean (NRCan 1998). A 1994 Environment Canada study of the impact of climate change on Fraser River salmon reported that altered flow regimes, aquatic temperatures, river hydrology, and seasonal runoff will intensify competition among water users in the watershed (Glavin 1996). And a recent US report on climate change impacts notes that a projected narrowing in the annual water temperature range in many estuaries may cause species' ranges to shift and increase the vulnerability of some estuaries to introduced species (USGCRP 2000).

---

trout were completed in 1999 and 2000. A total of 26 distinct groups are now listed as either threatened or endangered. Stakeholders, including government officials, state, local, and tribal officials, and the public, are working together to address habitat restoration and other concerns to aid salmon recovery (Buck, Corn, and Baldwin 2001). In December 2000, the United States released a comprehensive long-term federal strategy to help restore the 14 salmon subspecies in the Columbia River Basin listed on the ESA. It states that actions are necessary to restore health to the tributaries and estuaries where these species spawn in order for them to recover. It provided for four dams on the lower Snake River to be breached if a number of salmon

through hydropower systems, and better conditions in streams and reservoirs (Federal Caucus 2000).

Natural climatic regime shifts, climate change (see Box 21), and habitat loss and destruction are conspiring to threaten the continued viability of North America's Pacific salmon populations. As those dependent on them as a source of income also struggle to survive, both countries are taking additional measures, outlined in their national sustainable fisheries strategies, to help to restore these and other wild fish stocks to North America's coastal and marine waters and to enhance and maintain global biological diversity. Fisheries and Oceans Canada instituted a new Sustainable Development Strategy for 2001–03, which is built on the key economic, environmental, and social principles of sustainable development, including public participation, the precautionary approach, and expanded scientific knowledge about aquatic ecosystems (DFO 2001a).

The US Sustainable Fisheries Act of 1996 amended the Magnuson Fishery Conservation and Management Act to incorporate numerous provisions requiring science, management, and conservation action by the National Marine Fisheries Service (NMFS). The aims of the NMFS Strategic Plan are to maintain healthy stocks, eliminate over-fishing and rebuild over-fished stocks, increase long-term economic and social benefits from living marine resources, and promote the development of robust and economically sound aquaculture (OSF 2000). Recent restrictions, bilateral cooperation, and new ecosystem ap-

other North American fish stocks fare (DFO 2000c; DFO 2001a).

Nutrient Loading

Over the past 20 years, the introduction of excess nutrients has increasingly been recognized as causing a number of environmental problems in coastal ecosystems (NRCan 2000). Eutrophication, or the increased supply of organic matter to an aquatic system (see Box 22), is one of the most common effects and is now the most widespread problem affecting estuaries and coastal zones (Howarth, Anderson, and others 2000; NRCan 2000). Although an overabundance of nutrients in the environment due to human activities was recognized as a problem in North America's freshwaters as early as the 1970s (EC 2000), until the late 1990s, the severity and extent of the problem in coastal waters had

Box 22: Eutrophication and Hypoxia

Eutrophication refers to the gradual increase in nutrients such as nitrogen and phosphorus in a body of water due to natural processes, which can be accelerated by human activities. The process and symptoms vary from one region to another due to differences in underlying geology and soil types (EPA 1998).

Excessive nutrients encourage an abundant plant life that can lead to chronic over-enrichment with symptoms that include low dissolved oxygen, fish kills, murky water, and depletion of desirable flora and fauna. Lakes, estuaries, and bays subject to eutrophication can eventually become bogs and marshes (EPA 1998; EPA 2001). Elevated levels of chlorophyll indicate the onset of eutrophication while depleted dissolved oxygen indicates more serious or highly developed eutrophication (Clement, Bricker, and Pirhalla 2001). When the concentration of dissolved oxygen in water bodies falls below 2 ppm, the level generally accepted as the minimum required for most marine life to survive and reproduce, the condition is termed a state of hypoxia or hypoxic waters (EPA 1998).

proaches have contributed to improving the ocean survival of some important salmon stocks, but it remains to be seen if all Pacific salmon species rebound and how

not been adequately appraised due to the complexity of the phenomena and the lack of consistent national data sets (Bricker, Clement, and others 1999).

Nutrient additions to marine and coastal ecosystems increased dramatically over the past several decades due to large increases in population density, fossil fuel use, sewage inputs, animal production, and fertilizer use (EC 2001). These activities release nitrogen and phosphorus, which can enhance plant growth in aquatic systems causing oxygen depletion and multiple effects on the ecosystem: eutrophication can cause the alteration of food webs, decreased biological diversity, loss of seagrass, destroyed fish habitat, the closure of shellfish areas, degraded beaches, and site contamination (Carpenter, Caraco, and others 1998; EC 1999; EC 2001).

Over the past 30 years, North America has had notable success in stemming nutrient emissions from point sources, or localized inputs. Since the early 1970s, anti-pollution legislation has greatly reduced point sources of nitrogen and phosphorous—principally from the discharge of municipal sewage and industrial wastes—and successfully controlled phosphates in laundry detergents (NOAA 1998). During the early 1970s, half of the phosphorous found in US domestic wastewater came from laundry detergents, which contained some 12 percent phosphorous by weight. By 1982, the phosphorous content of detergents had dropped to about 5 percent and accounted for 35 percent of amounts in wastewater (Miller Jr.1985).

Today, non-point sources, or dispersed activities, are the major

concern. In many parts of North America non-point nutrient inputs to fresh and coastal waters come mainly from fertilizer and manure runoff. Over the past three decades, fertilizer use in the region rose by almost 30 percent (see Figure 27 in the land section).

A trend toward rearing livestock (cattle, hogs, chickens and other animals) in intensive feedlots has also resulted in the release of huge amounts of manure to surface and coastal waters (Mathews and Hammond 1999). In the United States, intensive feedlots are the third leading agricultural source of water pollution, and the issue of excess livestock manure has gained increased public attention, underscoring the need for better protection against non-point sources of water pollution. With ever more animals confined on fewer and larger feedlots, there is frequently not enough accessible cropland on which to use all the manure efficiently. Inadequate manure management has led to coastal water pollution in many regions and serious policy difficulties in addressing the growing problem (Harkin 1997) (see Box 23). Significant amounts of nitrogen are also deposited in aquatic ecosystems from airborne sources derived from manure, as well as from vehicles and electric utility power plants (NOAA 1998).

Sources of nutrients vary greatly from place to place. Along the north Atlantic coast, non-point sources of nitrogen are some ninefold greater than inputs from wastewater treatment plants (EC 2001). But in some coastal areas, wastewater treatment plants remain the primary sources of nutrient inputs. For example, much municipal wastewater discharged into Canada's coastal waters is still subject only to primary treatment (EC 2000).

Rather than in coastal or marine environments, however, Canada's most serious over-enrichment

Box 23: Intensive Hog Farming

Nutrients from hog production, which has increased in scale, intensification, and geographical concentration over the past 25 years, strongly affect the health of North America's marine and coastal areas (Welsh, Hubbell, and Carpentier 2000). In 1992, there were about 60 million swine in the United States, which represents an 18 percent increase from the previous decade. During the same period, the number of hog farms dropped by 72 percent (Copeland and Zinn 1998). Canada's hog population grew from about 6 million in 1976 to 11 million in 1996 while the number of hog farms decreased from 65,000 to 20,000 during the same 20-year period (EC 2000). This trend toward industrialization of hog farming was influenced by cost and production advantages such as economies of scale, new technologies, advances in animal genetics, and new and more efficient management practices (Furuseth 1997).

Operations also have become more regionally concentrated since the 1980s. The most notable concentration has occurred in North Carolina's low coastal flood plain. The number of hogs in the state increased threefold between 1987 and 1998. North Carolina was 14th in hog production in 1970, but by the end of the 1990s it ranked second (NPPC 1999). Most of Canada's hog farms are found in southern Ontario and Quebec and the Prairie provinces (EC 2000). Geographic concentration was influenced by a number of factors, including incentives such as tax breaks and subsidies offered by local governments in both countries to attract hog producers in order to create local financial and employment gains. In some cases, US states such as North Carolina offered inexpensive land to attract the industry to economically declining rural areas (CIBE 1999). Finally, states with no anti-corporate farming laws also influenced geographic concentration (Welsh, Hubbell, and Carpentier 2000).

The intensification and concentration of hog production has exacerbated the challenge of manure and other hog waste disposal. Almost all hog manure (like manure from other livestock) is applied to agricultural land. Rich in nitrates and phosphates, hog manure is a valuable fertilizer, but if applied to the land in amounts that exceed plant needs, excess nutrients leach through the soils to contaminate ground or surface waters. There is increasingly too little land for the amounts of hog manure produced in these regions of concentrated hog farming (Furuseth 1997).

Hog manure is mostly stored in open-air lagoons with relatively little treatment before being sprayed on land to irrigate forage crops. Both lined and unlined lagoons can leak contaminants into groundwater. In the United States, intensive feedlots are the third leading agricultural source of water pollution and in North Carolina, they are the biggest source of nutrient pollution (Environmental Defense 1998). In 1997, Hurricane Floyd flooded many of the large hog facilities that had been built on North Carolina's low coastal flood plain. Hog wastes from at least 46 waste lagoons flowed into the surrounding floodwaters, contaminating local drinking water and threatening human health (Taylor 2001). A two-year moratorium on new hog factories was instituted in 1997 to allow new and lasting solutions to the problems associated with the state's hog industry to be developed (Environmental Defense 1998).

problems are found in the rivers of the southern Prairie Provinces, where agricultural activity is intensive, and in southern Ontario and Quebec, where inputs from manure and fertilizer as well as from municipal sewage and industrial wastewater are heavy (EC 2000). Canadian estuaries in the North Atlantic are less severely affected by nutrient loading than more southerly ones

Area of Gulf of Mexico Low-Oxygen Zone, 1985-1998

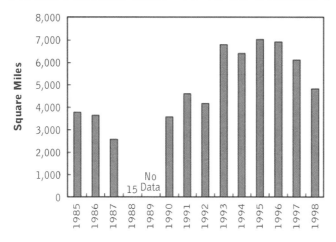

Source: Modified from Rabalais et al 1998

Figure 25
Area of Gulf of Mexico low-oxygen zone, 1985-1998.

Source: H. John Heinz III Center 1999.

thanks in part to a cooler climate and significant flushing of coastal waters (NOAA 1998).

Nutrient additions to the US coast have been increasing over the past two decades. In the mid-1990s, greater nutrient loading from municipal discharges and agricultural runoff contributed to the classification of some US estuarine and coastal waters as not 'fishable or swimmable' (CEQ 1996). In 1998, more than 60 percent of US coastal rivers and bays were moderately to severely degraded by nutrient contamination, and nitrogen was

found to be the single greatest environmental threat in some 'trouble' spots on the Atlantic coast (Howarth, Anderson, and others 2000). More recently, a 2001 report states that approximately 65 percent of the nation's estuarine surface area has moderate to high eutrophic conditions. A high level of human influence is associated with 36 of the 44 estuaries with high eutrophication (Clement, Bricker, and Pirhalla 2001). In the last 40 years, human activity has increased the flux of nitrogen in the Mississippi River some fourfold and in rivers in the northeastern US some eightfold (NRCan 2000).

The Mississippi River, which drains 40 percent of the continental United States, carries excess nutrients to the Gulf of Mexico where they contribute to an area of hypoxia (see Box 22) called the 'dead zone'. Nearly 12,950 km^2 in the Gulf of Mexico were affected with low oxygen conditions in 1998 (H. John Heinz III Center 1999) (see Figure 25). The region is now subject to intensive research. An EPA task force formed in 1997 examined the causes and consequences of Gulf hypoxia as part of the basis of an Action Plan to reduce, mitigate and control hypoxia in the northern Gulf of Mexico. In October 2000, a US $1 billion-per-year plan was agreed upon to revive some 30 percent of the dead zone by 2015 (NOS 2000).

The US Clean Water Act, last re-authorized in 1987, and the 1972 and 1980 Coastal Zone Management Act directed states to develop management plans for non-point contamination sources and provided funding and incentives to implement them. In addition, the US National Estuary Program (NEP) was established in 1987 to identify key problems in specific estuaries and to develop and implement management plans to address them (NOAA 1998). The 1987 Chesapeake Bay

algal blooms or red tides (CEC 2000). Harmful algal blooms (HABs) (see Box 24) are found in the waters of almost every US coastal state and most have experienced their environmental, human health, and economic impacts (NSTC 2000). The number of coastal and estuarine waters in the United States

Box 24: Harmful Algal Blooms (HABs) and Red Tides

The algae that form Harmful Algal Blooms or HABs are a very diverse group of organisms that range from single-celled microalgae or phytoplankton to large seaweed-like macroalgae. The most well known is the dinoflagellate *Pfiesteria piscicida*. Some species produce toxins and appear in great abundance in massive 'blooms'. Some contain pigments that tint the water red to produce what is commonly known as 'red tides', while others turn the water green or brown or have no color or massive concentration during the toxic phase. HABs are harmful because they produce highly potent toxins that can kill marine organisms directly or travel through the food chain as the algae are consumed by shellfish and other marine life, causing harm at multiple levels. Although the toxins may only slightly affect shellfish, the amount in one clam can kill a human (NSTC 2000; EC 2001).

Program, for example, was set up under the NEP. It is a federal-state-local partnership working to reduce nitrogen and phosphorous loading to the Bay by 40 percent. The Chesapeake Bay is the largest estuary in the United States and one of the most productive in the world. The region has a population of over 15 million and important commercial fish and shellfish harvests, and is a major stopover for migratory birds. By the late 1990s, only the phosphorous reduction goal had been met. Progress in reducing nutrients in the region is being hampered because of population growth and development (OECD 1996; EPA 1997).

Nutrient enrichment is a likely contributing factor in the recent dramatic increase in the number, intensity, frequency, and expanse of

that host major recurring incidents of HABs doubled between 1972 and 1995 (Harkin 1997) (see Figure 26). Along with nutrient enrichment, the recorded increase in several algal groups is likely to be due to improved methods of detection and greater monitoring efforts, introduction of exotic species, failure of grazers to control the algal species' growth, climate changes, natural events, and habitat degradation (Bushaw-Newton and Sellner 1999; NSTC 2000).

The impacts of HAB events can include human illness and death from eating contaminated fish or shellfish, mass mortalities of wild and farmed fish, restricted local harvests of fish and shellfish, and changes in marine food chains due to the negative effects on eggs,

young, and adult marine inverte-
brates, seabirds, sea turtles, and
mammals (NSTC 2000). The expansion of HABs in the United States
over the past 20 years has caused
losses of about US $100 million per
year in medical-related expenses
and impacts on the fishing and

Location of HAB-related Events in US Coastal Waters Before and After 1972

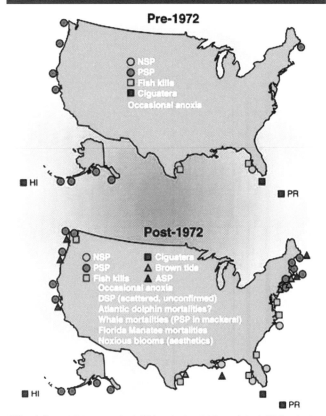

Abbreviations: NSP, neurotoxic shellfish poisoning; PSP, paralytic shellfish poisoning; ASP, amnesic shellfish poisoning; DSP, diarrheic shellfish poisoning.

Figure 26
Location of
HAB-related
events in US
coastal waters
before and after
1972.

Source: Bushaw-Newton and Sellner 1999.

tourism industries, among others
(Bushaw-Newton and Sellner 1999).

In response to incidents of human illness from contaminated
shellfish, both Canada and the
United States have developed testing
and water quality programs to
identify phytoplankton toxins and to
provide information about them to
the public. Recently, public concern

and research into marine toxins and
HABs has intensified due to increased incidences of fish kills and
fish with lesions in 1997 in Chesapeake Bay tributaries and in North
Carolina (NOAA 1998). The Ecology
and Oceanography of Harmful Algal
Blooms (ECOHAB), an interagency
program established in 1996, provides information on environmental
conditions that favor optimal growth
and toxicity of several noxious
species and supports numerous
research projects on HABs (CEQ
1996). The US Harmful Algal Bloom
and Hypoxia Research and Control
Act requires an examination of the
means to reduce, mitigate, and
control HABs, and of their social
and economic costs and benefits.
Controlling the human inputs that
stimulate nutrient enrichment is one
approach that may reduce the
incidence of HABs (NSTC 2000).

Canadian and US Ocean Acts
(1997 and 2000, respectively) establish frameworks for improving the
stewardship of North America's
coastal and ocean waters (EC 1999;
The White House 2000). As yet,
there is no binational strategy to
address nutrient loading in North
America's coastal waters, and coordination among the various agencies
responsible for their management is
still inadequate (NRCan 2000).
Evidence suggests that the situation
can be reversed, but the need remains for increased political action
and cultural and behavioral changes
to reduce human activities that emit
nutrients to the water- and airsheds
that feed coastal streams and rivers.

References

Alden, Robin (1999). A Troubled Transition for Fisheries: Sustaining Marine Fisheries. *Environment* 41 (4):25-8

ASF (2000). *The Wild Atlantic Salmon: State of the Populations in North America 2000.* The Atlantic Salmon Federation http://www.asf.ca/stateofsalmon/SOP2000E.pdf. Accessed 29 May 2002

Botkin, Daniel, and Edward A. Keller (1995). *Environmental Science: Earth As a Living Planet.* New York, John Wiley & Sons, Inc.

Bricker, S., C. Clement, D. Pirhalla, S.P. Orlando, and D.R.G. Farrow (1999). *National Estuarine Eutrophication Assessment: Effects of Nutrient Enrichment in the Nation's Estuaries,* National Ocean Service, NOAA

Brown, Kathryn (2000). Pacific Salmon Run Hot and Cold. *Science* 290 (5492):685-6

Buck, Eugene H., M. Lynne Corn, and Pamela Baldwin (2001). *IB10072: Endangered Species: Difficult Choices,* CRS Issue Brief for Congress, National Council for Science and the Environment http://cnie.org/NLE/CRSreports/Biodiversity/biodv-1.cfm#_1_1. Accessed 23 January 2002

Bushaw-Newton, K.L., and K.G. Sellner (1999). Harmful Algal Blooms. In *NOAA's State of the Coast Report.* US National Oceanic and Atmospheric Administration, Silver Spring, Maryland http://state-of-coast.noaa.gov/bulletins/html/hab_14/hab.html. Accessed 12 February 2002

Carlisle, John (1999). *Nature, Not Man, is Responsible for West Coast Salmon Decline.* National Policy Analysis http://www.nationalcenter.org/NPA254.html. Accessed 12 February 2002

Carpenter, Stephen, Nina F. Caraco, David L. Correll, Robert W. Howarth, Andrew N. Sharpley, and Val H. Smith (1998). Nonpoint Pollution of Surface Waters with Phosphorus and Nitrogen. *Issues in Ecology* (3)

CEC (1997). *Ecological Regions of North America: Toward a Common Perspective.* Montreal, Commission for Environmental Cooperation of North America http://www.cec.org/files/pdf/BIODIVERSITY/eco-eng_EN.pdf. Accessed 11 February 2002

CEC (2000). *Booming Economies, Silencing Environments, and the Paths to Our Future: Background Note by the Commission for Environmental Cooperation on Critical and Emerging Environmental Trends.* Montreal, Commission for Environmental Cooperation of North America http://www.cec.org/pubs_docs/documents/index.cfm?varlan=english&ID=66. Accessed 26 February 2002

CEQ (1996). *Environmental Quality: The Twenty-fifth Anniversary Report of the Council on Environmental Quality.* Washington DC, US Council on Environmental Quality

CIBE (1999). Industrial Hog Farming in Canada Becoming a Major Environmental Problem. *The Gallon Environment Letter Special (Canadian Institute for Business and the Environment)* 3 (30)

Clement, Chris, S.B. Bricker, and D.E. Pirhalla (2001). Eutrophic Conditions in Estuarine Waters. In *NOAA's State of the Coast Report.* Silver Spring MD, National Oceanic and Atmospheric Administration http://state-of-coast.noaa.gov/bulletins/html/eut_18/eut.html. Accessed 12 February 2002

Copeland, Claudia, and Jeffrey Zinn (1998). *Animal Waste Management and the Environment: Background for Current Issues.* The National Council for Science and the Environment http://cnie.org/NLE/CRS/abstract.cfm?NLEid=16293.Accessed 12 February 2002

Culliton, T.J., C.M. Blackwell, D.G. Remer, T.R. Goodspeed, M.A. Warren, and J.J. McDonough III (n.d.). *Fifty Years of Population Change Along the Nation's Coasts, 1960-2010. Coastal Trends Series, Report #2.* Rockville MD, Strategic Assessment Branch, Ocean Assessment Division, Office of Oceanography and Marine Assessment, National Ocean Survey, NOAA

DFAIT (2002). *Current Issues in Canada–US Relations.* Washington DC, Department of Foreign Affairs and International Trade, Embassy of Canada http://www.canadianembassy.org/foreignpolicy/report.asp. Accessed 11 February 2002

DFO (1999a). *1999 Agreement Between Canada and the US Under the Pacific Salmon Treaty.* Fisheries and Oceans Canada http://www.ncr.dfo.ca/pst-tsp/agree/toc_e.htm. Accessed 12 February 2002

DFO (1999b). *Backgrounder: Pacific Fisheries Adjustment and Restructuring Program.* Fisheries and Oceans Canada http://www.ncr.dfo.ca/COMMUNIC/BACKGROU/1999/hq29%28115%29_e.htm. Accessed 12 February 2002

DFO (2000a). *Canadian Aquaculture Production Statistics.* Fisheries and Oceans Canada http://www.dfo-mpo.gc.ca/communic/statistics/aquacult/aqua_e.htm. Accessed 12 February 2002

DFO (2000b). *Annual Summary Commercial Statistics, Salmon Landings in BC (1951-95).* Fisheries and Oceans Canada – Pacific Region http://www-sci.pac.dfo-mpo.gc.ca/sa/. Accessed 12 February 2002

DFO (2000c). Fisheries and Oceans Announces Rebuilding Efforts Result in Astounding Recovery of Upper Adams and Nadina Sockeye Runs. *News Release.* Fisheries and Oceans Canada http://www-comm.pac.dfo-mpo.gc.ca/english/release/p-releas/2000/nr00138e.htm. Accessed 12 February 2002

DFO (2001a). *Building Awareness and Capacity: An Action Plan for Continued Sustainable Development 2001-2003.* Fisheries and Oceans Canada http://www.dfo-mpo.gc.ca/sds-sdd/SDS01-03_e.pdf/susdev-e2.pdf. Accessed 11 February 2002

DFO (2001b). *Pacific Salmon Treaty: Canada and US Reach a Comprehensive Agreement under the Pacific Salmon Treaty.* Fisheries and Oceans Canada http://www.dfo-mpo.gc.ca/pst-tsp/main_e.htm. Accessed 11 February 2002

EC (1996). *The State of Canada's Environment – 1996.* Environment Canada http://www.ec.gc.ca/soer-ree/English/1996Report/Doc/1-1.cfm. Accessed 28 May 2002

EC (1999). *Canada's Oceans: Experience and Practices.* Canadian Contribution to the Oceans and Seas Dialogue, Paper for the Seventh Session of the United Nations Commission on Sustainable Development (UN CSD), 19-30 April

EC (2000). *Nutrient Additions and Their Impacts on the Canadian Environment: Reporting on the State of Canada's Environment.* Environment Canada http://www.durable.gc.ca/group/nutrients/report/index_e.phtml. Accessed 28 May 2002

EC (2001). *Nutrients in the Canadian Environment: Reporting on the State of Canada's Environment.* Environment Canada, Indicators and Assessment Office, Ecosystem Science Directorate, Environmental Conservation Service http://www.ec.gc.ca/soer-ree/english/national/nutrientseng.pdf. Accessed 31 January 2002

Environmental Defense (1998). *Environmental Defense Hog Watch* http://www.hogwatch.org/. Accessed 12 February 2002

EPA (1997). *Deposition of Air Pollutants to the Great Waters: Second Report to Congress.* Research Triangle Park NC, US Environmental Protection Agency, Office of Air Quality Planning and Standards

EPA (1998). *Terms of Environment, Revised Edition.* US Environmental Protection Agency http://www.epa.gov/OCEPAterms. Accessed 12 February 2002

EPA (2001). *Nutrient Criteria: Technical Guidance Manual,Estuarine and Coastal Marine Waters.* US Environmental Protection Agency, Office of Water http://www.epa.gov/ost/standards/nutrients/marine/. Accessed 11 February 2002

FAO (1990-1998). *Total Fish Catch (MT).* FAOSTAT Fisheries Data http://apps.fao.org/page/collections?subset=fisheries. Accessed 13 February 2002

Federal Caucus (2000). *Basinwide Salmon Recovery Strategy.* SalmonRecovery.gov http://www.salmonrecovery.gov/strategy.shtml. Accessed 13 February 2002

Fishstat (2001). *FISHSTAT Plus, Universal Software for Fishery Statistical Time Series.* FAO Fisheries, Software version 2.3 http://www.fao.org/fistatist/fisoft/fishplus.asp. Accessed 31 May 2002

Furuseth, Owen J. (1997). Restructuring of Hog Farming in North Carolina: Explosion and Implosion. *Professional Geographer* 49 (4):392-303

Glavin, Terry (1996). *Dead Reckoning: Confronting the Crisis in Pacific Fisheries.* Vancouver, Greystone Books

H. John Heinz III Center (1999). *Designing a Report on the State of the Nation's Ecosystem: Selected Measurements for Croplands, Forests, and Coasts and Oceans.* The H. John Heinz III Center for Science, Economics and the Environment http://www.heinzcenter.org/publications/Coasts.pdf. Accessed 12 February 2002

Hanfman, Deborah T. (1993). *The Status and Potential of Aquaculture in the United States: An Overview and Bibliography.* National Agricultural Library Aquaculture Information Center, National Agricultural Library Beltsville, Maryland http://ag.ansc.purdue.edu/aquanic/publicat/govagen/nal/status.htm. Accessed 12 February 2002

Hare, S.R., and N.J. Mantua (2000). Empirical Evidence for North Pacific Regime Shifts in 1977 and 1989. *Progress in Oceanography* 47 (2-4):103-46

Harkin, Senator Tom (1997). *Animal Waste Pollution in America: An Emerging National Problem.* Report Compiled by the Minority Staff of the United States Senate Committee on Agriculture, Nutrition, & Forestry for Senator Tom Harkin http://www.senate.gov/~agriculture/Briefs/animalw.htm. Accessed 13 February 2002

Howarth, Robert , Donald Anderson, James Cloern, Chris Elfring, Charles Hopkinson, Brian Lapointe, Tom Malone, Nancy Marcus, Karen McGlathery, Andrew Sharpley, and Dan Walker (2000). Nutrient Pollution of Coastal Rivers, Bays, and Seas. *Issues in Ecology* (7) http://esa.sdsc.edu/issues.htm

JISAO (2000). *The Pacific Decadal Oscillation (PDO).* Joint Institute for the Study of the Atmosphere and Ocean http://tao.atmos.washington.edu/pdo/. Accessed 12 February 2002

Kope, Robert G. (1999). Pacific Salmon. In *Our Living Oceans: Report on the Status of US Living Marine Resources, 1999.* US National Marine Fisheries Service, US Department of Commerce, NOAA Tech, Memo. NMFS-F/SPO-41, on-line version http://spo.nwr.noaa.gov/unit12.pdf. Accessed 13 February 2002

Mann, Charles, C., and Mark L. Plummer (2000). Can Science Rescue Salmon? *Science* 289 (5480):716-19

Mathews, Emily, and Allen Hammond (1999). *Critical Consumption Trends and Implications: Degrading Earth's Ecosystems.* Washington DC., World Resources Institute

Miller Jr., G. Tyler (1985). *Living in the Environment: An Introduction to Environmental Science.* Vol. 4. Belmont, CA, Wadsworth Publishing Company

Myers, J.M., R.G. Kope, G.J. Bryant, D. Teel, L.J. Lierheimer, T.C. Wainwright, W.S. Grand, F.W. Waknitz, K. Neely, S.T. Lindley, and R.S. Waples (1998). *Status Review of Chinook Salmon from Washington, Idaho, Oregon, and California.* US Department of Commerce, NOAA Tech. Memo. NMFS-NWFSC-35

NMFS (1998). *Factors Contributing to the Decline of Chinook Salmon: An Addendum to the 1996 West Coast Steelhead Factors For Decline Report.* Protected Resources Division, National Marine Fisheries Service http://www.nwr.noaa.gov/1salmon/salmesa/pubs.htm#Factors for Decline. Accessed 13 February 2002

NMFS (2000). *Fisheries Statistics & Economics, Commercial Fisheries, Annual Landings.* Silver Spring MD, National Marine Fisheries Service, Fisheries Statistics and Economics Division, http://www.st.nmfs.gov/. Accessed 27 February 2002

NOAA (1998). *1998 Year of the Ocean: Perspectives on Marine Environmental Quality Today.* US National Oceanic and Atmospheric Administration http://www.yoto98.noaa.gov/yoto/meeting/mar_env_316.html. Accessed 13 February 2002

NOAA (1999). *United States Announces Agreement With Canada On Pacific Salmon.* US Department of State, US Department of Commerce http://www.nwr.noaa.gov/1press/060399_1.html. Accessed 13 February 2002

NOS (2000). *National Centers for Coastal Ocean Science, Gulf of Mexico Hypoxia Assessment.* National Ocean Service, National Oceanic and Atmospheric Administration, US Department of Commerce http://www.nos.noaa.gov/products/pubs_hypox.html. Accessed 13 February 2002.

NPPC (1999). *1999/2000 Pork Issues Handbook.* National Pork Producers Council http://www.nppc.org/IssueHandbook/99_2000_handbook.pdf. Accessed 13 February 2002

NRCan (1998). *Sensitivities to Climate Change.* Natural Resources Canada, Geological Survey of Canada http://sts.gsc.nrcan.gc.ca/adaptation/sensitivities/map5.htm. Accessed 13 February 2002

NRCan (2000). *Clean Coastal Waters: Understanding and Reducing the Effects of Nutrient Pollution.* Committee on the Causes and Management of Coastal Eutrophication, Ocean Studies Board and Water Sicence and Technology Board; Commission on Geosciences, Environment, and Resources; National Research Council. Washington DC, National Academy Press http://books.nap.edu/books/0309069483/html/R1.html. Accessed 13 February 2002

NSTC (2000). *National Assessment of Harmful Algal Blooms in US Waters.* National Science and Technology Council, Committee on Environment and Natural Resources http://www.habhrca.noaa.gov/FinalHABreport.pdf. Accessed 11 February 2002

OECD (1996). *Environmental Performance Reviews: United States.* Paris, Organization for Economic Co-operation and Development

OSF (2000). *Office of Sustainable Fisheries Home Page.* Office of Sustainable Fisheries, NOAA Fisheries, National Marine Fisheries Service http://www.nmfs.noaa.gov/sfa/sfweb/index.htm. Accessed 11 February 2002

PSC (2000). *Pacific Salmon Commission.* Pacific Salmon Commission http://www.psc.org/Index.htm. Accessed 13 February 2002

Rabalais, Nancy N. (1999). *Oxygen Depletion in Coastal Waters: NOAA's State of the Coast Report.* Silver Spring MD, US National Oceanic and Atmospheric Administration http://state-of-coast.noaa.gov/bulletins/html/hyp_09/hyp.html. Accessed 12 February 2002

Statistics Canada (2000). *Human Activity and the Environment.* Ottawa, Minister of Industry

Strangway, David W., and William D. Ruckelshaus (1998). *Pacific Salmon Report to the Prime Minister of Canada and to the President of the United States.* Fisheries and Oceans Canada http://www.ncr.dfo.ca/pst-tsp/reports/report.htm. Accessed 13 February 2002

Taylor, David A. (2001). From Pigsties to Hog Heaven. *Environmental Health Perspectives* 109 (7):A328-31

The White House (2000). *Statement by the President on Oceans Act 2000.* Martha's Vineyard MA, The White House, Office of the Press Secretary http://clinton6.nara.gov/2000/08/2000-08-07-statement-by-the-president-on-oceans-act-of.html. Accessed 13 February 2002

TU / TUC (1999). *Resolving the Pacific Salmon Treaty Stalemate.* Seattle, Trout Unlimited USA in partnership with Trout Unlimited Canada http://www.tu.org/newsstand/library_pdfs/pacificsalmon99.pdf. Accessed 13 February 2002

USGCRP (2000). *Climate Change Impacts on the United States: The Potential Consequences of Climate Variability and Change.* Washington DC, National Assessment Synthesis Team, US Global Change Research Program http://sedac.ciesin.org/NationalAssessment/. Accessed 13 February 2002

Walters, Carl (1995). *Fish on the Line: The Future of Pacific Fisheries.* Vancouver, The David Suzuki Foundation

Welch, David (1999). What is the Most Alarming Potential Impact of Climate Change on Salmon Stocks? Panel at Climate Change and Salmon Stocks, 27 October, at Vancouver BC, Pacific Fisheries Resource Conservation Council

Welsh, R., B. Hubbell, and C.L. Carpentier (2000). Agro-Food System Restructuring and the Geographic Concentration of US Swine Production, 1975–1996. *Environment & Planning* unpublished manuscript currently under review

YCELP (1995). *A Request for a NACEC Secretariat Report on Opportunities for Forest Preservation and Sustainable Management.* Student Clinic, Yale Center for Environmental Law and Policy, Yale Environmental Policy Clinic for the Natural Resources Defense Council http://www.yale.edu/envirocenter/clinic/nacec.html. Accessed 27 February 2002

Freshwater

5

Freshwater

North America has abundant water resources and holds about 13 percent of the world's renewable freshwater (excluding glaciers and ice caps). Canada has about 10 times the per capita water resources and about half a million km³ more water in total than the United States. Freshwater is not evenly distributed, of course: for example, the Great Lakes, the world's largest system of fresh, surface water lies in the east, 60 percent of Canada's water flows north, and water supplies in the United States are far more abundant in the eastern states than those in the west, particularly the dry southwest (EC 1998a; De Villiers 2000; CEC 2002). Some regions, such as California, suffer from acute water deficits, and the frequency of extreme events like droughts and floods is expected to increase in areas such as the Great Plains.

Extensive water control projects, including dams and canals, have been built to compensate for water deficiencies, generate hydroelectric power, control floods, and improve navigation. Today, water in less than half of the region's rivers still flows in a course unaltered by humans, resulting in changed hydrologic flows, landscapes, and wildlife habitat. Canada has more water diversions than any other country, particularly in the province of Quebec (CEC 2002). As in other parts of the world, environmental and aboriginal groups have opposed large dams because of their ecological and social impacts (see Box 25).

With an abundant supply of fresh water, a growing population, extensive irrigated agriculture, and growing municipal and industrial demands, North Americans use more water per person per year than any other people (De Villiers 2000). At the end of the 1990s, they used 1,693 cubic meters of water per capita per year (Gleick 1998). In the United States, recent conservation measures have led to declines in both per capita and total water consumption (De Villiers 2000). Between 1980 and 1995, total water withdrawals declined by nearly 10 percent while the population increased by 16 percent (Solley, Pierce, and Perlman

1998). In Canada, on the other hand, water withdrawal rose by 80 percent between 1972 and 1991 while the population grew by only 3 percent (EC 2001a). Water pricing in Canada does not reflect the costs of water provision, with the result that water is overused, industrial water recirculation rates have been low, and until recently, there has been little reinvestment in municipal water systems (EC 1998a). There is also an overall paucity of data and knowledge about water in Canada, which hampers reporting efforts.

Agriculture accounts for the largest proportion of total water consumed in North America. The United States has over 75 percent of the continent's irrigated cropland, which consumes its largest amount of water by far. In Canada, by contrast, agriculture is the fourth largest user of water. As discussed below, one of North America's priority concerns is the quantity and quality of the region's groundwater resources, which provide most irrigation supplies and drinking water to rural communities (CEC 2002).

Box 25: James Bay Hydroelectric Development

The province of Quebec nationalized hydroelectric development in the 1960s and began to harness the power of the northern rivers of the James Bay territory in the 1970s to provide the province with clean energy, jobs, and economic growth. The first phase of the project on La Grande River, about 1,000 km north of Montreal, diverted five rivers and created a reservoir of 4,275 km^2. The second phase diverted another five rivers. Together, these projects vastly changed the watersheds of 10,000 km^2 of territory that was home to some 10,000 First Nations Cree. Having failed to stop the project through the courts, the Cree signed a historic comprehensive land claim agreement in 1975 that was meant to compensate them for the loss of traditional lands and livelihoods.

The next phase, the damming of the Great Whale River north of the La Grande complex, announced in 1989, would divert two more rivers and flood 3,400 km^2 for four reservoirs. In 1985, La Grande was producing large electricity surpluses, some of which were sold to the eastern United States. Environmental groups in the northeastern United States and the Cree in Quebec mounted a strong campaign against the Great Whale Project. Part of their campaign focused on the advantages of energy efficiency over new hydroelectric development. They initiated and won a court case that provoked a comprehensive environmental and social assessment of the project's impacts. The project was eventually delayed indefinitely in September 1991 in reaction to new energy efficiency practices in New York state, a drop in its projected energy demand, and the cancellation of its energy import contract with Hydro-Quebec, combined with the need for a full and lengthy impact assessment (Barr 1992).

In a recent and much more modest development project, the Quebec government entered into partnership with the Cree in February 2002 to allow hydro installations along the Eastmain and Rupert rivers, subject to environmental approval, closing a deal deemed favorable by the majority of the Cree community. It includes financial compensation, increased control of their own community and economy, more power over logging, and more hydro-related employment opportunities (Canadian Press 2002).

Gross-point source water pollution has been successfully reduced in North America since the 1970s thanks to effective anti-pollution laws and regulations and clean-up programs. The US Clean Water Act of 1970 and subsequent amendments were instrumental in declines in industrial wastewater emissions and untreated sewage dumping. Non-point sources, however, such as agricultural runoff and urban storm drainage have increased, causing serious pollution problems. By the end of the 1990s, an overwhelming majority of US citizens—some 218 million—lived within 16 km of a polluted lake, river, stream, or coastal area (EPA 2000a).

Thirty years ago, one of the gravest issues facing North America's freshwater resources was the precarious state of the Great Lakes Basin, which contains the world's largest freshwater system and North America's biggest urban-industrial complex. The story of how the region tackled its complex and serious water problems is a striking example of cooperation among nations and local users.

Box 26: Some Health Risks From Groundwater Pollution

Groundwater contains naturally occurring chemicals that sometimes exceed drinking water standards or render it unfit for consumption. It may be that as much as half the groundwater within 496 m of the surface is too saline for use as drinking water (Moody 1996). Human activities are further reducing the quality of groundwater resources through the large and growing number of toxic compounds used in industry and agriculture. Once it was thought the soil acted as an effective filter, preventing all contaminants from reaching the water table, but there is now evidence that pesticides and other contaminants reach groundwater resources that can slowly spread the contaminants over large areas. Polluted groundwater is extremely expensive and difficult, if not impossible, to clean up. In many cases contamination may only be recognized after users have been exposed to potential health risks (Waldron 1992; Moody 1996; EPA 1998; EC 1999a).

About 20 to 40 percent of all rural well water in Canada may be affected by contaminants, mostly in the form of coliform bacteria from livestock and septic systems and nitrates from fertilizer (EC 1996). The incidence of bacteria in well water in Ontario has almost doubled in the past 45 years (Fairchild, Barry, and others 2000).

A number of recent reports of localized well contamination have alerted the public to the health risks associated with polluted groundwater (EC 1999a). In May 2000, for example, seven Canadians in Walkerton, Ontario, died and more than 2,000 became sick from *E.coli* contamination in the town's water supply. The source of contamination was livestock manure that had been spread, according to proper practices, on a farm near the town. Provincial budget reductions had led to shortcomings in the approvals and inspections programs of the Ontario Ministry of the Environment and years of improper practices at the public water utility. The tragedy alerted the Canadian provinces to the need to correct serious drinking water problems related to animal waste encroachment into groundwater supplies and, in the case of Ontario, to the roles played by budget cuts, staff reductions, and greater reliance on municipalities for regulating environmental services (Gallon 2000; O'Connor 2002).

Groundwater

Most of the continent's (unfrozen) freshwater resources lie in groundwater, which fills the spaces below the soil surface. It is stored in, and moves through, water-saturated zones called aquifers. In response to dwindling supplies of unpolluted surface water in the decades leading up to the 1970s, municipalities in the United States turned to groundwater. Similarly, between the 1960s and 1980s, the proportion of Canadians drinking groundwater more than doubled (OECD 1995b). By the mid 1990s, about 51 percent of all drinking water for the total US population and 99 percent of drinking water for the rural population came from groundwater, while in Canada, groundwater supplied 30 percent of the population, or about 8 million people, and 90 percent of rural dwellers (EPA 1998; Statistics Canada 2000). In the mid-1990s, a total of 23.4 percent of all US freshwater withdrawals for all uses came from groundwater, while in Canada, groundwater supplied only 2.3 percent of total water withdrawals (OECD 1995a).

Groundwater is critical not only as a direct supply of water for human uses, but also as a crucial part of the hydrological cycle, and its gradual discharge to rivers helps to maintain stream flow in dry periods. It is important to wildlife and their habitats as well, which are also affected by contamination and depletion (GF 1996).

The large and growing number of hazardous compounds used in industry and agriculture are threatening groundwater quality. It is now known that contaminants from non-point sources are present in many shallow wells throughout large regions of North America (Moody 1996) and present risks to human health (see Box 26). Table 3 shows the presence of selected chemicals in US groundwater.

Agriculture is the dominant factor in groundwater quality impairment (EC 1996), primarily through the

Table 3: Groundwater Contamination in the United States, Selected Chemicals, 1990s

Chemical Group	Share of Groundwater Percent		
	Containing at least one chemical in group	Containing two or more chemicals in group	Above drinking water guidelines for a single chemical
Nitrates	71	Not applicable[1]	15
Pesticides	50	25	Not significant
Volatile Organic Compounds[2]	47[3]	29	6

[1] However, nitrates are typically found in aquifers where pesticides are detected.
[2] A small share of these VOCs are used as pesticides.
[3] Samples from urban areas only.

Source: Sampat 2000b, 26

widespread use of commercial fertilizer, the main non-point source of nitrogen and phosphorous contamination. Artificial fertilizer use rose from 13.6 to 20.4 million tons a year over the past 30 years (IIFA 2001), peaking in 1981 in the United States then rising again after 1995. This increase reflects the rise in maize acreage, which uses 40 to 45 percent of all fertilizers (CEQ 1997) (see Figure 27). The nitrogen content of commercial fertilizer

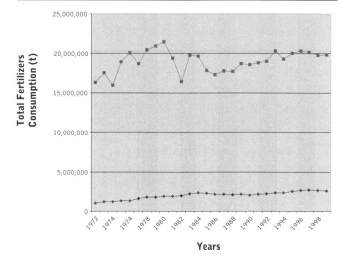

Total Fertilizer Consumption, 1972-1999

Years

Figure 27

Total fertilizer consumption, 1972-1999.

Source: FAO 1990-1998

applied on farmland also increased, growing in Canada by 451 percent between 1970 and 1995 (Statistics Canada 2000). Some consider nitrates to be the most widespread groundwater contaminant (EPA 1998). Consumed in high concentrations, this chemical can cause infant methemoglobinemia, or blue-baby syndrome (Sampat 2000a).

In the mid 1970s, elevated nitrate levels resulting from fertilizer infiltration in rural groundwater supplies began to be detected

(Gurganus and Engel 1989). Excessive nitrogen—that not taken up by crops—can leach into groundwater. This is increasingly the case in regions with concentrated industrial hog and other livestock operations using manure as a fertilizer (see Box 23 in the coastal and marine section). For example, between 1971 and 1991, the risk of nitrate contamination of aquifer waters in British Columbia is estimated to have doubled due to the concentration of animal production and some shifts to land uses with low nitrogen needs (MacLeod, Sanderson, and Campbell 2000).

Although nitrogen contamination rarely exceeds levels of potential health risk, some groundwater wells in Canada's Atlantic provinces, where about 90 percent of the rural population relies on groundwater, have elevated nitrate concentration (Statistics Canada 2000). And in Ontario alone, a study found that 37 percent of 1,300 farm wells surveyed contained bacteria or nitrate levels exceeding provincial water quality objectives (AAFC 1997). Nitrate-nitrogen concentrations greater than the Canadian drinking water quality guideline of 10 mg per litre occurred in anywhere from 1.5 percent to over 60 percent of the wells visited in a recent regional survey, and levels are continuing to rise (AAFC 1997; EC 2001b).

In the United States in the mid-1990s, nitrates polluted groundwater to some extent in 49 states, although nitrate contamination at levels of potential health risk affects fewer than 2 percent of wells (OECD 1996). Concentrations of nitrate that exceed the US EPA drinking water standard of 10 mg per liter (as nitrogen) were found in 15 percent of samples collected in shallow groundwater beneath agricultural and urban land, which may be of concern in those rural areas that rely on shallow aquifers for drinking water (USGS 1999). Concentrations that exceed the recommended level are found mostly in aquifers that are subject to high nitrogen inputs and are most vulnerable to leaching (Revenga, Brunner, and others 2000). The US Department of Agriculture and most Canadian provinces have initiated strategies to help farmers develop nutrient management plans (EPA 1998; EC 2001c).

Pesticides also enter groundwater, and several incidents of contamination from field applications of pesticides were confirmed in the 1980s in the United States (Gurganus and Engel 1989). In the 1993–95 and the 1999 National Water Quality Assessments (NWQA), about half of the wells sampled contained one or more pesticides, with the highest detection frequencies in shallow groundwater beneath agricultural and urban areas. The overall frequency of pesticide detection in these studies is considerably higher than those reported by previous large-scale studies of pesticide occurrence in groundwater across the United States. Herbicides account for about 70 percent of total US use of pesticides. Water-quality

standards and guidelines have been established for only about one-half of the pesticides measured in the study's water samples. Although concentrations of individual pesticides rarely exceed the current drinking water standards, some scientists suggest that the overall health and environmental risks of their combined effects are not adequately assessed (Kolpin, Barbash, and Gilliom 1998; USGS 1999).

In Canada, pesticide concentrations in groundwater are also mostly well below guidelines for drinking water. New application restrictions

for atrazine, the herbicide most often detected in groundwater, are expected to help reduce the concentrations found in the past due to long-term monoculture production in Ontario and Quebec (AAFC 2000).

Underground storage tanks (UST) containing, for example, petroleum products, acids, chemicals, and industrial solvents, and other types of waste, are leading sources of groundwater contamination by known or suspected carcinogens (Sampat 2000b). The tanks are often inappropriate containers for these substances or have been improperly installed. Prior to 1980, they were made of steel and many were not adequately protected against corrosion. Up to half of them leak by the time they are over 15 years old (EC1999a). In 1996, about 20 percent of US steel tanks were over 16 years old and some 25 to 30 percent were leaking petro-

Sectoral Share of Groundwater Withdrawals, 1987

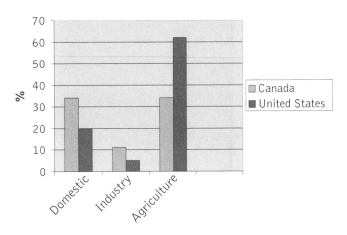

Sectoral Share

Figure 28
Sectoral share of groundwater withdrawals, 1987.

Source: UNEP, World Bank and WRI 2000, updated by White 2001.

leum products (Moody 1996). In 1998, over 100,000 petroleum USTs in the United States were found to be leaking. Environment Canada estimates that more than 20 percent of the 10,000 tank systems (underground and above ground) at federally owned or leased facilities in Ontario are currently leaking (EC n.d.). Tanks are leading sources of benzene, toluene, and xylene contaminants. Many contaminants are known or suspected carcinogens (Sampat 2000b). When MTBE, a

chemical added to gasoline to reduce carbon monoxide pollution, leaks from storage tanks, it causes widespread groundwater pollution and is shown in animal studies to cause cancer (Tenenbaum 2000). As of 1998, State Underground Tank Remediation Funds have helped to clean up many US sites (EPA 1998).

Septic tank systems, the largest source by volume of waste discharged to the land, contain many organic contaminants and are suspected to be one of the key sources of rural well contamination by nutrients and microbes. Septic systems have a normal 10-to-15 year design life, and many of those built during the 1970s may be failing and causing groundwater contamination. Between one-third and one-half of US septic systems may have been operating inadequately in 1996 due to their age and other design and management shortcomings (Moody 1996). Another high-priority source of groundwater contamination is landfills that operated prior to the establishment of legislation requiring them to adhere to strict standards (EPA 1998).

The long-term availability of groundwater in arid agricultural regions is another key concern. In general, use of stored groundwater declined since the 1980s, but still accounted for about 10 percent of all freshwater withdrawal in the United States in the mid-1990s (OECD 1996). Agriculture is the largest user of groundwater resources, supplying 62 percent of US irrigated farmland in 1985 (OECD 1996; Sampat 2000b) (see Figure

28). Groundwater withdrawals in 1995 were generally highest in the western states to supply a growing population and to sustain agricultural production (EPA 1998). The Ogallala Aquifer under the High Plains is being depleted, with withdrawals exceeding the rate of renewal despite recent conservation measures (see Box 27).

Widespread recognition of the need to protect groundwater has

Box 27: The Ogallala Aquifer

The Ogallala Aquifer, which contains about the same amount of water as Lake Erie, underlies about 580,000 square kilometers of the Great Plains in eight states, most of which are the portion called the High Plains (see Figure 29). Although semi-arid and subject to frequent droughts, the Ogallala states make up one of the world's major agricultural regions, producing almost half of US beef and a significant proportion of its grain exports (Dugan and Sharpe 1996; De Villiers 2000). Nearly 30 percent of all the groundwater used for irrigation in the nation comes from the aquifer, and in 1990, about 95 percent of the water withdrawn from it was devoted to agriculture (McGuire, Stanton, and Fischer 1999).

The number of irrigated areas expanded after 1940 and extensive groundwater irrigation development resulted in large water-level declines in many areas of the High Plains region (Blazs 2000). A trend of rapid aquifer decline rates of as much as 1.5 m a year in places slowed after the mid-1970s (Abramovitz 1996). Between 1980 and 1997, the decline was half the rate it had been between 1950 and 1980 (McGuire, Stanton, and Fischer 2000). A number of factors contributed to the declines: low well yields; improved water conservation irrigation equipment and management practices; conversion to crops requiring less irrigation; local regulation of groundwater withdrawals for irrigation; the geographic shift in irrigation away from areas of large potential rates of aquifer depletion; the withdrawal of some marginal lands from irrigated agriculture; rising energy costs; low farm prices; and above-normal precipitation (Dugan and Sharpe 1996; HPWD 1997/98). These are encouraging signs even though depletion continues (Abramovitz 1996).

The Ogalla Aquifer

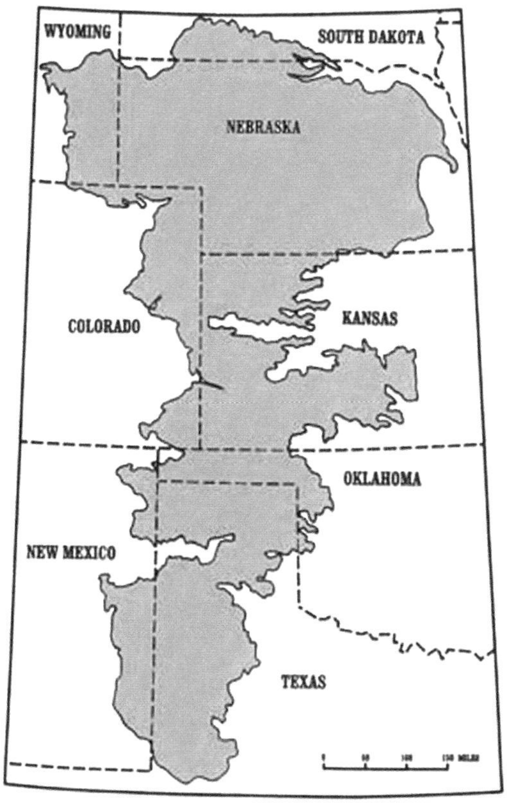

Figure 29 *Source: HPDW 2002*

Box 28: Water Use in the Las Vegas Valley

Las Vegas, Nevada's population began to grow with the opening of hotels and casinos during the boom in the gaming industry in the 1940s. Growth continued, fueled by tourism and migration toward the Sun Belt. By the 1980s and '90s, Las Vegas had become a major convention center. Over the past 20 years, the population in the Las Vegas Valley has increased dramatically (see Figure 30). Today, Las Vegas is the fastest-growing metropolitan area in the United States; its population is predicted to double by 2015.

The temperature in the Las Vegas Valley typically rises to 32.2 °C or more on over 125 days of the year and less than 1000 mm of rain fall annually to the valley floor. As the city grew (see figure 30a), so demand for water for residential, hotel, recreation, and industrial uses increased, and groundwater was withdrawn faster than it recharged, causing the land to subside in

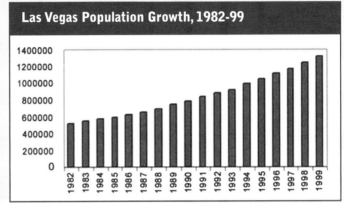

Las Vegas Population Growth, 1982-99

Figure 30 *Source: LVWCC n.d.*

places. Water has been imported from the Colorado River, and during the last decade, the main aquifer has been artificially recharged with water from nearby Lake Mead. Although water levels have risen as a result, growing demand for water and limits on imports have led to withdrawals often exceeding recharge by factors of two to three.

With some 6,000 newcomers a month relocating to the valley, huge hotels that feature water-related attractions, over 50 irrigated golf courses in the area, and watering of inappropriate landscaping features, Las Vegas water uses are straining supplies. The Southern Nevada Water Authority (SNWA) is implementing strategies to expand the future supply of water to southern Nevada and the Las Vegas Valley. Since 1989, water conservation awareness campaigns have helped to reduce per capita water consumption by 12 percent (Acevado, Gaydos, and others 1997; Bennet 1998, Pavelko, Wood, and Laczniak 1999).

only recently arisen. Given the greater reliance on this resource in the United States, that country has taken a more active role in protecting it than the Canadian government (TFGRR 1993). The individual states and provinces have the primary responsibility for groundwater and groundwater jurisdiction in North America is divided and often fragmented among federal, state/provincial, and local governments (Cosgrove and Rijsberman 2000). Although there are some 20 EPA programs addressing groundwater, there is no single comprehensive, coherent federal legislation covering this resource. During the late 1980s and early 1990s, all US States enacted groundwater legislation

(TFGRR 1993; Gobert 1997). As shown in the Ogallala example in Box 27, an increase in dry farming practices and improved and more efficient irrigation techniques contributed to declines in ground-water withdrawals in the United States between 1980 and 1995 (EPA 1998).

Canada's 1987 Federal Water Policy, currently under revision, calls for the sustainable use of freshwater and recently, the Cana-dian federal government initiated new national legislation on the environment, trade, and groundwa-ter issues (EC 1998a; EC 1999a). The US Geological Survey and the Canadian Geological Survey also undertook the task of examaning and reporting on issues affecting groundwater (DOI and USGS 1998; EC 1998a). Rights to groundwater are more complex than those for surface water because it is a transboundary resource and is used by a common pool of users (Rogers 1996). Recent dramatic population growth in the dry US interior (see Box 28), for example, has increased city-farm competition for groundwa-ter as demands by an affluent and growing population increase (Rogers 1996, CEC 2000). At the international level, boundary water agreements lack specific guidelines regarding transboundary aquifers, complicating jurisdiction of shared groundwater resources.

Traditionally, groundwater management has focused on sur-face and groundwater separately (USGS 1999). Yet interactions

1972

2000

between them have direct effects on regional water quality and availabil-ity, as well as on the health of wetlands, riparian ecology, and aquatic ecosystems in general (Cosgrove and Rijsberman 2000).

Figure 30a

These satellite images show the population growth that occurred in Las Vegas, Nevada USA from 1972 to 2000.

Source: NASA, Landsat

To evaluate the quantity and quality of water resources, coordination between surface and groundwater programs is essential (EPA 1998). To address this need, and to better detect the sources of non-point pollution, the US EPA introduced a river basin approach through its Index of Watershed Indicators (IWI), using 18 indicators of the health of the nation's water resources in 2,111 watersheds. The IWI shows that 15 percent of watersheds have relatively good water quality; 36 percent have moderate problems; 22 percent of the watersheds have more serious water

Great Lakes Water Quality

The Great Lakes Basin is one of the Earth's largest freshwater systems, containing 18 percent of the world's fresh surface water (see Box 29). Less than 1.0 percent of the water is renewed annually by precipitation, surface water runoff, and groundwater inflow (EC 2000a).

As the region's economy shifted from a rural-agrarian one to North America's largest urban-industrial complex, the lakes became subject to a polluting mix of effluents resulting from inadequate sewage treatment and fertilizer and wastewater effluent. By the early 1970s, beaches were

Box 29: The Great Lakes

The Great Lakes lie within eight US states and the Canadian province of Ontario and span over 1,200 km from east to west, covering an area of 750,000 km² (EC 2000a). They form a transportation route from the Atlantic Ocean to the middle of the continent and part of the boundary between Canada and the United States. Half of the trade between the two countries crosses the region and they share the lakes' bountiful resources and services, which include diverse and abundant fish; water for shipping, municipal, industrial, and agricultural uses; hydroelectric power supplies; recreational playgrounds; and water for 27 percent of Canadians and 11 percent of US citizens. The region's waters also play a major role in North America's ecology and climate and the Basin supports extensive forests, huge mineral reserves, fertile agricultural areas, and an abundant and diverse wildlife (EC n.d; EC 1999b; EC 2000a).

quality problems; and 27 percent do not have enough information to be characterized. One in 15 watersheds are also highly vulnerable to further degradation (IWI 1999). Canada, too, adopted an ecosystem approach for watershed management and together with other levels of government and stakeholders is developing basin-wide action plans to restore numerous polluted aquatic ecosystems (EC 1998a).

smothered with algae and the water was unfit for drinking unless extensively purified. Lake Erie suffered from excess phosphorus, algal blooms, and serious declines in some fish populations. Aboriginal communities, which relied heavily on the lakes' resources for their subsistence, were most affected. Newspaper headlines in 1970 declared that 'Lake Erie is Dead' (EC n.d.; EC 1999b).

Other clues pointed to more insidious problems. In the early 1970s, eggshells of the Double-crested Cormorant, a bird that is high on the aquatic food chain and subject to the effects of bioaccumulation, were some 30 percent thinner than normal (EC 1999b). Some species of bird populations crashed.

In 1970, the International Joint Commission (IJC), an independent organization of Canadian and US representatives that has existed since 1909 (see Box 30) released a report on the pollution problem in the lower Great Lakes.

The IJC report led to the 1972 signing of the Great Lakes Water Quality Agreement (GLWQA) (see Box 31) and the beginning of concerted efforts on the part of both countries to restore the Basin's water quality.

Public consultation and involvement were critical to the enactment of the GLWQA and to regional action plans, bringing together various interest groups to achieve consensus on issues and actions (EC

Box 30: Binational Cooperation, the IJC

Established under the Boundary Waters Treaty of 1909, the IJC has been in charge of preventing and resolving disputes over, and assessing and reporting on, water quantity and quality along the boundary between Canada and the United States. The IJC is an independent organization consisting of six members, three appointed by each head of government. Today, there are more than 20 boards made up of experts from both governments that carry out its work (IJC 2000a).

1999b; EC n.d). The numbers of NGOs dedicated to improving the Great Lakes environment grew substantially in the 1980s, and they took on roles in educating the public, lobbying governments, and serving as 'watchdog' to governmental progress. In 1982, Great Lakes United was formed and became the region's foremost and most influential basin-wide NGO (EC 1999b).

The call to action led to one of the notable success stories in the history of pollution reduction in the Basin. The 1970s IJC's report showed the link between increasing phosphorus concentrations and the

---

Box 31: Binational Cooperation, the GLWQA

Canada and the United States signed the Great Lakes Water Quality Agreement (GLWQA) in 1972. This milestone event committed the two countries to controlling and cleaning up pollution in the Great Lakes from industrial and municipal wastewaters. The major issue was phosphorus over-enrichment. In 1978, the GLWQA was renewed and made more comprehensive with the introduction of the ecosystem approach, in which the interactions among water, air, land, biota, and humans are considered together. The agreement was also expanded to address persistent toxic chemical discharges to the ecosystem. The 1987 protocol to the GLWQA set out targets or strategies for phosphorus load reductions, airborne pollutants, pollution from land based activities, and the problems of contaminated sediment and groundwater. Amendments required the two countries to develop Remedial Action Plans (RAPs) to clean up 43 Areas of Concern (AOCs) (see Figure 31) (EC n.d.; IJC 1989).

appearance of nuisance algae and suggested that the loadings would need to decline from about 28,000 tons a year to about 11,000 tons. Strict control of phosphates in detergents, sewage treatment plant upgrades and other pollution controls led to a 50 percent reduction in phosphorus levels in Lake Erie by the mid-1980s. Since then, it has continued to oscillate around the recommended level of 9,979 tons annually (AAFC 2000). Municipal phosphorus loadings to Lakes Erie and Ontario have been reduced by almost 80 percent since the 1970s, slowing algal growth and decreasing the extent of oxygen depletion in bottom waters. Once

thought 'dead', Lake Erie now boasts the world's largest walleye fishery (EC n.d.; EC 1999b).

Another success story in reversing Great Lakes pollution is the reduction in production and use of a number of persistent toxic chemicals through legislated controls. For example, large quantities of wastewater from the pulp and paper mills located on the Lakes' shores were being discharged directly into the Basin's waters. These effluents carry dioxins and furans from bleaching agents, among other polluting constituents (EC 1999c). Since the late 1980s, government regulations have achieved an 82 percent reduction in chlorinated toxic substances

Figure 31
Areas of Concern (AOCs) in the Great Lakes

Source: EC 2000b

Areas of Concern (AOCs) in the Great Lakes

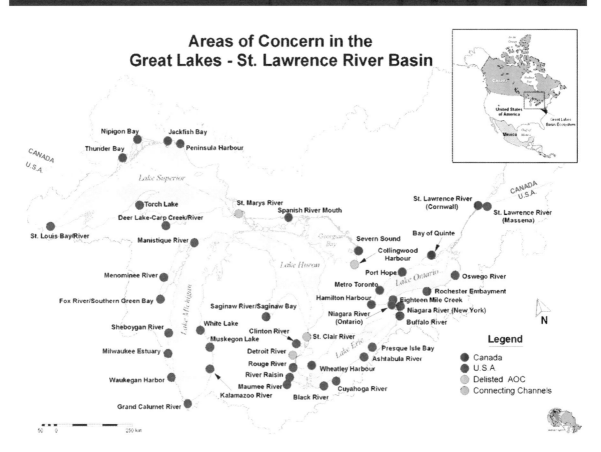

Areas of Concern in the
Great Lakes - St. Lawrence River Basin

discharged from pulp and paper
mills and reduced the dioxins and
furans in effluents, resulting in their
virtual elimination from the mills'
wastewater. Since 1972, there has
been an overall cutback of 71 percent in the use, generation, and
release of seven priority toxic chemicals and a significant reduction in
the number and magnitude of
chemical spills (EC n.d.; EC 1999b).

DDT and PCB residues, once
exceptionally high in cormorant
eggs in the Great Lakes Basin,
decreased by as much as 91 percent
and 78 percent respectively between
the early 1970s and 1998 (EC
2001b). Cormorant populations are
breeding successfully again (see
Figure 32) and other bird populations, such as the Osprey and Bald
Eagle, are growing (EC 1998b;
EC 1999b).

As government legislation and
public participation addressed these
problems, rapid urban and industrial development continued to
cause environmental damage to the
watershed during the 1990s. By
1990, the population in the Great
Lakes Basin had reached 33.4
million, an 8 percent increase since
1970 (EC n.d.). During the 1990s,
scientific studies pointed to new
issues of concern.

By the mid-1990s, sediment
contamination was identified as a
key environmental problem in all
Areas of Concern and the IJC
named it a priority issue for the
1995–1997 biennial cycle (IJC 1997).
Sediment accumulates in harbors
and river mouths, which also receive

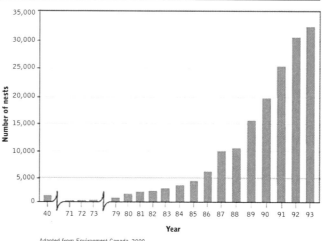

Double-crested Cormorant Population in the Great Lakes, 1971-1993

Adapted from Environment Canada, 2000

urban and agricultural effluent.
Animals and humans can be affected by the contaminants through
contact with sediment or the consumption of fish from contaminated
areas. The viability of commercial
ports is threatened by contaminated
sediment because of restrictions on
vessel traffic and delays and costs
related to dredging navigation
channels and disposing of the
dredged sediments. It is also costly
to treat water taken from contaminated areas (IJC 1997).

Persistent toxic chemicals were
also a concern. During the 1980s,
the IJC noted a leveling out of the
downward trend in contaminant
concentrations (Bandemehr and
Hoff 1998). As a result of the continued cycling of these substances in
the ecosystem and the release from
sediments, persistent toxic substances remained in the Basin even
though many of them had been
banned in North America. But
during the 1990s, evidence revealed

Figure 32
Double-crested
Cormorant
population in
the Great
Lakes, 1971-
1993.

*Source: AAFC
2000*

that pollutants carried in the air drift down onto the lakes, contributing significantly to water pollution (EPA 1997). One study reported

that up to 96 percent of PCBs in the Great Lakes came from the atmosphere (Bandemehr and Hoff 1998). In 1990, the two countries developed an integrated network to address the problem of atmospheric deposition (see Box 32).

with stressful situations, and displayed slightly delayed neuromuscular development during infancy (Health Canada 1997). A 2001 study found that even the health of mature adults could be affected by exposure to contaminated fish. Adults who ate large amounts of fish from Lake Michigan and who had the highest levels of PCBs in their blood were found to suffer from memory and learning impairment (Schantz, Gasior, and others 2001). Those relying most heavily on food from the lakes and less likely to be reached by fish advisories are the most vulnerable to the threat of adverse health risks from toxic pollution in the Basin (IJC 2000b). Today, there is increasing concern about, and research into, the potential for exposure to persistent toxic substances from the Great Lakes to cause reproductive and hormonal

---

Box 32: Binational Cooperation, Toxics and Atmospheric Deposition

Canada and the United States developed the Integrated Atmospheric Deposition Network (IADN) in 1990 through which they cooperate to assess the importance of atmospheric deposition relative to other inputs; identify the trends, sources, and distribution of deposition; and make the information available (Bandemehr and Hoff 1998). Then in 1997, they signed the Great Lakes Binational Toxics Strategy, in which they agreed to targets for eliminating persistent, bioaccumulative toxic substances and committed to continue assessing atmospheric deposition to the Basin (EC 2000a). The ultimate goal is for virtual elimination, to be achieved through a variety of actions focused primarily on pollution prevention from 1997 to 2005 (BNS 1999).

Although exposure to persistent toxic contaminants has decreased significantly over the past 20 years, some studies show that children of mothers who ate large quantities of Great Lakes fish were slightly smaller, somewhat less able to deal

disruption and learning disabilities (EPA 1996).

Despite the progress that has been made in a number of pollution issues in the Great Lakes, more remains to be done. The IJC's 2000 report on Great Lakes Water Quality urged both governments to take further action to meet the GLWQA's goals, stating that neither one had committed adequate funding or taken the necessary decisive steps to ensure that the Lakes' waters are safe for drinking, swimming, and fishing. The report detailed the need to address the impacts of urbanization in the Basin, such as the nutrients, pathogens, chemicals, pesticides, and sediment introduced to waterways by runoff from cities, towns, and suburbs. It also expressed concern over the rate of progress in cleaning up sediments containing persistent toxic substances. The IJC further warned that existing regulations and guidelines for ballast exchange are inadequate to protect the lakes from exotic invasive species (see the biodiversity section) and urged the development of appropriate standards (IJC 2000b).

Other problems that remain in the Basin relate to the impact of urban development on sensitive tributary and near-shore habitats and acid rain in areas on the Canadian Shield (EC 1999b; EC 2000a). In addition, previous contamination continues to affect fish consumption due to persistent pollutants (EPA 1998)

The Great Lakes will face still other environmental challenges in the future. Over the past several decades, the Basin has experienced changes in hydrological conditions that are consistent with those projected by climate change models and global warming enhanced by human activity. Global climate change could lower lake levels by a meter or more by the middle of this century, causing severe economic, environmental, and social impacts. Water shortages throughout North America may also increase pressure to divert and/or remove water in bulk from the lakes, threatening the sustainable use of the Basin's surface and groundwater (IJC 2000c).

In the future the effects of climate change on North America's freshwater resources may include lower water levels in inland lakes and streams as well as increased demand for water for irrigation (EC 1998a). Both countries are undertaking studies to examine the potential effects of warming and adaptation strategies to changing water conditions. They are also aware that more needs to be done to understand the links between surface and ground water and to fully account for the total cost of water use and pollution.

References

AAFC (1997). *Profile of Production Trends and Environmental Issues in Canada's Agriculture*. Ottawa, Agriculture and Agri-Food Canada

AAFC (2000). *The Health of Our Water: Toward Sustainable Agriculture in Canada*. Agriculture and Agri-Food Canada, Research Branch http://res2.agr.ca/research-recherche/science/Healthy_Water/e07d.html. Accessed 4 February 2002

Abramovitz, Janet N. (1996). Sustaining Freshwater Ecosystems. In *State of the World 1996: A Worldwatch Institute Report on Progress Toward a Sustainable Society*. New York, W.W. Norton & Company

Acevedo, William, Leonard Gaydos, Janet Tilley, Carol Mladinich, Janis Buchanan, Steve Blauer, Kelley Kruger, and Jamie Schubert (1997). *Urban Land Use Change in the Las Vegas Valley*. US Geological Survey http://geochange.er.usgs.gov/sw/changes/anthropogenic/population/las_vegas/. Accessed 30 January 2002

Bandemehr, Angela, and Raymond Hoff (1998). *Monitoring Air Toxics: The Integrated Atmospheric Deposition Network of the Great Lakes*. (unpublished report to the CEC Secretariat) Montreal, Commission for Environmental Cooperation of North America

Barr, Jane (1992). Beaching the Great Whale Project: The Role of NGOs in Delaying the Construction of James Bay II. Paper read at the Proceedings of the Joint Meetings of the New England-St. Lawrence Valley Geographical Society (NESTVAL) and the Atlantic Division of the Canadian Association of Geographers, October 9-10, at Portland, Maine

Bennett, Paul (1998). Bounty of the Desert. *Landscape Architecture* 38 (3):39-43.

Blazs, Robert L. (2000). *Water-Level Monitoring in the High Plains Aquifer*. US Geological Survey http://csdokokl.cr.usgs.gov/public/proj/proj_ok090.html. Accessed 4 February 2002

BNS (1999). *The Great Lakes Binational Toxics Strategy: Canada-United States Strategy for the Virtual Elimination of Persistent Toxic Substances in the Great Lakes*. Binational Toxics Strategy http://www.epa.gov/glnpo/p2/bns.html. Accessed 4 February 2002

Canadian Press (2002). James Bay Cree Approve $3.4-Billion Power Deal. *The Globe and Mail*, Toronto, 3 February. http://www.globeandmail.ca/. Accessed 4 February 2002

CEC (2000). *Background State of the Environment Report for the Fourth Advisory Group Meeting in Critical and Emerging Trends* (unpublished report). Montreal, Commission for Environmental Cooperation of North America

CEC (2001). *The North American Mosaic: A State of the Environment Report*. Montreal, Commission for Environmental Cooperation of North America

CEQ (1997). *Environmental Quality, The World Wide Web: The 1997 Report of the Council on Environmental Quality*. Washington DC, The White House

Cosgrove, William J., and Frank R. Rijsberman (2000). *World Water Vision: Making Water Everybody's Business*, World Water Council, Earthscan Publications

De Villiers, Marq (2000). *Water: The Fate of Our Most Precious Resource*. Toronto, Mariner Books

DOI, and USGS (1998). *Strategic Direction for the US Geological Survey Groundwater Resources Program, A Report to Congress*. US Department of the Interior and US Geological Survey http://water.usgs.gov/ogw/gwrp/stratdir/contents.html. Accessed 4 February 2002

Dugan, Jack T., and Jennifer B. Sharpe (1996). *Water-Level Changes in the High Plains Aquifer, Predevelopment to 1994*. US Geological Survey http://ne20dnelnc.cr.usgs.gov/virtual/hightext.html. Accessed4 February 2002

EC (n.d.). Tabs for Tanks: Technical Assistance Bulletins. Environment Canada, Ontario Region, Environmental Protection Branch http://www.on.ec.gc.ca/pollution/fpd/tabs/5002-e.pdf. Accessed 29 May 2002

EC (1996). *The State of Canada's Environment – 1996*. Environment Canada http://www.ec.gc.ca/soer-ree/English/1996Report/Doc/1-1.cfm. Accessed 28 May 2002

EC (1998a). *Canada and Freshwater: Monograph No. 6.* Ottawa, Environment Canada, Minister of Public Works and Government Services Canada

EC (1998b). *Toxic Contaminants in the Environment: Persistent Organochlorines.* Environment Canada, Indicators and Assessment Office, Ecosystem Science Directorate, Environmental Conservation Service http://www.ec.gc.ca/ind/English/Toxic/default.cfm. Accessed 31 January 2002

EC (1999a). *Groundwater – Nature's Hidden Treasure: Freshwater Series A-5.* Environment Canada http://www.ec.gc.ca/water/en/info/pubs/FS/e_FSA5.htm. Accessed 4 February 2002

EC (1999b). *Rising to the Challenge: Celebrating the 25th Anniversary of the Great Lakes Water Quality Agreement.* Environment Canada http://www.on.ec.gc.ca/glimr/data/celebrate-glwqa/. Accessed 4 February 2002

EC (1999c). *The Canada-Ontario Agreement Respecting the Great Lakes Basin Ecosystem.* Environment Canada http://www.on.ec.gc.ca/coa/. Accessed 4 February 2002

EC (2000a). *Our Great Lakes, Working Towards a Healthy and Sustainable Great Lakes Basin Ecosystem.* Environment Canada http://www.on.ec.gc.ca/glimr/intro-e.html. Accessed 4 February 2002

EC (2000b). *Binational Remedial Action Plans (RAPs).* Environment Canada http://www.on.ec.gc.ca/glimr/raps/intro.html. Accessed 4 February 2002

EC (2001a). *The Management of Water.* Environment Canada http://www.ec.gc.ca/water/. Accessed 1 February 2002

EC (2001b). *Nutrients in the Canadian Environment: Reporting on the State of Canada's Environment.* Environment Canada, Indicators and Assessment Office, Ecosystem Science Directorate, Environmental Conservation Service http://www.ec.gc.ca/soer-ree/english/national/nutrientseng.pdf. Accessed 31 January 2002

EC (2001c). *Tracking Key Environmental Issues.* Ottawa, Environment Canada http://www.ec.gc.ca/tkei/main_e.cfm. Accessed 28 May 2002

EC (n.d.). *Great Lakes Water Quality Agreement.* Environment Canada http://www.on.ec.gc.ca/glwqa/. Accessed 4 February 2002

EPA (1996). *The Effects of Great Lakes Contaminants on Human Health: Report to Congress.* US Environmental Protection Agency http://www.epa.gov/glnpo/health/atsdr.htm. Accessed 4 February 2002

EPA (1997). *Deposition of Air Pollutants to the Great Waters: Second Report to Congress.* Research Triangle Park, NC, US Environmental Protection Agency, EPA-453/R-977-011

EPA (1998). *National Water Quality Inventory: 1998 Report to Congress.* US Environmental Protection Agency, Office of Water http://www.epa.gov/305b/98report. Accessed 31 January 2002

EPA (2000a). *Liquid Assets 2000: America's Water Resources at a Turning Point.* US Environmental Protection Agency, Office of Water http://www.epa.gov/ow/liquidassets/. Accessed 1 February 2002

EPA (2000b). *Great Lakes Areas of Concern.* US Environmental Protection Agency http://www.epa.gov/glnpo/aoc/index.html. Accessed 4 February 2002

Fairchild, G.L., Barry, D.A.J., M.J. Goss, A.S. Hamill, P. Lafrance, P.H. Milburn, R.R. Simard, and B.J. Zebarth (2000). Groundwater Quality. In *The Health of Our Water: Toward Sustainable Agriculture in Canada,* edited by D. R. Coote and L. J. Gregorich. Research Branch, Agriculture and Agri-Food Canada, http://res2agr.ca/research-recherche/science/Healthy_Water/e06.html. Accessed 4 February 2002

FAO (1990-1998). *Total Fertilizer Consumption.* FAOSTAT Fertilizer Data http://apps.fao.org/page/collections?subset=agriculture. Accessed 30 May 2002

Gallon, Gary (2000). The Real Walkerton Villain. *The Globe and Mail,* Toronto, 20 December

GF (1996). *Welcome to the Groundwater Foundation.* The Groundwater Foundation http://www.groundwater.org/index.htm. Accessed 4 February 2002

Glantz, Michael, ed. (1989J. *The Ogallala Aquifer Depletion: Forecasting by Analogy: Societal Responses to Regional Climatic Change.* Summary Report, Environmental and Societal Impacts Group NCAR http://www.iitap.iastate.edu/gccourse/issues/society/ogallala/ogallala.html. Accessed 4 February 2002

Gleick, P.H. (1998). *The World's Water 1998–1999.* Washington DC, Island Press

Gobert, Christopher (1997). Groundwater Contamination: A Look at the Federal Provisions. *The Compleat Lawyer,* Spring, American Bar Association. http://www.abanet.org/genpractice/compleat/sp97gr.html. Accessed 4 February 2002.

Gurganus, James, and Bernard Engel (1989). *Groundwater Education System.* Agricultural and Biological Engineering, Purdue University http://abe.www.ecn.purdue.edu/~agenhtml/agen521/epadir/grndwtr/menu.html. Accessed 4 February 2002

Health Canada (1997). *State of Knowledge Report on Environmental Contaminants and Human Health in the Great Lakes Basin.* Edited by D. Riedel, N. Tremblay and E. Tompkins. Ottawa, Minister of Public Works and Government Services Canada

HPWD (1997/98). *The Ogallala Aquifer.* High Plains Underground Water Conservation District No.1. http://www.hpwd.com/ogallala.html. Accessed 4 February 2002

IIFA (2000). *Fertilizer Nutrient Consumption, by Region, 1970/71 to 1998/99.* International Industry Fertilizer Association http://www.fertilizer.org/STATSIND/cnnam.htm. Accessed 4 February 2002

IJC (1989). *Great Lakes Water Quality Agreement of 1978.* International Joint Commission, http://www.ijc.org/agree/quality.html. Accessed 4 February 2002

IJC (1997). *Overcoming Obstacles to Sediment Remediation in the Great Lakes Basin.* White Paper by the Sediment Priority Action Committee, Great Lakes Water Quality Board, International Joint Commission. http://www.ijc.org/boards/wqb/sedrem.html#preface. Accessed 4 February 2002

IJC (2000a). *International Joint Commission: United States and Canada.* International Joint Commission http://www.ijc.org/agree/water.html. Accessed 4 February 2002

IJC (2000b). *Tenth Biennial Report on Great Lakes Water Quality.* International Joint Commission http://www.ijc.org/comm/10br/en/indexen.html. Accessed 4 February 2002

IJC (2000c). *Protection of the Waters of the Great Lakes: Final Report to the Governments of Canada and the United States.* International Joint Commission http://www.ijc.org/ijcweb-e.html. Accessed 4 February 2002

IWI (1999). *Index of Watershed Indicators.* US Environmental Protection Agency, Index of Watershed Indicators http://www.epa.gov/iwi/. Accessed 1 February 2002

Kolpin, Dana W., Jack E. Barbash, and Robert J. Gilliom (1998). *Occurrence of Pesticides in Shallow Ground Water of the United States: Initial Results from the National Water-Quality Assessment Program.* US Geological Survey http://water.wr.usgs.gov/pnsp/ja/est32/. Accessed 1 February 2002

LVWCC (n.d.). *About the Las Vegas Wash.* Las Vegas Wash Coordination Committee http://www.lvwash.org/thewash/urbandevelopment.html. Accessed 30 January 2002

MacLeod, J.A., J.B. Sanderson, and A.J. Campbell (2000). Groundwater Quality: Nitrate. In *The Health of Our Water: Toward Sustainable Agriculture in Canada,* edited by D. R. Coote and L. J. Gregorich. Research Branch, Agriculture and Agri-Food Canada http://res2.agr.ca/research-recherche/science/Healthy_Water/e06b.html. Accessed 5 February 2002

McGuire, V.L., C.P. Stanton, and B.C. Fischer (1999). *Water-level Changes in the High Plains Aquifer – 1980 to 1996.* US Geological Survey http://ne20dnelnc.cr.usgs.gov/highplains/hp96_web_report/hp96_factsheet.htm. Accessed 4 February 2002

McGuire, V.L., C.P. Stanton, and B.C. Fischer (2000). *Water-level Changes, 1980 to 97, and Saturated Thickness, 1996-97, in the High Plains Aquifer.* US Geological Survey http://ne20dnelnc.cr.usgs.gov/highplains/hp97_web_report/fs-124-99.htm. Accessed 4 February 2002

Moody, David W. (1996). Sources and Extent of Groundwater Contamination. In *North Carolina Cooperative Extension Service*, Publication Number: AG-441-4. Division of Pollution Prevention and Environmental Assistance http://www.p2pays.org/ref/01/00065.htm. Accessed 4 February 2002

O'Connor, The Honourable Dennis R. (2002). *Report of the Walkerton Inquiry: The Events of May 2000 and Related Issues.* Ontario Ministry of the Attorney General http://www.walkertoninquiry.com/. Accessed 1 February 2002

OECD (1995a). *OECD Environmental Data: Compendium 1995.* Paris, Organization for Economic Co-operation and Development

OECD (1995b). *Environmental Performance Reviews. Canada.* Paris, Organization for Economic Co-operation and Development

OECD (1996). *Environmental Performance Reviews: United States.* Paris, Organization for Economic Co-operation and Development

Pavelko, Michael T., David B. Wood, and Randell J. Laczniak (1999). Las Vegas, Nevada: Gambling with Water in the Desert. In *Land Subsidence in the United States: US Geological Survey Circular 1182*, edited by D. Galloway, D. R. Jones and S. E. Ingebritsen. US Department of the Interior, US Geological Survey, http://water.usgs.gov/pubs/circ/circ1182/pdf/08LasVegas.pdf. Accessed 30 January 2002

Revenga, Carmen, Jake Brunner, Norbert Henninger, Richard Payne, and Ken Kassem (2000). *Pilot Analysis of Global Ecosystems: Freshwater Systems.* Washington DC, World Resources Institute

Rogers, Peter (1996). *America's Water: Federal Roles and Responsibilities.* Cambridge MA, MIT Press

Sampat, Payal (2000a). *Deep Trouble: The Hidden Threat of Groundwater Pollution.* Washington DC, Worldwatch Institute

Sampat, Payal (2000b). Groundwater Shock: The Polluting of the World's Major Freshwater Stores. *World Watch* 13 (1):10-22.

Schantz, Susan L., Donna M. Gasior, Elena Polverejan, Robert J. McCaffrey, Anne M. Sweeney, Harold E.B. Humphrey, and Joseph C. Gardiner (2001). Impairments of Memory and Learning in Older Adults Exposed to Polychlorinated Biphenyls Via Consumption of Great Lakes Fish. *Environmental Health Perspectives* 109 (6).

Solley, Wayne B., Robert R. Pierce, and Howard A. Perlman (1998). *Estimated Use of Water in the United States in 1995.* US Department of Interior, US Geological Survey http://water.usgs.gov/watuse/pdf1995/html/ Accessed 4 February 2002

Statistics Canada (2000). *Human Activity and the Environment 2000.* Ottawa, Minister of Industry

Tenenbaum, David J. (2000). Moving Beyond MTBE. *Environmental Health Perspectives* 108 (8):A351.

TFGRR (1993). *Groundwater Issues and Research in Canada.* Task Force on Groundwater Resources Research, A Report Prepared For The Canadian Geoscience Council http://www.env.gov.bc.ca/wat/gws/gwdocs/gweddocs/GW_IandR_in_Canada.html. Accessed 4 February 2002

UNDP, UNEP, World Bank, and WRI (2000). *World Resources 2000-2001: People and Ecosystems, the Fraying Web of Life.* Washington DC, World Resources Institute

USGS (1999). *The Quality of Our Nation's Waters: Nutrients and Pesticides.* US Department of the Interior, US Geological Survey, Circular 1225 http://water.usgs.gov/pubs/circ/circ1225/pdf/front.pdf. Accessed 31 January 2002

Waldron, Dr. Acie C. (1992). *Pesticides and Groundwater Contamination: Bulletin 820.* Ohio State University http://ohioline.ag.ohio-state.edu/b820/index.html. Accessed 4 February 2002

White, Robin (2001). *Annual Groundwater Withdrawals, Data Update* World Resources Institute, Update Printout

Land

6

Land

North America harbors about 11 percent of the world's agricultural croplands, which produce ample amounts of food, fiber, and other products both for the region's own needs and for export around the world. Almost 20 percent of the United States is covered by arable and permanent cropland and 26 percent by permanent grassland or pastures, totaling about 46 percent of all land used for agricultural production (OECD 1999). Although only 7 percent of Canada's land is devoted to agriculture, this represents virtually all the undeveloped land that is amenable to cultivation (EC 1996). Highly differentiated by region, the largest extensions of croplands are found in the states and provinces of the Great Plains regions, extending from central Canada to the southern United States. About 82 percent of Canada's agricultural land lies in the Prairie Provinces of the Central Plains (Wilson and Tyrchniewicz 1994).

Agricultural productivity has greatly increased with more intense land use and agricultural inputs—including irrigation, agro-chemicals, and multiple cropping—while the amount of cropland has remained fairly stable since World War II (Ervin, Runge, and others 1998). Agricultural activity contributes significantly to the North American economy, representing 2 percent of Canada's GDP and 3 percent of GDP in the United States (CEC 2000). Agricultural expansion, intensification, and industrialization have also contributed to land degradation, however, reducing the organic content of the soil and exacerbating its exposure to wind and water (CEC 2001a). Land degradation has been an issue of concern in North America.

Another issue of high priority for the region is the use of agricultural pesticides. While pesticides help expand food production, many have important environmental effects. Particularly harmful pesticides known as persistent organic pollutants (POPs) have received considerable attention because of their links to reproductive failure in animals and health effects in humans.

Land Degradation

Land degradation is difficult to define (see Box 33) but in general, it refers to unsustainable or poor land use that leads to the irreversible decline in its productivity (Eswaran, Lal, and Reich 2001).

Socioeconomic factors that sometimes can drive unsustainable agriculture and land degradation may include large federal subsidies,

use of chemical fertilizers and pesticides, and uniform high-yield hybrid crops (Dregne 1986; Gold 1999).

Pressures to extract ever more produce from agricultural soils over the past 30 years often left them bare and exposed to wind and water erosion. For example, the shift to large, heavy equipment and sprinkler irrigation systems required field enlargement and the consequent elimination of many wind-breaking hedgerows and other natural features that help to reduce wind and

---

Box 33: Definition of Land Degradation

There are many different definitions of land degradation. In general terms, it refers to the processes that negatively affect the land's or soil's natural functions of water, energy, and nutrient acceptance, storage, and recycling, leading to a decline in soil productivity. Humans are the major drivers of land degradation through socioeconomic and political pressures that lead to land clearing and deforestation, unsustainable agricultural activities, land conversion to urban uses, and contamination (Eswaran, Lal, and Reich 2001, IUSS 2001).

Physical, chemical, and biological processes are direct impacts that begin land degradation. Physical processes include the decline in soil structure, which leads to crusting, compaction, erosion, desertification, anaerobism, and contamination by pollutants. Soil structure affects all degradation processes. Chemical processes include acidification, leaching, salinization, reduced soil retention capacity, and fertility depletion. Biological processes include carbon reduction and decline in land biodiversity. Carbon loss leads to soil erosion and reduced fertility. Desertification refers to land degradation in arid, semiarid, and dry, sub-humid areas (Eswaran, Lal, and Reich 2001, IUSS 2001).

---

growing global demand for agricultural products, and increased trade liberalization (MacGregor and McRae 2000). Some of the human pressures leading to degradation over the last 30 years have been rapid technological change in production methods, fewer but larger farms, single and row cropping systems over many seasons, overgrazing in arid lands, extensive

water erosion (Miller 1982). Erosion reduces soil productivity by removing the finer soil particles so the soil becomes more compact and loses nutrients and the capacity to store water and organic matter (IISD 2001). Lessons learned after the Dust Bowl experiences of the 1930s, when about 3.6 million ha of farmland were destroyed and another 32 million ha severely damaged led to

Box 34: Conservation Strategies to Curb Soil Erosion

Erosion control practices include conservation tillage, which involves either zero tillage or keeping tillage to a minimum. In the former, crops are seeded into the previous crop's stubble. Both systems provide for minimal soil disturbance and by maintaining a cover of plants or crop residues on the soil, protect it from the erosive power of flowing water and the impact of heavy rain. Another method is to extend crop rotations to include forages by alternating them with cereals and oilseeds or legumes. Forages can be grown on poorer soils or steep slopes not suitable for other crops. When planted as a perennial crop or plowed back into the soil, forages return residue to the soil, increasing organic matter and nutrients. This improves the soil structure, allowing it to absorb more water and thus reduce runoff and erosion. Other strategies include planting shelterbelts, strip-cropping, contour cultivation, and restructuring the landscape with terraces, diversions, and grassed waterways (Acton and Gregorich 1995; Vandervel and Abday 2001).

Figure 34

Changes in erosion in the United States, 1982-1997.

Source: NRCS 1997

the adoption of various soil conservation strategies that decreased water and soil erosion, such as contour plowing, no-till methods, reduced summer fallow, and increased crop residues (see Box 34) (Miller 1982).

In the late 1970s and early 1980s, both countries reported on the declining status of their nations' soil, and the messages in these reports led to the US Soil and Water Resources Conservation Act of 1977 and Canada's 1989 National Soil Conservation Program (Vaisey, Weins, and Wettlaufer 1996). They

also adopted strategies that took fragile lands out of agricultural production to protect them from erosion (see Box 35, next page).

Conservation measures have led to significant declines in erosion over the past 30 years (see Figures 34 and 35). Between 1987 and 1997, soil erosion declined by about one-third in the United States. In addition to idling land, US agro-environmental programs included other cost-sharing schemes, such as those that paid farmers to construct field terraces, ponds to retain runoff laden with sediment, or windbreaks (Ervin, Runge, and others 1998). In the United States, 30 percent of croplands had highly erosion-prone conditions in 1982 compared to 24 percent in 1992 (H. John Heinz III Center 2001).

In Canada's agricultural regions, between 1981 and 1996 the average number of days soil was left bare declined by 20 percent while the share of cultivated land at high-to-severe risk of wind erosion declined from 15 percent to 6 percent thanks

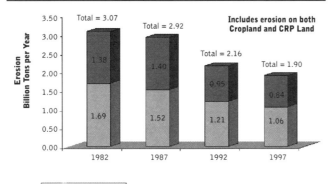

Changes in Erosion in the United States, 1982-1997

Includes erosion on both Cropland and CRP Land

- Wind
- Sheet & Rill

to improved management practices. In the Prairies reduced tillage technologies and summer fallow practices led to an overall decline of 30 percent in the risk of wind erosion between 1981 and 1985 (Padbury and Stushnoff 2000) (see Figure 35). In general, conservation practices spurred at least an 11 percent decline in the overall risk of water erosion over this period(Acton and Gregorich 1995).

Despite promising conservation measures, erosion continues to be a serious problem in many parts of North America, however. Excessive erosion occurs on more than 23.2 million ha of fragile, highly erodible cropland in the United States, while erosion exceeding the tolerable soil

Risk of Wind Erosion on Cultivated Land in the Prairie Provinces under Prevailing Management Practices, 1981-1996

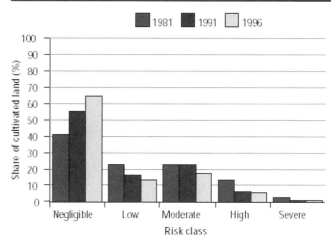

Water and Wind Erosion Vulnerability, 1998

Water erosion

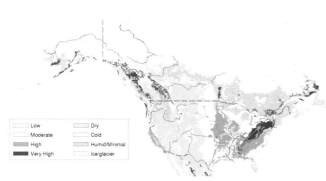

Wind erosion

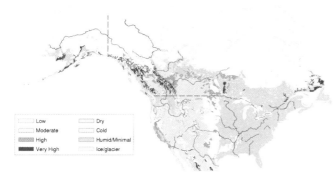

loss rate (a measure indicating the maximum rate of annual soil erosion that will permit crop productivity to be sustained economically and indefinitely) occurs on nearly 20.4 million ha of cropland that is not highly erodible (NRCS 2001b). In total, erosion, threatens productivity on about one-third of US cropland. Twenty percent of Canada's agricultural land was at high-to-severe risk of inherent (bare soil) water erosion in 1995 (USDA 1996, Shelton, Wall, and others 2000). Figure 36 shows the area of risk for wind and water erosion in North America in 1998.

Data for other indices of land degradation are somewhat scarce: consistent US data for the national level of organic matter, the degree of soil

Figure 35
Risk of wind erosion on cultivated land in the prairie provinces under prevailing management practices, 1981-1996.

Source: Padbury and Stushnoff 2000

Figure 36
Water and wind erosion vulnerability, 1998.

Source: USDA 2001a and 2001b

Box 35: Conservation Programs

The US Conservation Reserve Program (CRP) of 1985, which came to dominate federal spending on conservation, was prompted by a farm crisis related to export market contraction, surpluses, falling commodity prices, and a growing environmental consciousness (Ervin, Runge, and others 1998; USDA 2001a). The aim was to reduce erosion and excess production by helping farmers to retire highly erodable or environmentally sensitive cropland for 10 years in return for rental and cost-sharing payments and technical assistance. Reversed economic conditions in the mid-1990s led many farmers to leave the program. It was re-authorized in 1996 under the Federal Agricultural Improvement and Reform Act (FAIR), which added more environmental and water quality goals (USDA 2000a), but participation remained voluntary (Ervin, Runge, and others 1998). In all, about 13 percent of US cropland was idled under federal programs between 1982 and 1997 compared to 11 percent of cropland between 1950 and 1970 (see Figure 33) (Zinn 1994; H. John Heinz III Center 2001). As of October 2000, more than 13.4 million ha were enrolled in the CRP, making it the most extensive US agricultural conservation program (USDA 2000a).

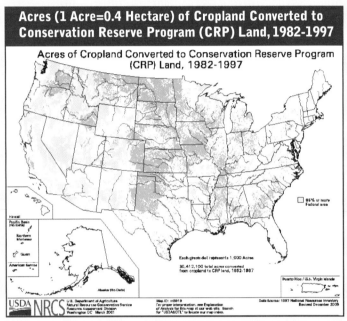

Figure 33 *Source: NRCS 2001a*

The CRP produces a wide range of environmental and economic effects (USDA 2000a). Allowing trees and vegetation to grow on what was once cropland not only prevents erosion but also can improve the amount and suitability of wildlife habitat and the abundance of species. Species that consume insects and plants pests can help to increase the commercial value of crops, while game species provide recreational economic benefits (Ervin, Runge, and others 1998).

In Canada, the Permanent Cover Program (PCP), first delivered in 1989 by the federal Prairie Farm Rehabilitation Administration (PFRA), aims to reduce soil deterioration on cropland at high risk for soil damage by maintaining a permanent cover of grass and trees. About 555,000 ha of marginal prairie agricultural land was removed from annual cultivation under the program. Despite the PCP's shortcomings—it had limited funds, only applied for a short time period, restricted the amount of land each farmer can retire, and left some 4.9 million ha of land at risk of soil degradation under annual cultivation after it ended—between US $1.3 and 3.3 million dollars of soil productivity were saved by permanent cover on 320,000 ha of land (Wilson and Tyrchniewicz 1994; Vaisey, Weins, and Wettlaufer 1996; AAFC 1997a).

compaction, and the amount of land affected by salt are lacking (H. John Heinz III Center 2001). Levels of organic matter in Canadian soils in general have been maintained or increased in some croplands with the help of erosion-reducing practices (Acton and Gregorich 1995). There is some indication that conservation practices have led to a decline in the rate of organic carbon loss from 70 kg/ha in 1970 to 43 kg/ha in 1990 (Smith, Wall, and others 2000). On the other hand, the risk of soil compaction increased in eastern Canada and there has been an overall national decrease in the amount of land under cropping systems that improve soil structure (McBride, Joosse, and Wall 2000).

Desertification, which refers to land degradation in arid, semi-arid, and dry sub-humid areas, has generally been stabilized over the past 30 years as plant cover on rangelands improves and erosion and water logging are controlled (Dregne 1986; UNCCD 2001). In the mid-1980s, increasing salinity (salinization) was estimated to affect adversely about 25 percent of the irrigated land in the United States, and by 1992, at least 19.4 million ha of crop and pasturelands were affected by salinity. Conditions in heavily irrigated agricultural areas of the dry US southwest continue to worsen (De Villiers 2000).

In Canada, only 2 percent of agricultural land has more than 15 percent of its area affected by salinity (EC 1996). Dry land agricultural soil in some parts of the Prairie Prov-

inces is subject to salinization, a significant problem (IISD 2001). In 1995, 7 percent of farmland in the Prairie Provinces was at high risk of salinization under 1991 management practices (Acton and Gregorich 1995).

Traditional policies to address land degradation in the United States have focused on land retirement (see Box 35). The US Department of Agriculture now recognizes that many emerging environmental problems on agricultural land can only be addressed by changing management practices, and it is looking at achieving cost-effective environmental benefits from conservation spending on working lands (USDA 2001a).

Furthermore, government agricultural policy in North America historically focused on economic and production goals, but more recently, sustainability has guided policy reforms (MacGregor and McRae 2000; USDA 2001a). The Canadian Agri-Environmental Indicator Project, completed in 2000, contributed to a more informed debate about agricultural sustainability. A major step forward in judging the environmental sustainability of agriculture in the nation, it introduces two criteria: how well agriculture conserves natural resources that support agricultural production, and how

compatible agricultural systems are with natural systems and processes (McRae, Smith, and Gregorich 2000).

The Prairie Farm Rehabilitation Administration (PFRA), established in response to the drought and conditions of the 1930s, seeks to make large-scale dry land agriculture sustainable over the long term and has promoted sustainable development on the rural prairies for six decades (AAFC 2001a). The Canadian government set out its Sustainable Development Strategy for agriculture in 1997, with the objective of working cooperatively with all sectors to integrate environmental goals into decision-making and management (AAFC 1997b). To support the strategy, the National

Soil and Water Conservation Program (NSWCP) was set up between 1997 and 1999, with the goal of advancing environmental sustainability initiatives across the country (AAFC 1999). A federal framework was put in place to guide the 1997 strategy and a new strategy was published in 2001 (AAFC 2001c).

The 1985 and 1990 US Farm Bills also led to more sustainable stewardship by farmers and landowners (McRae, Smith, and Gregorich 2000; NRCS 2000). In 1994, the US Task Force on Sustainable Agriculture set out recommendations to achieve environmentally and socially sound agricultural production, and two years later, the Federal Agriculture Improvement and Reform Act was signed expanding on earlier conservation themes (PCSD 1996; Gold 1999). Also, the US Food and Agricultural Policy calls for redefining 'output'—now limited to food, fiber, and timber production—to include environmental amenities, such as rural landscapes, wildlife habitat, wetlands, and improved water and air quality (USDA 2001a).

Canada and the United States have ratified the 1996 United Nations Convention to Combat Desertification, which commits participating nations to research, prevent, and reverse the transformation of fertile farm and pasture lands into arid deserts. Although as developed countries they do not have to prepare a National Action Plan under the Convention, they have committed themselves to properly addressing issues of drought and land degradation (CIDA 2000; ENN 2000).

Pesticides

Pesticides are part of the package of agricultural inputs that have contributed to the production of an abundant and affordable food supply (Gold 1999). Chemical pesticides include human-made herbicides, insecticides, algaecides, and fungicides. They are applied to crops to control unwanted insects, weeds, and diseases and to ensure crop quality and quantity (Statistics Canada 2000). About 10 percent of US land area is treated annually with pesticides (Muir 1998). This includes the use by forest companies to clear unwanted trees and vegetation and to fight forest insects and the use on lawns, playgrounds, parks, and golf courses, mostly for cosmetic reasons, although these uses represent a fraction of total application. Homeowners use between 5 and 10 percent of the total amount of pesticides sold in North America to keep lawns weed-free (Aspelin and Grube 1999; EC 2000).

North America leads the world in the consumption and use of pesticides, accounting for 36 percent of world pesticide use. The pesticide market has been growing at about 6 percent a year since 1990 (CEC 2000). The pesticide industry is worth about US $65.5 million yearly in sales in Canada and in 1995 in the United States, sales totalled US $10.4 billion (Benbrook 1997; Mulholland 2001). However, the benefits af-forded by pesticides have come at a cost to the health of people, wildlife, and the environment.

By far the most common and widespread use of pesticides in North America is agricultural applications, which accounted for 76 to 77 percent of US pesticide use through 1990 to 1991, with corn and soybeans using 62 percent of all crop applications (Schmitt 1998). Over the past 30 years, the area treated with chemical pesticides has rapidly expanded. For example, in Canada it increased 3.5 times between 1970 and 1995 (Statistics Canada 2000). In 1996, Canada used an average of 644 kg of pesticides per ha of cropland while average use in the United States was more than twice as intensive at 1,566 kg per ha (UNDP, UNEP, World Bank, and WRI 2000).

Since 1979, the total annual amount of pesticides (all types, by all sectors) used in the United States has fluctuated somewhat but overall has remained fairly steady while in Canada, pesticide use in agriculture leveled off since the mid-1980s (AAFC 1997). Scientists are increasingly advocating the use of biological and cultural pest management methods (USDA 2000a). Safer pesticide products, new management techniques for eliminating crop pests, and training and certification programs for pesticide users help to account for recent reductions in agricultural pesticide applications. Major developments include genetically

Box 36: POP Pesticides

Persistent Organic Pollutants (POPs) are a family of chemicals generally used as insecticides or industrial chemicals. They are very toxic and persist in the environment, taking decades or longer to break down. Some are also highly soluble in fat, bioaccumulating in food webs as they increase in concentration in the bodies of top predators (EC 1998). Of the 12 worst POPs called 'the dirty dozen', nine are pesticides. They include DDT, hexachlorobenzene (HCB), toxaphene, chlordane, and dieldrin (Statistics Canada 2000).

Because they last so long and can travel great distances in air and water currents, even those persistent, toxic organochlorine pesticides that have been banned in North America are still found in the food supply. Persistent residues of POPs pesticides used in the 1960s and 1970s remain in the soil, for example, and continue to be taken up in crops (Schafer, Kegley, and Patton 2000). They also travel long distances northward because of the 'grasshopper' effect as they migrate in repeated cycles of evaporation and condensation.

Entering the food chain, POPs pesticides can threaten human health. Exposure to dieldrin and DDE, a breakdown product of DDT, has been associated with breast and other types of cancer and nervous system disorders. Several POPs pesticides are present in the breast milk of Canadian women, with levels of the pesticide chlordane 10 times higher in the breast milk of Inuit women in the north than in women in southern Canada (Statistics Canada 2000).

Given their persistence and ability to travel, POPs need to be regulated and managed at a global level. After years of negotiation, during the fifth POPs negotiating session in December 2000, the international community finalized the text of a new legally binding treaty. Signed by both Canada and the United States in Stockholm in May 2001, the POPs Convention requires governments to eliminate or severely restrict the use and production of an initial list of 12 POPs of which eight are pesticides. Included in the treaty are commitments to the precautionary approach that move chemical regulation and management from a 'regulate and reduce' approach to one in which a lack of scientific certainty is no longer regarded as a reason to avoid taking preventive action (UNEP 2000).

engineered herbicide-tolerant varieties and plant pesticides, which reduce the need for chemical applications (USDA 2000a).

In the 1960s and '70s, the damaging effects on wildlife of persistent, toxic organochlorine pesticides included in the class of chemicals known as POPs (see Box 36) became known. As shown in the section on the Great Lakes, extremely high residues of some of these pesticides in a number of bird species were causing populations to crash. The freshwater section of this report highlights the trends in pesticide contamination in North America's groundwater.

As a result of their effects on wildlife, dieldrin and DDT pesticides were banned in the 1970s, and by the early 1990s, all exempted uses and the manufacture of DDT in North America had been phased out (CEC 1997; Schafer, Kegley, and Patton 2000). Pesticide rulings by the US EPA in the 1970s ended 25 percent of insecticide applications in use at that time and since then, 43 pesticides have been banned and 10 severely restricted (OECD 1996; Benbrook 1997). Because of these bans, concentrations of POP pesticides in biota have declined significantly since the 1990s (Schmitt 1998).

The use of insecticides declined markedly in the United States from the 1976 peak due largely to the implementation of Integrated Pest Management (IPM) programs (see below) and the use of new pyrethroid insecticides, which can be applied at about a tenth the rate of traditional insecticides (Muir 1998; Schmitt 2000). For a period of time, herbicide use grew as a way to control weeds, due in part to the increase in conservation tillage, which leaves crops and residue on the land to help control soil erosion (see Box 34): as a share of total pesticides applied, herbicides rose from 33 percent in 1966 to 70 percent in 1986. But there has been a more recent decline in herbicide use in US agriculture—about 25 percent from its 1982 peak—due to a reduction in farmed land, increased herbicide costs, and the greater potency of herbicides, which give greater control with lower levels of active ingredients (Ervin, Runge, and others 1998; Muir 1998). The use of fungicides and other compounds has risen steadily for the last 40 years (Ervin, Runge, and others 1998).

Farm workers risk direct exposure to pesticides, but accurate national and comparative data about their exposure is sparse. In the United States today, more than 85 percent of fruits and vegetables are hand harvested by disenfranchised workers who often lack access to the proper information about controlling their exposure to agricultural pesticides (Acury, Quandt, and McCauley 2000). This is often because of the migratory nature of their activities, which also affects the ability to monitor and treat pesticide-related illness (OECD 1996).

Recent evidence suggests that some pesticides may be linked to immune system suppression, reproductive damage, and hormonal system disruption (Colburn, Myers, and Dumanoski 1996). Children are more vulnerable than adults to the effects of pesticides, which impair their neurological development, growth, and immune and endocrine systems (as shown in the human health section).

With increased public concern about the health effects of pesticides and recognition of the special vulnerability of children and indigenous peoples living in (see Box 54 in the human health and the environment section) the north, pesticide regulation in North America became more stringent during the 1990s. Re-registration of existing pesticides, initiatives to help replace old and dangerous pesticides with newer, safer ones, reviews of high-risk pesticides, accelerated registration for reduced-risk compounds, and improved consumer information were introduced.

The 1996 US Food Quality Protection Act eliminated a previous prohibition against wording that pertained to all residues that might cause cancer, streamlined the approval process for new, safer pesticides, targeted children for protection, and required more pesticide information on food products (Ervin, Runge, and others 1998). In response to the risks faced by migratory farm workers, worker protection standards and worker outreach efforts were extended (OECD 1996).

Canada's regulatory system was reformed with the 1995 Pest Management Regulatory Agency, which assesses the human health and environmental safety of pest control products prior to their use (PMRA 2001). Inactive ingredients in pesticides were recently brought to the attention of Canadians when it was found that the list of these ingredients was outdated and that many were dangerous to human health. Legislation was subsequently introduced requiring manufacturers either to remove them or to list them on product labels (Mittelstaedt 2001a).

Canada and the United States now work together in a number of ways to reduce the risks associated with pesticides and other POPs (see Box 37). In addition, heeding public demand to protect children from lawn pesticides, many North American municipalities are now restrict-

---

Box 37: Bilateral Cooperation

In 1996, Canada's Pest Management Regulatory Agency (PMRA) and the US EPA developed a joint process to divide between them the review applications made simultaneously on both sides of the border for reduced-risk pesticides and biopesticides. Through these initiatives, an increasing number of these chemicals were brought forward for evaluation and registration. In 1998, procedures were revised to broaden the process to include chemicals that do not meet reduced-risk requirements but qualify as organophosphate alternatives or NAFTA (North American Free Trade Agreement) priority chemicals (e.g., methyl bromide alternatives) (PMRA 1999; PMRA 2000).

The two countries also work together (with Mexico) under the Commission for Environmental Cooperation of North America's Sound Management of Chemicals initiative to reduce the risks of toxic substances to human health and the environment. Begun in 1995, the project focuses on persistent and bioaccumulative toxic substances. It provides a forum for identifying priority chemical pollution issues of concern to all three NAFTA countries; developing North American Regional Action Plans (NARAPs) to address the issues; overseeing the implementation of approved NARAPs; and facilitating and encouraging capacity building to support the project's goals. Action plans for three POPs (PCBs, DDT, Chlordane) are being implemented. A fourth plan for mercury is also underway. An action plan on dioxins, furans, and hexachlorobenzene as well as one for environmental monitoring and assessment are currently being developed (CEC 2001b). Consideration is also being given to developing a NARAP for lindane. Lead is currently undergoing a scientific review to see whether it is of mutual concern to the three countries.

ing pesticide use on public land and some have instituted total bans (see the example in Box 38).

Although some new pesticides that are used in higher volumes today are safer than their predecessors (OECD 1996), pesticides still pose a number of problems. 'Soft' pesticides produced since 1975 are shorter-lived than POPs and do not accumulate, but they are fast-acting and highly toxic to terrestrial and aquatic inverte-brates in the short term; in some places they have led to higher fish and wildlife kills (OECD 1996, Schmitt 1998). In some agricultural regions, the intensity of pesticide use has grown in the last decade. In California, which produced 11.7 percent of total US market value of agricultural products in 1997 (NASS 1997) and accounted for 25 percent of its pesticide use between 1991 and 1995 (Liebman 1997), the quantity of applied active ingredients per unit area rose 60 percent between 1991 and 1998 (Kegley, Orme and Neumeister 2000).

Pests have also become resistant to pesticides. One report estimates that more than 500 insect pests, 270 weed species, and 150 plant diseases are now resistant to one or more so that more applications are needed today to accomplish the same level of control effected by one application made in the early 1970s (Benbrook 1997). While crops of Genetically Modified Organisms (GMOs) have the potential to enhance yields while using fewer pesticides, the conse-quences for non-target organisms and the development of pest resistance to the toxic effects of some

bioengineered crops are still being debated. The United States and Canada are leaders in the produc-tion and export of GMOs.

In response to pest resistance, consumer concerns, scientific advice, and environmental regula-tion of chemical pesticides, recent

---

Box 38: Cosmetic Use of Pesticides in Canada

In June 2000, Canada's Supreme Court unanimously ruled that towns and cities have the right to enact bylaws banning the purely cosmetic use of pesticides (Makin 2001). The Quebec community of Hudson initiated a court case leading to the decision, which was followed by Toronto's Board of Health endorsing a similar bylaw, making it the first large city to begin steps to phase out the use of pesticides on lawns for cosmetic purposes. Against concerns that weeds will proliferate and jobs will be lost, municipalities across the country now have the right to impose the restrictions long sought after by residents worried about the health consequences of lawn and park applications of herbicides and insecticides, particu-larly on children (Mittelstaedt 2001b).

---

government programs encourage the development and use of biologi-cal and cultural methods, including Integrate Pest Management (IPM) and national organic standards (USDA 2000a). IPM combines a range of different control options: biological tools in which pests are controlled by the release of predator insects, for example; cultural tools such as crop rotation; physical tools such as cultivating corn weeds; genetic tools such as planting disease-resistant varieties; and chemical tools, such as conventional pesticides (NIPMN, Western Region

2000). One of IPM's key characteristics is that action is not taken against pests routinely, but rather when their numbers or effects warrant it (PMRA 2001). IPM therefore continues to rely, to a reduced extent, on chemical pesticides. In the biointensive IPM approach, the most stringent form, reduced-risk chemical pesticides are used only when other methods fail (Benbrook 1997).

Canada's PMRA is working through Partnership Projects and other initiatives to help establish IPM as the basis of pest management in a variety of pesticide user sectors. The US goal is to implement IMP on 75 percent of its crops (Jacobsen 1996, PMRA 2001). Strategies are based on voluntary implementation and a participatory process involving many stakeholders (Jacobsen 1996; PMRA 1998).

These governmental initiatives allow for greater flexibility than organic agriculture, in which chemical pesticides are shunned. North

Box 39: Organic Produce

Organic produce is usually understood to be foods grown without the use of chemical fertilizers and pesticides, and not derived through genetic engineering or treated by irradiation. It also refers to food grown with sustainable agricultural practices, including the promotion of soil health and biodiversity (AAFC 2001b; Cunningham 2001).

Active since the 1970s, the market in organics is growing in North America. The organic sector was the fastest-growing agricultural sector in the 1990s in the United States, with private and state certified organic cropland more than doubling between 1992 and 1997 (see Figure 37) (ERS 2000). In 1999, the value of retail sales of organic foods was an estimated US $6 billion. By 2000, the number of organic farmers in the United States was rising by about 12 percent per year, with about 12,200 mostly small-scale producers nationwide (USDA 2000b). Still, the area of certified organic cropland accounts for only about 0.2 percent of all US cropland (Halweil 2001). At the end of 2000, the US Department of Agriculture released its final version of national standards to govern the certification of farming and production practices and regulate the use of the term 'organic' on foods. The standards create a uniform definition of organic foods and standardize product-labeling guidelines, bringing consistency to a network of private and public organic certification agencies' standards. It specifically prohibits the use of genetic engineering methods, ionizing radiation, and sewage sludge for fertilization (USDA 2000b).

The Canadian organic market has also expanded since the 1970s, growing at a rate of 15 percent per year between 1989 and 1999. Organic items accounted for 1 to 2 percent of all food sales at the end of that period (Roberts, MacRae, and Stahlbrand 1999). Canada had about 1 million ha under organic production in 2000. The industry anticipates it will represent 10 percent of the country's retail market by 2010 (AAFC 2001b). Certified organic cropland accounts for about 1.3 percent of Canada's cropland (Halweil 2001). Canada's National Standard for Organic Agriculture, published in 1999, is voluntary and does not mandate certification or endorse any one certifying body, but two Canadian provinces have established organic standards (Quebec and BC) that require third-party certification (AAFC 2001b; ERS 2001; Shaw 2001).

American consumers are increasingly seeking organic produce, however, because many of them are concerned about potential pesticide residues in food (see Box 39).

Now that strong legislation for point source pollution has been enacted and gross emissions to the land have declined, it is becoming clear that more needs to be done to curb non-point pollution from pervasive and long-lasting agricultural chemicals—both nutrients from fertilizer and pesticides—which travel in the air and water to environments far from emission sources. North America's soil conservation measures and its commitment to the continued phase-out of POPs are positive trends. However, there is a

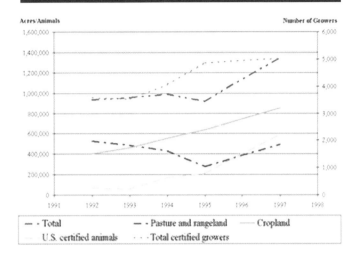

Expansion in US Organic Agriculture, 1991-1997

lack of reliable data on soil erosion and other measures of land degradation, and improved tracking of pesticide use and impact monitoring are still needed.

Figure 37
Expansion in US organic agriculture, 1991-1997.

Source: ERS 2000

References

AAFC (1997a). *Profile of Production Trends and Environmental Issues in Canada's Agriculture.* Ottawa, Agriculture and Agri-Food Canada

AAFC (1997b). *Agriculture in Harmony with Nature: Strategy for Environmentally Sustainable Agriculture and Agri-food Development in Canada.* Agriculture and Agri-Food Canada http:// www.agr.ca/policy/envharmon/docs/strat_e.pdf. Accessed 5 February 2002

AAFC (1999). *National Soil and Water Conservation Program.* Agriculture and Agri-Food Canada http://www.agr.gc.ca/pfra/nswcpe.htm. Accessed 4 February 2002

AAFC (2001a). *Prairie Farm Rehabilitation Administration (PFRA).* Agriculture and Agri-Food Canada http://www.agr.gc.ca/pfra/aboutuse.htm. Accessed 4 February 2002

AAFC (2001b). Canada's Organic Industry. *Agriculture and Agri-Food Canada Factsheets.* Agriculture and Agri-Food Canada http://www.agr.gc.ca/cb/factsheets/2industry_e.phtml. Accessed 5 February 2002

AAFC (2001c). *Agriculture in Harmony with Nature: Agriculture and Agri-food Canada's Sustainable Development Strategy 2001-2004.* Agriculture and Agri-Food Canada http://www.agr.gc.ca/policy/ environment/eb/public_html/ebe/sum_sds.html. Accessed 28 May 2002

Acton, D.F., and L.J. Gregorich (1995). Executive Summary. In *The Health of Our Soils: Toward Sustainable Agriculture in Canada,* edited by D. F. Acton and L. J. Gregorich. Centre for Land and Biological Resources Research, Research Branch, Agriculture and Agri-Food Canada http:// sis.agr.gc.ca/cansis/publications/health/intro.html Accessed 4 February 2002

Arcury, Thomas A., Sara A. Quandt, and Linda McCauley (2000). Farmworkers and Pesticides: Community-Based Research. *Environmental Health Perspectives* 108 (8):787-92

Aspelin, Arnold L., and Arthur H. Grube (1999). *Pesticides Industry Sales and Usage: 1996 and 1997 Market Estimates.* Biological and Economic Analysis Division, Office of Pesticide Programs, Office of Prevention, Pesticides and Toxic Substances, US Environmental Protection Agency http://www.epa.gov/oppbead1/pestsales/97pestsales/index.htm. Accessed 4 February 2002

Benbrook, Charles M. (1997). *Pest Management at the Crossroads.* Consumers Union http:// www.pmac.net/aboutpm.htm. Accessed 5 February 2002

CEC (1997). *North American Regional Action Plans on DDT and Chlordane: North American Working Group For The Sound Management of Chemicals Task Force on DDT And Chlordane.* Montreal, Commission for Environmental Cooperation of North America http://www.cec.org/ programs_projects/pollutants_health/smoc/smoc-rap.cfm?varlan=english. Accessed 5 February 2002

CEC (2000). *Background State of the Environment Report for the Fourth Advisory Group Meeting in Critical and Emerging Trends* (unpublished report). Montreal, Commission for Environmental Cooperation of North America

CEC (2001a). *The North American Mosaic: A State of the Environment Report.* Montreal, Commission for Environmental Cooperation of North America

CEC (2001b). *Sound Management of Chemicals.* Montreal, Commission for Environmental Cooperation of North America http://www.cec.org/files/PDF/POLLUTANTS/321_e_EN.PDF. Accessed 5 February 2002

CIDA (2000). *Combatting Desertification.* Canadian International Development Agency http:// www.acdi-cida.gc.ca/cida_ind.nsf/. Accessed 4 February 2002

Colborn, Theo, John Peterson Myers, and Diane Dumanoski (1996). *Our Stolen Future: How We Are Threatening Our Fertility, Intelligence, and Survival.* New York, Dutton

Cunningham, Rosalie (2001). *The Organic Consumer Profile,* Alberta Agriculture, Food and Rural Development, Strategic Information Services Unit

De Villiers, Marq (2000). *Water: The Fate of Our Most Precious Resource.* New York, Mariner Books

Diamond, H.L., and P.F. Noonan (1996). *Land Use in America.* Washington DC., Island Press

Dregne, H.E. (1986). Desertification of Arid Lands. In *Physics of Desertification*, edited by F. El-Baz and M. H. A. Hassan. Dordrecht, The Netherlands, Martinus, Nijhoff, http://www.ciesin.org/docs/002-193/002-193.html. Accessed 5 February 2002

EC (1996). *The State of Canada's Environment – 1996.* Environment Canada http://www.ec.gc.ca/soer-ree/English/1996Report/Doc/1-1.cfm. Accessed 28 May 2002

EC (1998). *Toxic Contaminants in the Environment: Persistent Organochlorines, National Environmental Indicator Series, SOE Bulletin No. 98-1.* Ottawa, Environment Canada, State of the Environment Reporting Program, http://www.ec.gc.ca/Ind/english/Toxic/default.cfm. Accessed 5 February 2002

EC (2000). *The Pros and Cons of Pesticides.* Environment Canada http://www.mb.ec.gc.ca/pollution/pesticides/ec00s09.en.html. Accessed 5 February 2002

ENS (2000). *United States Ratifies Treaty to Halt Desert Expansion.* Environment News Service http://ens.lycos.com/ens/oct2000/2000L-10-20-07.html. Accessed 4 February 2002

ERS (2000). US Organic Agriculture Gaining Ground. In *Agricultural Outlook* (April). United States Department of Agriculture, Economic Research Service http://www.ers.usda.gov/publications/agoutlook/apr2000/ao270d.pdf. Accessed 5 February 2002

ERS (2001). *Harmony Between Agriculture and the Environment: Current Issues.* US Department of Agriculture, Economic Research Service http://www.ers.usda.gov/emphases/harmony/issues/organic/organic.html. Accessed 5 February 2002

Ervin, David E., C. Ford Runge, Elisabeth A. Graffy, Willis E. Anthony, Paul Faeth Sandra S. Batie, Tim Penny, and Tim Warman (1998). Agriculture and the Environment: A New Strategic Vision. *Environment* 40 (6):8-15, 35-9

Eswaran, H., R. Lal, and P. F. Reich (2001). Land Degradation: An Overview. Paper read at Responses to Land Degradation. Proceedings of the Second International Conference on Land Degradation and Desertification, at Khon Kaen, Thailand. New Delhi, India, Oxford Press http://www.nhq.nrcs.usda.gov/WSR/papers/land-degradation-overview.htm

Gold, Mary V. (1999). *Sustainable Agriculture: Definitions and Terms: Special Reference Briefs Series* (no. SRB 99-02, Updates SRB 94-05). Alternative Farming Systems Information Center, National Agricultural Library http://warp.nal.usda.gov/afsic/AFSIC_pubs/srb9902.htm. Accessed 5 February 2002

H. John Heinz III Center (2001). *Designing a Report on the State of the Nation's Ecosystem: Selected Measurements for Croplands, Forests, and Coasts and Oceans.* The H. John Heinz III Center for Science, Economics and the Environment http://www.us-ecosystems.org/index.html. Accessed 5 February 2002

Halweil, Brian (2001). Organic Gold Rush. *WorldWatch* 14 (3):22-32

IISD (2001). *On the Great Plains: 11 Key Issues for Sustainability.* International Institute for Sustainable Development http://iisd1.iisd.ca/agri/default.htm. Accessed 4 February 2002

IUSS (2001). *The Land Degradation and Desertification Website.* The Working Group on Land Degradation and Desertification of the International Union of Soil Sciences http://www.nhq.nrcs.usda.gov/WSR/Landdeg/papers.htm. Accessed 4 February 2002

Jacobsen, Barry (1996). *USDA Integrated Pest Management Initiative.* Regents of the University of Minnesota http://ipmworld.umn.edu/chapters/jacobsen.htm. Accessed 4 February 2002

Kegley, Susan, Stephan Orme, and Lars Neumeister (2000). *Hooked on Poison: Pesticide Use in California, 1991–1998.* Pesticide Action Network North America http://www.panna.org/resources/documents/hookedSum.pdf. Accessed 5 February 2002

Liebman, James (1997). *Rising Toxic Tide: Pesticide Use in California, 1991–1995.* Pesticide Action Network & Californians for Pesticide Reform http://www.igc.org/panna/risingtide/textoftide.html. Accessed 5 February 2002

MacGregor, R.J., and T. McRae (2000). Driving Forces Affecting the Environmental Sustainability of Agriculture. In *Environmental Sustainability of Canadian Agriculture: Report of the Agri-Environmental Indicator Project. A Summary*, edited by T. McRae, C. A. S. Smith and L. J. Gregorich. Ottawa, Ont., Agriculture and Agri-Food Canada

Makin, Kirk (2001). Municipalities Can Ban Pesticides. *The Gazette*, 29 June, A3

McBride, R.A., P.J. Joosse, and G. Wall (2000). Indicator: Risk of Soil Compaction. In *Environmental Sustainability of Canadian Agriculture: Report of the Agri-Environmental Indicator Project. A Summary*, edited by T. McRae, C. A. S. Smith and L. J. Gregorich. Ottawa, Ont., Agriculture and Agri-Food Canada

McRae, T., C.A.S. Smith, and L.J. Gregorich eds. (2000). *Environmental Sustainability of Canadian Agriculture: Report of the Agri-Environmental Indicator Project. A Summary*. Ottawa, Agriculture and Agri-Food Canada

Miller Jr., G. Tyler (1982). *Living in the Environment: An Introduction to Environmental Science.* 4th ed. Belmont, CA, Wadsworth Publishing Company.

Mittelstaedt, Martin (2001a). Federal Pesticide List Outdated. *The Globe and Mail*, 17 July, A4

Mittelstaedt, Martin (2001b). Toronto Takes Steps to Ban Pesticides Within Two Years. *The Globe and Mail*, Tuesday 17 July, A1

Muir, Patricia S. (1999). *Agriculture: Pesticides.* Oregon State University http://www.orst.edu/instruction/bi301/agpestic.htm. Accessed 4 February 2002

Mulholland, Angela (2001). The Pesticide Debate. *CBC News In Depth* http://cbc.ca/consumers/indepth/lawn.html. Accessed 4 February 2002

NASS (1997). *1997 Census of Agriculture.* National Agricultural Statistics Service http://www.nass.usda.gov/census/. Accessed 5 February 2002

NIPMN, Western Region (2000). *Integrated Pest Management in the Western Region.* The Western Region IPM Network http://www.colostate.edu/Depts/IPM/. Accessed 5 February 2002

NRCS (1997). *Changes in Erosion, 1982–1997.* Natural Resources Conservation Service, Resource Assessment Division, US Department of Agriculture http://www.nhq.nrcs.usda.gov/land/meta/m5852.html. Accessed 5 February 2002

NRCS (2000). *Summary Report: 1997 National Resources Inventory, Revised December 2000.* US Department of Agriculture, Natural Resources Conservation Service http://www.nhq.nrcs.usda.gov/NRI/1997/summary_report/original/body.html. Accessed 5 February 2002

NRCS (2001a). *Acres of Cropland Converted to Conservation Reserve Program (CRP) Land, 1982–1997.* Natural Resources Conservation Service, Resource Assessment Division, US Department of Agriculture http://www.nhq.nrcs.usda.gov/land/meta/m5919.html. Accessed 5 February 2002

NRCS (2001b). *National Resources Inventory: Highlights.* Natural Resources Conservation Service, US Department of Agriculture http://www.nhq.nrcs.usda.gov/land/pubs/97highlights.pdf. Accessed 5 February 2002

OECD (1996). *Environmental Performance Reviews: United States.* Paris, Organisation for Economic Co-operation and Development

OECD (1999). *OECD Environmental Data Compendium.* Paris, Organization for Economic Co-operation and Development

Padbury, G., and C. Stushnoff (2000). Indicator: Risk of Wind Erosion. In *Environmental Sustainability of Canadian Agriculture: Report of the Agri-Environmental Indicator Project. A Summary*, edited by T. McRae, C. A. S. Smith and L. J. Gregorich. Ottawa, Ont., Agriculture and Agri-Food Canada http://www.agr.gc.ca/policy/environment/eb/public_html/pdfs/aei/Chap07.pdf. Accessed 4 February 2002

PCSD (1996). *Sustainable Agriculture: Task Force Report.* President's Council on Sustainable Development http://clinton2.nara.gov/PCSD/Publications/TF_Reports/ag-top.html. Accessed 5 February 2002

Pembina Institute (n.d.). Agricultural Sustainability. *GPI Background Report* http://www.pembina.org/green/gpi/. Accessed 26 September 2001

PMRA (1998). *Sustainable Pest Management.* Pest Management Regulatory Agency http://www.hc-sc.gc.ca/pmra-arla/english/spm/spm-e.html. Accessed 5 February 2002

PMRA (1999). *Procedures for Joint Review Applications for Chemical Pesticides.* Pest Management Regulatory Agency http://www.hc-sc.gc.ca/pmra-arla/english/pdf/nafta/naftajr/nafta-jr_pest-e.pdf. Accessed 4 February 2002

PMRA (2000). *Government Response to the Report of the House of Commons Standing Committee on the Environment and Sustainable Development, Pesticides: Making the Right Choice for the Protection of Health and the Environment.* Pest Management Regulatory Agency http://www.hc-sc.gc.ca/pmra-arla/english/pdf/hlawns/hl-GovtResp-e.pdf. Accessed 4 February 2002

PMRA (2001). *About PMRA.* Pest Management Regulatory Agency http://www.hc-sc.gc.ca/pmra-arla/english/aboutpmra/about-e.html. Accessed 4 February 2002

Roberts, Wayne, Rod MacRae, and Lori Stahlbrand (1999). *The Growing Trend Away From Pesticides: A Brief to the House of Commons Standing Committee on the Environment.* World Wildlife Fund http://www.wwf.ca/satellite/prip/resources/presentation-roberts.pdf. Accessed 4 February 2002

Schafer, Kristin S., Susan E. Kegley, and Sharyle Patton (2000). *Nowhere to Hide: Persistent Toxic Chemicals in the US Food Supply.* PANNA: Pesticide Action Network North America http://www.igc,org/panna/resources/documents/nowheretohide.pdf. Accessed 4 February 2002

Schmitt, Christopher, J. (1998). Environmental Contaminants. In *Status and Trends of the Nation's Biological Resources,* edited by M. J. Mac, P. A. Opler, C. E. Puckett Haecker and P. D. Doran. Washington DC, US Department of the Interior and US Geological Survey

Shaw, Hollie (2001). *Canada Braces for Frenzied Growth of Organic Food: US Outlets Expand.* National Post Online, 6 July http://www.nationalpost.com/financialpost/story.html?f=/stories/20010706/610607.html. Accessed 26 July 2001

Shelton, I.J., G. J. Wall, J.-M. Cossette, R. Eilers, B. Grant, D. King, Padbury G., H. Rees, J. Tajek, and L. van Vliet (2000). Indicator: Risk of Water Erosion. In *Environmental Sustainability of Canadian Agriculture: Report of the Agri-Environmental Indicator Project. A Summary,* edited by T. McRae, C. A. S. Smith and L. J. Gregorich. Ottawa, Ont., Agriculture and Agri-Food Canada

Smith, C.A.S., G. Wall, R. Desjardins, and B. Grant (2000). Indicator: Soil Organic Carbon. In *Environmental Sustainability of Canadian Agriculture: Report of the Agri-Environmental Indicator Project. A Summary,* edited by T. McRae, C. A. S. Smith and L. J. Gregorich. Ottawa, Ont., Agriculture and Agri-Food Canada

Statistics Canada (2000). *Human Activity and the Environment 2000.* Ottawa, Minister of Industry

UNCCD (2001). *United Nations Secretariat of the Convention to Combat Desertification.* United Nations http://www.unccd.int/main.php. Accessed 5 February 2002

UNDP, UNEP, World Bank, and WRI (2000). *World Resources 2000-2001: People and Ecosystems, the Fraying Web of Life.* Washington DC, World Resources Institute

UNEP (2000). *Stockholm Convention on Persistent Organic Pollutants (POPs).* United Nations Environment Programme http://www.chem.unep.ch/sc/. Accessed 5 February 2002

USDA (1996). *Part 407 – Sustainable Agriculture (Subpart A – General).* US Department of Agriculture, Natural Resources Conservation Service Electronic Directives System http://policy.nrcs.usda.gov/national/gm/title180/part407/subparta/. Accessed 5 February 2002

USDA (2000a). *Agricultural Resources and Environmental Indicators, 2000.* US Department of Agriculture, Economic Research Service, Resource Economics Division http://www.ers.usda.gov/briefing/arei/newarei/. Accessed 4 February 2002

USDA (2000b). *Glickman Announces National Standards for Organic Food.* US Department of Agriculture News Release No. 0425.00 http://www.usda.gov/news/releases/2000/12/0425.htm. Accessed 4 February 2002

USDA (2001a). *Food and Agricultural Policy: Taking Stock for the New Century*. US Department of Agriculture http://www.usda.gov/news/pubs/farmpolicy01/content.pdf. Accessed 4 February 2002

USDA (2001b). *Water Erosion Vulnerability*. Washington DC, US Department of Agriculture, Natural Resources Conservation Service, Soil survey Division, World Soil Resources http://www.nrcs.usda.gov/technical/worldsoils/mapindx/erosh2o.html. Accessed 31 May 2002

USDA (2001c). *Wind Erosion Vulnerability*. Washington DC, US Department of Agriculture, Natural Resources Conservation Service, Soil survey Division, World Soil Resources http://www.nrcs.usda.gov/technical/worldsoils/mapindx/eroswind.html. Accessed 31 May 2002

Vaisey, Jill S., Ted W. Weins, and Robert J. Wettlaufer (1996). The Permanent Cover Program – Is Twice Enough? Paper read at Soil and Water Conservation Policies: Successes and Failures, September 17-20, at Prague, Czech Republic

Vanderwel, Douwe, and Syd Abday (2001). *An Introduction to Water Erosion Control*. Alberta Agricluture, Food and Rural Development http://www.agric.gov.ab.ca/agdex/500/72000003.html. Accessed 4 February 2002

Wilson, Art, and Allen Tyrchniewicz (1994). *Sustainable Development for the Great Plains: Policy Analysis*. Winnipeg, International Institute for Sustainable Development http://www.iisd.org/pdf/sd_for_gp.pdf. Accessed 4 February 2002

Zinn, Jeffrey (1994). *Conservation Reserve Program: Policy Issues for the 1995 Farm Bill*. Congressional Research Service, Report for Congress http://cnie.org/NLE/CRS/abstract.cfm?NLEid=1599. Accessed 5 February 2002

Forests

Forests

Figure 38

Forest extent.

Source: FAO 2001a

orests spread over roughly 26 percent of North America's land area (see Figure 38) and represent 12 percent of the world's forests. North America has over one-third of the world's boreal forests (see Box 40) as well as a wide range of other forest types. Over 96 percent is natural forest. After Russia and Brazil, Canada has more forest than any other country, with 244.6 million ha covering 26.5 percent of the total land area. The United States is the fourth most forested country, with 226 million ha, representing about 25 percent of the country's land area (FAO 2001a).

While Canada's forest area remained virtually unchanged during 1990–2000, the United States forest area increased by almost 3.9 million ha—or approximately 1.7 percent. Recent estimates (late-1990s) show that North America grows 255.5 million m^3 more timber annually than is harvested (see Figure 39) (UN-ECE and FAO 2000).

In Canada, 94 percent of forests are publicly owned, with the provinces responsible for 71 percent of total forested land (NRCan 2000a). In contrast, some 60 percent of US forests are privately owned, 35 percent are publicly owned and managed by the federal government, while the 50 states own and manage 5 percent (UN 1997).

The number of plantations (usually considered closely planted trees in neat rows) and areas replanted more randomly with seed-

Forest Extent

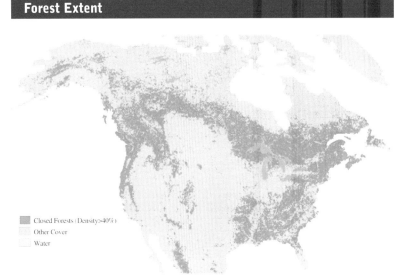

Closed Forests (Density>40%)
Other Cover
Water

Box 40: Boreal Forests

The boreal forest is one of the world's largest terrestrial ecosystems. It is a belt of coniferous forest around the northern hemisphere covering about 17 percent of the earth's land. North America's boreal forests stretch across the northern part of continent from the province of Newfoundland on the east coast, over half the Prairie Provinces, and throughout the Yukon territories and the state of Alaska. It covers 341 million ha in Canada, representing about 30 percent of the world's boreal forest, and 46 million ha in Alaska, which makes it the largest North American forest ecosystem (TRN 1998; Gawthrop 1999).

The boreal landscape, called *taiga* in Russia, is characterized by a diverse mosaic of forests of various ages and composition, relatively few tree species, large peat bogs, and a web of shrubs, mosses, lichens, and other organisms. The plants and animals are adapted to the cold climate, a short growing season, and repeated naturally occurring forest fires (BFW 1997; Gawthrop 1999).

Over the past 30 years, there has been a large increase in global consumption of wood products, primarily paper, and the boreal forest is a major supplier of wood and fibers to world markets. Over the last three decades some areas have been subject to increased environmental threats: large-scale industrial forestry has rapidly moved into previously un-logged areas of the boreal forest, oil and gas exploitation has grown, and the number and scale of forest fires has increased (TRN 1998). Only about 2.66 percent of Canada's Boreal Shield ecozone (the largest of seven subdivisions of Canada's boreal forests) is strictly protected from all forms of large-scale industrial activities (Urquizo, Bastedo and others 2000).

Unlike the temperate and tropical forests of the south, where trees are more majestic and grow in close stands, the boreal forest and potential threats to its sustainability have not inspired the same public interest as the forests of the Pacific Northwest (Gawthrop 1999).

lings or seed after harvesting is increasing. For example, the area successfully regenerated by planting and seeding in Canada expanded from 10,090 ha in 1975 to 297,820 ha in 1997 (NFDP 1998). The United States has about 21 million ha of plantations or about 4.5 percent of its forested land base (UN-ECE and FAO 2000).

Large tracts of North American forests have been designated as protected areas. In 1995, Canada had protected about 32 million hectares (7.6 percent) of its forested lands (not counting those under provincial protection), and 67 million ha (30 percent) of US forests enjoyed some status of protection

(University of Waterloo 1998; FAO 2001a).

Human intervention is the principal driving force behind forest degradation, and human demand for wood products such as timber

Figure 39
Annual timber increment and annual removals on available forest land, late 1990s

Source: UN-ECE and FAO 2000

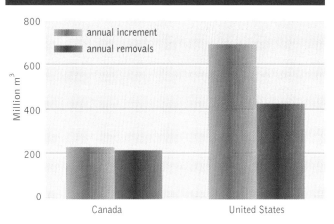
Annual Timber Increment and Annual Removals on Available Forest Land, Late 1990s

Box 41: Forest Health

In the past, a forest was deemed healthy if it was free of insects and disease and was growing vigorously (NRCan 1999). Over the past 20 years, however, the long-term sustainability of the forest ecosystem has become the primary measure of forest health (UN-ECE and FAO 2000). A forest may be considered healthy when it maintains biodiversity and resiliency; provides wildlife habitat, ecological services, and aesthetic appeal; and maintains a sustainable supply of timber and non-timber resources (NRCan 1999). Some level of fire, insects, and disease is recognized as a natural component of healthy forests. By these measures, past harvesting practices, the introduction of exotic species, and suppression of natural disturbances have created large forested landscapes with an unnatural tree distribution and age structure, which has increased the forest's vulnerability to drought, wind, insects, disease, and fire (UN 1997; USDA 1997). For example, as shown in the disasters section, decades of aggressive fire suppression contributed to major ecological change in some of North America's forest ecosystems so that the structural homogeneity of many new tree stands render them less diverse and resilient than their natural predecessors (Stuart 1998).

and paper is the primary driver of forest modification. The region accounts for about 40 percent of the world's production and consumption of industrial wood products (Mathews and Hammond 1999). In some areas, forests are becoming increasingly fragmented, biologically impoverished, and weakened or stressed, and the resulting changes in forest ecosystem structure and age appear to be factors in increased forest damage by fire, drought, pests, and air pollution (Bryant, Nielsen, and Tangley 1997). Maintaining healthy forest ecosystems is a priority issue.

One region in which new forests cannot replace the economic, cultural, or ecosystem value of previous growth is the Pacific Northwest coast of North America. The region's old-growth forests have become an issue of priority concern in North America, in some part due to campaigns against logging over the past 30 years that brought the issue to international attention.

Forest Health

Although North America's forest area is now relatively stable, a mixture of changing conditions in the semi-natural forests in many areas may be responsible for deteriorating health (see Box 41). For example, a significant warming trend and increased lightning, tree age factors, fire-fighting policy, harvesting, forest fragmentation, pollution, and invasion of non-native species are likely to be implicated in the doubling of the area annually disturbed by fire and insects in the boreal forests of central and northwestern Canada over the past 20 to 30 years compared to the previous 50-year period (Urquizo, Bastedo and others 2000; Bruce, Burton, and Egener 1999).

In the United States, the results of a number of reports from the mid-1990s show that northeastern forests were generally healthy, although particular species in localized areas showed cause for concern. Chronic and quite extensive decline was noted in the high-elevation spruce-fir forests of the northeast US, and serious declines for red spruce in the 1980s across the northeastern Appalachian Mountains and in some regions of the southern Appalachians were reported (McLaughlin 1996).

Invasive exotic diseases have been a principal cause of changes to North American forest ecosystems and continue to threaten forests (Mattoon 1998). For example, the American chestnut and elm are now functionally extinct due to exotic pathogens while the mellaleuca and miconia have invaded large areas of Florida and Hawaii, respectively, displacing native vegetation and transforming wildlife habitat (UN 1997, USDA 1997). The hemlock woolly adelgid is attacking the eastern hemlock, and entire stands are disappearing in parts of New England. And a fungal pathogen, the butternut canker, is affecting the butternut while the eastern and western flowering dogwoods are being affected by another fungal pathogen, the dogwood anthracnose (Mattoon 1998).

One of the most widespread and damaging invasive insects has been the gypsy moth caterpillar, which caused between 25 and 100 percent defoliation of more than 608,000 ha of northeastern forests in 1971 and destroyed about US $764 million worth of timber in 1981. It now occurs throughout the Northeast (Porter and Hill 1998). In all, it has been estimated that resource values on some 9.72 million ha of national

forest in the United States are at high risk of loss over the next 15 years due to insects and disease, with mortality potentially exceeding 25 percent of expected background rates (or average rate of probability of death) (Bartuska 2000).

Exotic invasives are now second to habitat loss and human modification of forest ecosystems as the largest threat to biodiversity. Logging, suburban development, and other land use changes have continued to destroy or modify forest ecosystems over the past 30 years, threatening forest-dwelling species. About two-thirds of Canada's 140,000 species of plants, animals, and microorganisms live in forest habitats. One-quarter of all its species-at-risk are forest dependent. The abundance and distribution of the woodland caribou and wolverine, two of Canada's flagship wilderness species, decline with just low levels of forest disturbance and fragmentation (GFW2000). Of the 1,049 species of plants and animals listed under the US Endangered Species Act (ESA) in 1997, all of 332 occur in national forests. In the southern Appalachian forest ecosystem, 260 aquatic species are at risk. Key salmon and trout species inhabit decreasing areas of their former range in the forested interior Columbia River Basin (USDA 1997). And it is estimated that about 198 tree species are threatened in the United States (UNDP, UNEP, World Bank, and WRI 2000).

Human modification of forest ecosystems through unsustainable harvesting methods can also contribute to degraded forest quality. For example, the Acadian mixed wood forest in the province of New Brunswick is gradually disappearing due to more than a century of high-grade logging. Late-successional species that require protection to regenerate are being replaced by lower-value, short-lived species. Appropriate silviculture has had considerable success in restoring 'protection-requiring' species, however, and if implemented could begin to replace present clear-cutting methods (see Box 45), allowing for the return of complex species assemblages and a more diverse ecosystem (Salonius 2001).

Exotic species and modifications to forest age and structure are part of a complex mix of pressures that affect the health of North America's forest ecosystems. Air pollution is increasingly recognized as a contributing factor in some areas (Bright 1999). It has played a role in the major die-off of high-elevation spruce-fir forests in the southern Appalachians, a region that has been the focus of concern for the US Forest Service (USDA 1997; Mattoon 1998) (see Box 42).

Although pollution regulation over the past 30 years has reduced acid rain in the northeast, evidence is now linking reduced growth in some tree species to its long-term effects (Driscoll, Lawrence, and others 2001). Research conducted by the Acid Rain Action Plan (see Box 43) shows acid deposition in areas of relatively poor soils resulted in both

Box 42: Stresses to the Eastern Forests

Evidence of declining tree health in North America's eastern forests illustrates the impact of overlapping stresses on forest ecosystems. Here, second-growth woodlands have spread over old woodlots and abandoned farms and fields in the past century. One of the major factors affecting their health is human amplification of the nitrogen cycle, which has been boosted by fertilizers, fossil fuel combustion from cars and power plants, and wetland drainage. Nitrogen oxides help to form ozone pollution (see Box 4 in the atmosphere section), which is responsible for significant tree damage in this region. Exposure to ozone correlates with die-offs of hickory and oak and injuries to the tulip poplar and magnolia. Ozone exposure also appears to play a role in reducing photosynthesis, leading to chronic leaf damage and, in turn, root failure and a syndrome of 'falling forest' (Bright 1999).

Nitric acid also contributes to acid rain. Essential minerals have been leached from the soil from past decades of acid rain, impairing the ability of the needles of the region's most important conifers to function properly in the winter. It is thought that this has contributed to the death of 75 percent of mature red spruce in the higher elevations of Vermont's Green Mountains. Nitrogen pollution is also making forests more vulnerable to native and exotic insects and disease. Such conditions have played a role in the mortality of sugar maple, and threats to the American beech and eastern hemlock (Bright 1999). Together with other biotic and abiotic stresses, acidic cloud water has contributed to predisposing red spruce in the high elevations of the northeast US Appalachians to winter injury, causing mortality and regional decline (McLaughlin 1996). A survey of five eastern US states found that overall, tree mortality may be three to five times historical levels (Mattoon 1998).

acidification and the depletion of calcium and magnesium, which are essential for tree growth (EC 2000). In Canada, the sugar maple has been the focus of studies on forest decline. Although the balance of evidence has shown no regional sugar maple decline, it is also evident that increasing crown transparency noted in southern Quebec and central Ontario is spatially correlated with the regional pollution gradient (McLaughlin 1996). A trend, albeit somewhat inconsistent, showed that where acid deposition was high,

Monitoring and Assessment Network, and the 1984 Acid Rain National Early Warning System (ARNEWS), as well as through a number of bilateral initiatives (see Box 43).

Another underlying cause of changing forest conditions is the historical lack of recognition in forest policy of the ecological, recreational, spiritual, aesthetic, and non-timber values of forest ecosystems and of the importance of working with natural disturbance rather than in opposition to it (see

Box 43: Bilateral Cooperation

Canada and the United States cooperate to assess the health of their forests. Established in 1958, the North American Forestry Commission, (NAFC) is one of FAO's six regional forestry commissions. NAFC supports research and natural resource management activities of mutual concern through seven working groups: atmospheric change, fire management, forest products, insects and diseases, silviculture, forest inventory and monitoring, and forest genetic resources. The atmospheric change group, for example, promotes the collection, exchange, and dissemination of information and techniques for monitoring forest health and evaluating the effects of atmospheric change on forests (NAFC 2000).

Canada and the United States also cooperate to assess the impacts of air pollution and acid deposition on forest ecosystems through a forest-mapping initiative included in the Acid Rain Action Plan adopted by the Conference of New England Governors and Eastern Canadian Premiers (NEG/ECP)(EC 2000). Forestry Canada and the US Forest Service work together as part of the North American Maple Project (NAMP) established in 62 locations in 11 states and four provinces. A system was erected to identify the types and extent of damage to forests as well as its natural and anthropogenic causes (NRCan 1995, CAS 2002).

especially as a result of nitrates, crowns were thinner (Hopkin, Lachance, and others 1996).

The long-term response to the impact of tropospheric ozone, acid rain, and other stressors is being monitored nationally by programs such as the US Forest Health Monitoring Program, Canada's Ecological

the section on wildfire in the environmental disasters chapter) (USDA 1997; WRM 1998). Since the 1992 United Nations Conference on the Environment and Development (UNCED), North American governments have changed the definition of sustainable forestry from promoting a sustained yield of fiber to addressing the health and sustainability of forest ecosystems. The new definition focuses on the stewardship and use of forest land at local, regional, national, and global levels in a way and at a rate that maintains their health—their biodiversity, productivity, regeneration capacity, and vitality—and their potential to fulfil relevant ecological, economic, and social functions now and in the future, without damaging other ecosystems. This shift has meant changes in how forestlands are examined, policy is formulated, and programs are designed and implemented (UN 1997; Apsey, Laishley, and others 2000).

Both countries are part of the Montreal Process on Criteria and Indicators for the Conservation and Sustainable Management of Temperate and Boreal Forests (The Montreal Process), an international agreement signed in 1994. Its Working Group agreed on a common definition of sustainable management and identified seven criteria and 67 associated indicators that define its characteristics. Their use should ensure the compatibility of national criteria and indicators with internationally recognized scientific standards (MPCI 1998). In the United States, the US Forest Service (USFS) has incorporated the concept of sustainable forestry and in 1999, it strengthened this emphasis with the development of sustainability criteria and indicators for management of the National Forest System. As part of the Montreal Process, the USFS is

producing a major technical evaluation of the state of the Nation's forests and of progress toward sustainable forest management to be ready in 2003, with input from public workshops held by the Roundtable on Sustainable Forests (UN 1997; USDA 2002).

Canada's commitment to sustainable forestry is reflected in its 1992 Forest Accord and National Forest Strategy, which introduced a multi-use forest management perspective recognizing the non-timber values of forests and the need for information that transcends political boundaries. The 1998–2003 strategy includes the Canadian Council of Forest Ministers' set of criteria and indicators of sustainable forest management, which was reinforced by the Montreal Process, as well as ongoing research conducted by Natural Resources Canada (NRCan 2000a; NRCan 2000b).

Many state and provincial initiatives also reflect a shift to sustainable ecosystem management, including a legislated requirement to integrate economic, environmental, and social interests in forest management; decreases in the size of harvesting areas; new harvesting methods for better natural regeneration; improved silviculture methods; the use of natural resource inventories; and public participation (UN 1997). Largely in response to public pressure, forest management over the past 20 years has incorporated a new emphasis on maintaining wildlife habitat, protecting soils, and retaining natural landscape characteristics and natural disturbances such as wildfires. In addition, as shown below in the old-growth section, some timber companies have also incorporated new forms of management to sustain economic activity, local communities, forest resources, wildlife habitat, and ecosystem functions.

An emerging issue in maintaining healthy forests is the potential impact of climate change and consideration of the connections between climate change and other damaging influences (NRCan 1999). Higher temperatures could lead to an increase in insect populations and outbreaks of fire, which can have devastating effects. For example, during an outbreak of the spruce budworm in eastern Canada between 1970 and the mid-1980s, some 55 million ha of forest were defoliated. Previously unknown in the forests north of the Alaska mountain range, this insect has defoliated some 23,000 ha (Gawthrop 1999).

Existing conditions in many forest stands throughout North America make them less resistant to catastrophic outbreaks of insects, diseases, and fires, which in turn reduces habitat diversity and utilizable timber, adding CO_2 to the atmosphere (Taylor 1997). North America's forests, particularly its broadleaf ecosystems, which appear to have a large capacity for carbon absorption, are unlikely to maintain their absorption attributes in an unhealthy state (Bright 1999). Evidence suggests that until about 1970, Canada's boreal forests took up more than half of the carbon emitted by that country, but by the end of the 1990s, they had begun to

lose carbon as natural and human disturbance that increased forest fires and insect infestations turned the boreal region from a sink to a source of atmospheric carbon. The International Panel on Climate Change has reported that higher temperatures are likely to lead to

Distribution of Coastal Temperate Rain Forest by State/Province

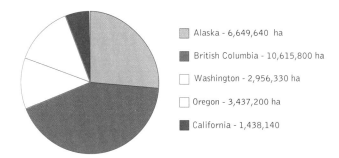

☐ Alaska - 6,649,640 ha

■ British Columbia - 10,615,800 ha

☐ Washington - 2,956,330 ha

☐ Oregon - 3,437,200 ha

■ California - 1,438,140

Figure 40
Distribution of coastal temperate rain forest by state/province.

Source: BC Ministry of Forests 1998

the eventual replacement of much of the boreal forest by grasslands, temperate forest, or tundra (Gawthrop 1999; NRCan 2000c).

As management practices place greater value on non-timber attributes, as more forested lands are protected from logging, and as a weakened forest's ability to absorb carbon is questioned, the importance of reducing North America's consumption of both wood products and fossil fuels should become ever more apparent.

Old-Growth Forests in the Pacific Northwest

Old-growth (see Box 44) forests once occurred in all North America's ecosystems. Although lack of historical data and inventory definitional problems make it difficult to determine exactly how much old growth there was, remnant old-growth forests and stands still remain in many ecosystems throughout the region, but especially in the Pacific Northwest, the Rocky Mountains, and the Pacific Southwest. Most of the remaining old-growth forests occur in the Pacific Northwest along the coast from Alaska through British Columbia (BC) and the states of Washington and Oregon to California. The classic old-growth forest in this area contains redwoods, cedars, Douglas fir, hemlock, or spruce. The region probably still (in 1998) contained about half the world's remaining un-logged coastal temperate rainforest, with the

Box 44: Old Growth

There is no broadly accepted definition of old growth, but it generally refers to ecosystems characterized by stands of very large and old trees, a distinct species composition, a multi-layered canopy, and a large buildup of organic matter (Lund 2000). The forests may or may not have been disturbed by humans. Old-growth forests supply high-value timber, contain large amounts of carbon, harbor a large reservoir of genetic diversity, provide habitat for many species of fauna and flora, regulate hydrologic regimes, protect soils and conserve nutrients, and have substantial recreational and aesthetic value (Marchak, Aycock, and Herbert 1999). Their trees have many nest cavities for birds and small mammals and the forest is littered with decaying trees and debris that provide habitat for rodents, insects, and reptiles (Dietrich 1992). Some 40 of 118 known vertebrate species that live primarily in old-growth forests may not be able to nest, breed, or forage anywhere else (PBS 1999). Temperate old-growth forests have been and still are home to many indigenous and tribal peoples. Much of the interest in old-growth forests stems from the powerful images they project of rich biodiversity and timeless stability. Many visitors sense a form of spirituality and grandeur in such forests, and most people place a high value on them.

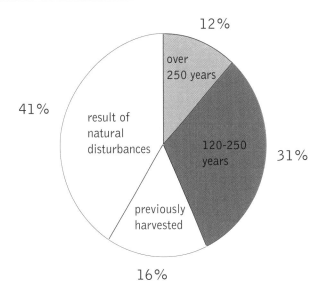

Old-Growth Forest in British Columbia

12%

over 250 years

41%

result of natural disturbances

120-250 years

31%

previously harvested

16%

greatest share in BC (see Figure 40). Old growth makes up 31 to 43 percent of the province's forests (see Figure 41) (BC Ministry of Forests 2001a).

The majority of old-growth losses in the eastern and lower elevations of North America came about through conversion of lands to agriculture and urban environments. In the west and mountainous regions, loss has resulted from harvesting of timber and conversion to younger, more vigorously growing stands along with recent catastrophic events like the eruption of Mt. St. Helens and the Yellowstone fires (see Box 52 in the environmental disasters section) (Harmon 1993; H. John Heinz III Center 1999). Figure 42 shows the decline in the percentage of total old-growth forest area in US west coast states. The remaining old-

growth forests in these states are characterized by highly fragmented stands of clear-cuts, thinned areas, young plantations, stands of mature growth, and extensive road systems (Turner, Carpenter, and others 1998).

With population growth, demand for timber, and technological improvements in the logging industry, the rate of logging in the Pacific Northwest increased dramatically after the 1950s. The introduction of

Figure 41
Old-growth forest in British Columbia.

Source: BC Ministry of Forests 2001a

Figure 42
Change in old-growth forest area in California, Oregon, and Washington, 1933-45 to 1992.

Source: H. John Heinz II Center 2001

Change in Old-Growth Forest Area in California, Oregon, and Washington, 1933-45 to 1992

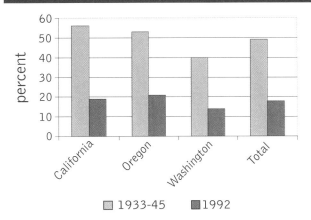

☐ 1933-45   ■ 1992

Box 45: Clear-Cutting

Clear-cutting is a simple, efficient, and cost-effective means to extract timber, whereby all trees in a given area are cut down and the saleable stock removed (Jones, Griggs, and Fredricksen 2000). Earlier, clear-cuts were thought to mimic forests gaps formed by natural disturbances. But today, many environmentalists consider clear-cutting to be destructive, unsightly, and unsustainable. They argue that it is practiced more frequently than the natural large-scale disturbances it has been said to mimic (Hammond 1993). The new vegetation does not maintain the complexity and stability of old forests that makes the latter storehouses for a diversity of genetic codes and uncommon species (Maser 1993). Furthermore, clear-cutting in sensitive ecosystems can cause soil erosion, landslides, and silting, which in turn can damage watersheds, lead to flooding, and inhibit the reproductive success of fish eggs, which is especially important to the wild salmon of the Pacific Northwest (see the coastal and marine section) (May 1998). It opens large gaps, fragmenting the forest and exposing more kilometers of 'edge' to the wind and increasing the chances of blowdown (Dietrich 1992). With high-profile NGO campaigns against the practice, there has been considerable public outcry over the perceived threats of clear-cutting, which also include the loss of aesthetic and recreational value (PFC 2000).

the chainsaw, the logging truck, and clearcutting (see Box 45) as the dominant harvesting method were important factors in this trend. Tree farming was also introduced at this time, and many clearcut areas began to be reforested with managed stands of short-rotation trees, resulting in blocks of forests of uniform age (Dietrich 1992).

A growing worldwide demand and higher prices in the 1970s drove the rapid harvesting of old-growth timber (Mathews and Hammond 1999). Old-growth losses and the practice of clear-cutting in the 1970s provoked ENGOs in both countries to launch intensive local campaigns to protect the mature forests from harvest (see Boxes 46 and 47).

Box 46: The Spotted Owl

In the United States, the spotted owl, which depends entirely on large tracts of old-growth habitat, became the focus of a much-publicized debate. In 1973, the year the federal Endangered Species Act (ESA) (see Box 10 in the biodiversity section) was passed, the spotted owl was listed as potentially endangered. With each new scientific discovery about the unique needs of this bird, owl researchers, followed by ENGOs attempted to secure protection of ever-larger amounts of old growth to ensure the species' survival. The owl's predicament gave ENGOs the means to seek its protection as an endangered species and to file lawsuits against clear-cutting. In a series of court decisions in 1988 and 1989, they challenged government science and its owl protection plans. Grassroots campaigns in which protesters blocked logging roads and sat in trees soon grew into strategic campaigns by national organizations. Finally, the Forest Service undertook a rigorous impact statement and after a court order in 1991, the US Fish and Wildlife Service declared the owl a threatened species and designated 4.7 million ha outside of parks as 'critical owl habitat' (Dietrich 1992).

Box 47: Clayoquot Sound

In British Columbia, the controversy over old growth focused on sensitive remaining rain-forest areas. Clayoquot Sound, a 1,000 km^2 wilderness on Vancouver Island, became the focus of a debate over old-growth logging. Beginning in 1984, environmentalists and the Nuu-chah-nulth First Nation protested clear-cutting in the rain forest by blocking logging roads, among other tactics. Between 1989 and 1993, government task forces attempted to resolve the conflict, and large tracts of coastal temperate rain forest were set aside for protection (MSRM 2002). In 1994, the 4,000 km^2 Long Beach Model Forest, which encompasses Clayoquot Sound, was established, with the vision of maintaining healthy ecological conditions while safeguarding the well-being of communities, including traditional, non-industrial, and industrial users. As one of 11 model forests in the Canadian Model Forest Network, research is being conducted to develop and test indicators to address old-growth forest issues (NRCan 2000d). Protests continued, however, with claims that logging was still permitted on 70 percent of Clayoquot Sound, bringing national and international attention to the issue (May 1998).

In 1995, in recognition that the Nuu-chah-nulth had not been adequately consulted, public negotiations toward a comprehensive treaty settlement with the First Nation peoples began, and recommendations regarding forest management that recognize other forest values than timber were formulated and adopted by the provincial government (May 1998).

In ensuing years, more progress was made in resolving remaining conflicts and protecting the forests. One of Canada's largest forest products companies announced in 1998 that it would phase out clear-cut harvesting in all its BC operations and design a new stewardship strategy focusing on old-growth conservation and variable retention harvesting instead of clear-cutting (PR Newswire 1998). An agreement was struck between First Nations and environmentalists to set aside most of the western coast of Clayoquot Sound, and to promote economic development through small-scale logging, non-timber forest products, and eco-tourism. With the January 2000 designation of Clayoquot Sound as a UNESCO Biosphere Reserve, industry, environmentalists, governments, and First Nations established a new form of governance based on shared responsibility for the ecosystem (ENS 1999; CNW 2000).

In the 1980s, new forest mechanization technologies improved efficiency (Apsey, Laishley, and others 2000). By the end of the 1980s, old growth was nearly gone from both private and public lands in the US Northwest (Dietrich 1992). Inventory done in 1989 and 1991 showed that 47 percent of coastal BC was still covered with old forest and 9 percent of the coast (678,000 ha of old forest) was in protected areas by the end of the 1980s (McKinnon and Eng 1995). Most industrial-scale logging in Canada took place less than 100 years ago. And since there is little second-growth forest that has reached maturity, most logging today occurs in mature natural forests, except in the coastal region where an increasing proportion of the harvest now comes from second-growth forests (British Columbia Ministry of Forests 2001a). Mature forests are therefore still deemed to be essential to Canada's industrial timber supply.

During the 1990s, the environmental lobby's campaign to protect British Columbia's old growth broadened to the international arena. ENGOs in the United States focused on persuading lumber and paper consumers in Europe and the Unites States to avoid purchasing products from the region, beginning an international boycott of western Canadian timber products (CBD 2000).

The forestry industry includes large corporations, independent loggers, truckers, pulp and paper mills, and log exporters, who are naturally concerned about jobs and timber revenues in the face of heated public protest. Some logging

communities became polarized over the dispute (Pace 1993), reflecting the complex nature of the issue and the difficulty in finding 'win-win' solutions. Timber-related jobs did in fact decline. In Oregon, where timber was the biggest industry in 1988, and Washington, where it was the second biggest, timber employment fell by 30,000 between 1979 and 1989. According to the 1991 spotted owl ruling (see Box 46), the main reasons for loss of timber jobs and mill closures in the Pacific Northwest were modernization, changes in product demand, and

Box 48: Certification, The Forest Stewardship Council

Certification emerged in the past six to seven years in response to international NGO pressure to promote sustainable forestry practices. It is designed to allow consumers and participants to measure forest management practices against approved standards. While enabling consumers to support responsible forestry, certification also provides forest owners with an incentive to maintain and improve forest management practices (Ghazalie 1994).

The Forest Stewardship Council (FSC) is the international leader in setting up a legitimate process to evaluate certifiers for the purposes of accreditation. Founded in 1993, FSC is an international, non-profit NGO formed of representatives from environmental and social groups, the timber industry, the forestry profession, indigenous peoples' organizations, community forestry groups, and certification bodies from at least 25 countries. Its purpose is to support ecologically appropriate, socially responsible, and economically viable management of the world's forests. It provides a model for the development of national and regional standards for evaluating whether and how well a forest is being managed according to a set of global principles and criteria that apply to all forests worldwide.

The FSC certification program is carried out by independent, third-party organizations and is the only one that verifies claims in a 'chain of custody' from the forest through to the final product. Products bearing the FSC label come from a forest managed according to FSC Principles (FSC-Can 1996; FSC-US 2001; NRCan 2001). The FSC's principles and criteria form the model for the development of national initiatives in over 20 countries, which coordinate the development of regional and local standards. The US and Canadian programs were created in 1996, and both countries are developing regional standards. The two countries have 1.8 million ha natural forests certified by FSC-accredited certification bodies (UNDP, UNEP, World Bank and WRI 2000). According to information collected by FAO about the area of forest certified under various certification schemes including FSC, a total of about 30.5 million ha have been certified in the region (FAO 2001b).

competition from elsewhere (Dietrich 1992; Marchak, Aycock, and Herbert 1999).

In response to public pressure, in the 1980s forest policies changed to reflect broader concerns for forest biodiversity and other values. As shown above, until recently, governmental management of forests in both Canada and the United States was based on the doctrine of sustained yield, which had been adopted in the United States and Canada in the first half of the 20th century. It established an upper limit on annual timber harvests, with increased yield to be obtained by controlling cutting on virgin forests and cultivating trees on cutover areas. Management focused on production for timber.

In 1978, the Canadian mandate was redefined to include management of all forest values, including timber, and soon thereafter the Forest Practices Code outlined in great detail how to protect other forest assets. It limited cutblock size, required strips to be reserved along streams, and restricted harvests on unstable soils on steep slopes (Apsey, Laishley, and others 2000; FPB 2002). In BC, sustained yield was replaced by new forest practices that made management more inclusive, such as 'multiple use' and 'integrated resource management'. Similarly, the US 1976 National Forest Management Act reinforced the idea of 'multiple use' and considered other forest values (Dietrich 1992). In addition, more forests were set aside for protection. By about

2000, almost 4 million hectares, or 15 percent, of BC's old growth were fully protected (BC Ministry of Forests 2001a).

Research began into alternative approaches, such as the *Montane Alternative Silvicultural Systems* (MASS) study, a multi-agency cooperative partnership in Canada that built on past silviculture experiences to test new approaches to harvesting and regeneration in mid- to high-elevation montane forests (PFC 2000). And timber companies on the BC coast introduced new methods, such as variable retention, in which individual trees or small plots of trees are left behind, depending on ecological conditions and objectives. The vegetation retained within the cutover areas provides habitat for a variety of insects, birds, mammals, and other plant species. Some operators abandoned clear-cutting altogether (NRCan 2000a; NRCan 2001).

In May 2000, all of 16 Canadian home building supply companies announced their commitment to phase out wood and wood products from forests managed unsustainably, including old growth from BC's North Coast (Sierra Club 2000). Certification, in which labels are applied to products from well-managed forests (see Box 48), is an emerging response to the growing demand for wood that is sustainably harvested, and increasingly, export markets require the certification of timber products from the Pacific Northwest. Today, certified wood accounts for only 1.0 percent of global supply and companies cannot keep up with demand (McKenna 2000).

Stakeholders in the Pacific Northwest continue to come together to resolve contentious issues. In November 2000, for example, a number of key ENGOs and logging companies, the BC government, and First Nations reached a consensus agreement in the largest rainforest conservation measure in North American history. The Great Bear Rainforest Agreement protects 603,000 ha of coastal temperate rainforest and defers logging on another 800,000 ha for two years of studies. It is based on developing a locally administered ecosystem and land use planning approach between the BC government and First Nations. Some 4,500 people live in the area, most of them First Nations. The agreement is a landmark sign of cooperation among previously conflicting interests (Sierra Club 2001; Judd 2001; BC Ministry of Forests 2001b).

Over the past 30 years, the timber industry and the governments responsible for North America's old-growth forests have gradually been influenced by the combined power of scientific knowledge, the action of voluntary groups, public awareness, and market pressures (Dietrich 1992; Apsey, Laishley, and others 2000). At the same time, society continues to demand forest products and the associated economic benefits from harvesting timber, such as direct and indirect jobs, government revenues, and the host of forest products in everyday use (FPB 2002). Adopting a new paradigm in managing North America's old-growth forests while continuing to compete to supply a growing worldwide demand for wood has been a challenge for both governments and the forest industry (NRCan 2000a). Using North America's forests sustainably will still require the maintaining and improving of government intervention, industry compliance, market incentives, scientific knowledge, watchfulness of civil society groups, public education, and resource use efficiency.

References

Apsey, Mike, Don Laishley, Vidar Nordin, and Gilbert Paillé (2000). *The Perpetual Forest: Using Lessons from the Past to Sustain Canada's Forests in the Future*, Natural Resources Canada

Bartuska, Ann (2000). *Statement of Ann Bartuska Director of Forest Management Forest Service, United States Department of Agriculture, before the Subcommittee on Forests and Forest Health, Committee on Resources United States House of Representatives, July 25, 2000 Concerning The Future of National Forest Timber Sales.* Committee on Resources, Subcommittee on Forests & Forest Health http://resourcescommittee.house.gov/106cong/forests/00jul25/bartuska.htm. Accessed 4 March 2002

BC Ministry of Forests (1998). *Coastal Temperate Rainforests of British Columbia.* BC Ministry of Forests http://www.for.gov.bc.ca/PAB/PUBLCTNS/International/three/three.htm

BC Ministry of Forests (2001a). Old Growth Forests. *Growing Together: Forest Management in British Columbia.* Government of British Columbia http://www.growingtogether.ca/facts/old_growth.htm. Accessed 4 March 2002

BC Ministry of Forests (2001b). Central Coast (Great Bear Rainforest). *Growing Together: Forest Management in British Columbia.* Government of British Columbia http://www.growingtogether.ca/centralcoast/index.htm. Accessed 20 February 2002

BFW (1997). Boreal Forest Ecology Basics. *The Boreal Ecosystem.* Boreal Forest Watch http://www.bfw.sr.unh.edu/html/files/bor-cco.html. Accessed 19 February 2002

Bright, Chris (1999). The Nemesis Effect. *World Watch* 12 (3):12-23

Bruce, James P., Ian Burton, and I.D. Mark Egener (1999). *Disaster Mitigation and Preparedness in a Changing Climate: A Synthesis Paper Prepared for Emergency Preparedness Canada, Environment Canada, and the Insurance Bureau of Canada.* Ottawa, Minister of Public Works and Government Services http://www.epc-pcc.gc.ca/research/down/DisMit_e.pdf. Accessed 13 February 2002

Bryant, Dirk, Daniel Nielsen, and Laura Tangley (1997). *The Last Frontier Forests: Ecosystems & Economies on the Edge: What is the Status of the World's Remaining Large, Natural Forest Ecosystems?* Washington, DC, World Resources Institute, Forest Frontiers Initiative

CAS (2002). *The North American Maple Project.* Penn State, College of Agricultural Sciences http://research.cas.psu.edu/research_programs/north_american_maple.htm. Accessed 29 February 2002

CBD (2000). The Clayoquot Sound Challenge: Protecting Ancient Temperate Rainforests While Providing Sustainable Resources For The Nuu Chah Nulth Indian Nation. *Real Stories.* Conservation Based Development http://www.explorecbd.org/stories/clayoquot/default.html. Accessed 4 March 2002

CNW (2000). *British Columbia Community Celebrates Designation of Clayoquot Sound as an International Biosphere Reserve.* Canadian News Wire http://www.newswire.ca/releases/May2000/05/c2312.html. Accessed 4 March 2002

Dietrich, William (1992). *The Final Forest: The Battle for the Last Great Trees of the Pacific Northwest.* New York, Simon & Schuster

Driscoll, Charles T., Gregory B. Lawrence, Arthur J. Bulger, Thomas J. Butler, Christopher S. Cronan, Christopher Eagar, Kathleen F. Lambert, Gene E. Likens, John L. Stoddard, and Kathleen C. Weathers (2001). Acidic Deposition in the Northeastern United States: Sources and Inputs, Ecosystem Effects, and Management Strategies. *BioScience* 51 (3):180-98

EC (2000). *Canada–United States Air Quality Agreement 2000: Progress Report.* Environment Canada http://www.ec.gc.ca/special/aqa_2000_e.pdf. Accessed 14 February 2002

ENS (1999). Natives, Enviros, MacMillan Bloedel Sign Clayoquot Truce. *Environment News Service,* E-Wire Press Release http://ens.lycos.com/ens/jun99/1999L-06-17-03.html. Accessed 4 March 2002

FAO (2001a). *Global Forest Resources Assessment 2000.* FAO Forestry Paper 140. Rome, Food and Agricultural Organization http://www.ers.usda.gov/emphases/harmony/issues/organic/table4graph.htm. Accessed 31 May 2002

FAO (2001b). State of the World's Forests 2001. Rome, Food and Agricultural Organization of the United Nations http://www.fao.org/forestry/fo/sofo/SOFO2001/sofo2001-e.stm. Accessed 29 May 2002

FPB (2002). *Alternatives to Conventional Clearcutting*. Forest Practices Branch, Ministry of Forests, Government of British Columbia http://www.for.gov.bc.ca/hfp/pubs/standman/atcc/atcc.htm. Accessed 27 February 2002

FSC–Can (1996). *Forest Stewardship Council of Canada* http://www.fsccanada.org/. Accessed 18 February 2002

FSC–US (2001). *FSC–US National Indicators for Forest Stewardship*. Forest Stewardship Council United States http://www.fscstandards.org/. Accessed 18 February 2002

Gawthrop (1999). *Vanishing Halo: Saving the Boreal Forest*. Vancouver/Toronto, Greystone Books

GFW (2000). *Canada's Forests at a Crossroads: An Assessment in the Year 2000, Global Forest Watch Canada*. Washington, DC, World Resources Institute

Ghazali, Baharuddin Haji (1994). *Timber Certification: an Overview*. FAO Corporate Document Repository http://www.fao.org/docrep/v7850e/V7850e04.htm. Accessed 18 February 2002

H. John Heinz III Center (1999). *Designing a Report on the State of the Nation's Ecosystem: Selected Measurements for Croplands, Forests, and Coasts and Oceans*. The H. John Heinz III Center for Science, Economics and the Environment http://www.heinzcenter.org/publications/Coasts.pdf. Accessed 12 February 2002

Hammond, Herb (1993). Clearcutting: Ecological and Economic Flaws. In *Clearcut: The Tragedy of Industrial Forestry*. San Francisco, Sierra Club Books and Earth Island Press

Harmon, Frances (1993). Acres of Late-Successional and Old-Growth Forest: The Wealth of Humboldt and the Klamath-Siskiyou Region. In *Forest Ecosystem Management: An Ecological, Economic, & Social Assessment, A Report of the Forest Ecosystem Management Assessment Team*, http://www.humboldt.edu/~envecon/Indicators/acresofoldgrowth.htm. Accessed 15 March 2002

Hopkin, A.A., D. Lachance, B. Pendrel, and J.P Hall (1996). Condition of Sugar Maple in Canada: Results of the North American Maple Project. Paper read at EMAN Second National Meeting. Abstracts of Papers and Posters, Ecological Monitoring and Assessment Network, Environment Canada http://www.eman-rese.ca/eman/reports/meetings/national96/hopkina.html. Accessed 28 February 2002

Jones, Laura , Laura Griggs, and Liv Fredricksen (2000). *The Fraser Institute Environmental Indicators*. The Fraser Institute http://oldfraser.lexi.net/publications/critical_issues/2000/env_indic/. Accessed 4 March 2002

Judd, Neville (2001). *Peace Breaks Out in War Over Canadian Rainforest*. Environmental News Service (ENS) http://ens.lycos.com/ens/apr2001/2001L-04-04-10.html. Accessed 20 February 2002

Lund, H. Gyde (2000). *Definitions of Old Growth, Pristine, Climax, Ancient Forests, and Similar Terms. (Definitions Of Forest State, Stage, and Origin)*. H. Gyde Lund, Forest Information Services http://home.att.net/~gklund/pristine.html. Accessed 4 March 2002

MacKinnon, A., and M. Eng. (1995). Old Forests Inventory for Coastal British Columbia. *Cordillera* 2 (1):20-33

Marchak, M. Patricia, Scott L. Aycock, and Doborah M. Herbert (1999). *Falldown: Forest Policy in British Columbia*. Vancouver, David Suzuki Foundation and Ecotrust Canada

Maser, Chris (1993). Sustainable Forestry. In *Clearcut: The Tragedy of Industrial Forestry*. San Francisco, Sierra Club Books and Earth Island Press

Mathews, Emily, and Allen Hammond (1999). *Critical Consumption Trends and Implications: Degrading Earth's Ecosystems*. Washington DC, World Resources Institute

Mattoon, Ashley T. (1998). Paper Forests. *World Watch* 11 (2):20-28

May, Elizabeth (1998). *At the Cutting Edge: The Crisis in Canada's Forests*. Toronto, Key Porter Books

McKenna, Barrie (2000). US Environmentalists Swing Axe at Canadian Forest Industry. *The Globe and Mail*, 22 January

McLaughlin, D. (1996). A Decade of Forest Health Monitoring in Canada: Evidence of Air Pollution Effects. Paper read at the Second National Science Meeting, Ecological Monitoring and Assessment Network (EMAN), 19 January, at Halifax, Nova Scotia

MPCI (1998). *The Montreal Process/ Le Processus de Montreal* http://www.mpci.org/. Accessed 19 February 2002

MSRM (2002). *Special Projects – Clayoquot Sound*. Government of British Columbia, Ministry of Sustainable Resource Management http://www.luco.gov.bc.ca/specialprojects/clayquot/index.htm. Accessed 4 March 2002

NAFC (2000). *North American Forest Commission: Working Groups*. North American Forest Commission http://www.fs.fed.us/global/nafc/welcome.html. Accessed 29 February 2002

NFDP (1998). *REGEN: A Program for Reporting Regeneration Results*. National Forestry Database Program http://nfdp.ccfm.org/regen/english/regen-frame.htm. Accessed 4 March 2002

NRCan (1995). *ARNEWS and North American Maple Project (NAMP)*. Natural Resources Canada http://nrcan.gc.ca/cfs/proj/sci-tech/arnews/abstract_e.html. Accessed 29 February 2002

NRCan (1999). *Forest Health: Context for the Canadian Forest Service's Science Program*. Science Branch, Canadian Forest Service, Natural Resources Canada http://www.nrcan.gc.ca/cfs/proj/sci-tech/context_health/mainpage_e.html. Accessed 4 March 2002

NRCan (2000a). *The State of Canada's Forests: 1999–2000 Forests in the New Millennium*. Natural Resources Canada http://www.nrcan.gc.ca/cfs/proj/ppiab/sof/sof00/toc.shtml. Accessed 4 March 2002

NRCan (2000b). *Defining Sustainable Forest Management: A Canadian Approach to Criteria and Indicators*. Natural Resources Canada, Canadian Forest Service, Canadian Council of Forest Ministers http://www.nrcan.gc.ca/cfs/proj/ppiab/ci/framain_e.html. Accessed 19 February 2002

NRCan (2000c). *The State of Canada's Forests: 1998–1999 Innovation, Protected Areas: Safeguarding Canada's Biodiversity*. Natural Resources Canada http://www.nrcan.gc.ca/cfs/proj/ppiab/sof/sof99/spart1.shtml. Accessed 4 March 2002

NRCan (2000d). *Long Beach Model Forest Network*. Natural Resources Canada, Canadian Forest Service http://www.lbmf.bc.ca/. Accessed 19 February 2002

NRCan (2001). *The State of Canada's Forests: 2000–2001*. Natural Resources Canada http://www.nrcan-rncan.gc.ca/cfs-scf/national/what-quoi/sof/latest_e.html. Accessed 29 February 2002

Pace, Felice (1993). Cultural Clearcuts: The Sociology of Timber Communities in the Pacific Northwest. In *Clearcut: The Tragedy of Industrial Forestry*. San Francisco, Sierra Club Books and Earth Island Press

PBS (1999). *Newton's Apple Teacher's Guides: Spotted Owl/Old-Growth Forests*. Twin Cities Public Television, Public Broadcasting Service http://www.pbs.org/ktca/newtons/11/oldgrwth.html#VOCAB. Accessed 4 March 2002

PFC (2000). *Ecology and Ecosystems: Montane Alternative Silviculture Systems (MASS)*. Pacific Forestry Centre, Natural Resources Canada http://www.pfc.forestry.ca/ecology/ferns/mass/index_e.html. Accessed 27 February 2002

Porter, William F., and Jennifer A. Hill (1998). Regional Trends of Biological Resources: Northeast. In *Status and Trends of the Nation's Biological Resources*, edited by M. J. Mac, P. A. Opler, C. E. Puckett Haecker and P. D. Doran. Washington DC, US Department of the Interior and US Geological Survey

PR Newswire (1998). *MacMillan Bloedel to Phase Out Clearcutting*. Forests.org http://forests.org/archive/canada/moreonbc.htm. Accessed 4 March 2002

Salonius, P. (2001). Management for Acadian Mixedwoods in New Brunswick. *Forest Health and Biodiversity News* 5 (2):3, 5-6

Sierra Club (2000). *Forest Policy & Economics: Sustainable Forests, Sustainable Communities.* Sierra Club British Columbia http://www.sierraclub.ca/bc/campaigns/forest_policy/#Cutting for the Economy's Sake. Accessed 4 March 2002

Sierra Club (2001). *Environmental Groups Express Cautious Optimism About Government Plans for British Columbia's Coast.* The Sierra Club http://bc.sierraclub.ca/News/Media_Releases/Cautious.html. Accessed 20 February 2002

Stuart, John D. (1998). Effects of Fire Suppression on Ecosystems and Diversity. In *Status and Trends of the Nation's Biological Resources*, edited by M. J. Mac, P. A. Opler, C. E. Puckett Haecker and P. D. Doran. Washington DC, US Department of the Interior and US Geological Survey

Taylor, Charles (1997). *Summary Report on Forest Health of the United States by the Forest Health Science Panel.* The US House of Representatives http://www.house.gov/resources/105cong/fullcomm/apr09.97/taylor.rpt/tay-sum.pdf. Accessed 20 February 2002

TRN (1998). The Boreal Forest: A Brief Status Report. Background Paper for the 4th Taiga Rescue Network Conference, "Boreal Forests of the W orld IV: Integrating Cultural Values into Local and Global Forest Protection", October, at Tartu, Estonia, October

Turner, Monica G., Stephen R. Carpenter, Eric J. Gustafson, Robert J. Naiman, and Scott M. Pearson (1998). Land Use. In *Status and Trends of the Nation's Biological Resources*, edited by M.J. Mac, P.A. Opler, C.E. Puckett Haecker and P.D. Doran. Washington DC, US Department of the Interior and US Geological Survey

UN (1997). *Institutional Aspects of Sustainable Development.* United Nations Sustainable Development: UN System-Wide Web Site on National Implementation of the Rio Commitments http://www.un.org/esa/agenda21/natlinfo/index.html. Accessed 4 March 2002

UN-ECE, and FAO (2000). *Forest Resources of Europe, CIS, North America, Australia, Japan and New Zealand (industrialized temperate/boreal counties).* Vol. UN-ECE/FAO Contribution to the Global Forest Resources Assessment 2000; Geneva Timber and Forest Study Papers, No. 17. New York and Geneva, United Nations

UNDP, UNEP, World Bank, and WRI (2000). *World Resources 2000-2001: People and Ecosystems, the Fraying Web of Life.* Washington DC, World Resources Institute

University of Waterloo (1998). *World Wide Web Resources on Parks and Protected Areas.* University of Waterloo, Faculty of Applied Health Sciences, Department of Recreation and Leisure Studies http://www.ahs.uwaterloo.ca/rec/parksoption/parkslinks99.htm. Accessed 4 March 2002

Urquizo, Natty, J. Bastedo, Tom Brydges, and Harvey Shear (2000). Ecological Assessment of the Boreal Shield Ecozone. A State of the Environment Report. Ottawa, National Indicators and Assessment Office, Environment Canada http://www.ec.gc.ca/soer-ree/English/National/craengfin.pdf. Accessed 28 May2002

USDA (1997). *America's Forests: 1997 Health Update.* US Department of Agriculture, Forest Service http://www.fs.fed.us/foresthealth/fh_update/update97/index.htm. Accessed 4 March 2002

USDA (2002). *Sustainable Resource Management.* US Department of Agriculture, Forest Service http://www.fs.fed.us/sustained/msie4.html. Accessed 19 February 2002

WRM (1998). *The Underlying Causes of Deforestation and Forest Degradation.* World Rainforest Movement http://www.wrm.org.uy/. Accessed 4 March 2002

Disasters

8

Disasters

Disasters as a result of human activity—both intentional actions, such as the illegal discharge of oil, and accidental ones, such as toxic spills or nuclear meltdown—can expose people, ecosystems, and animals to dangerous substances. Such vast quantities of hazardous materials are moved about by a variety of transportation modes that spills and other accidents are inevitable. Despite strong regulations governing the handling of hazardous material in North America, serious accidents that threaten human and environmental health and safety occasionally occur, prompting further preventive legislation.

In the United States, the number of incidents reported to the Hazardous Materials Incidents System (HMIS) rose from about 8,880 in 1990 to 13,853 in 1997. Most occurred on highways, with rail and aviation sectors reporting the next largest number of incidents. The incident rate is uncertain, however, since improved reporting or expanded economic activity may account for part of the increase (EPA 1999).

Oil spills during marine transport can cause severe harm to coastal and

Box 49: The Exxon Valdez Oil Spill

In March 1989, the Exxon Valdez oil tanker ran aground, spilling almost 50 million liters of crude oil into Prince William Sound. It was North America's worst oil spill and caused an ecological disaster: oil washed onto 2,092 km of Alaska's pristine and biologically rich coast, killing some 250,000 seabirds, 2,800 sea otters, 300 harbor seals, 150 bald eagles, and about 22 killer whales as well as millions of salmon eggs and plants and other organisms (EVOSTS 1999). Ten years later, oil is still leaching from beaches, and some populations of plants and animals have yet to completely recover. The disaster prompted new federal regulations to prevent oil spills, more severe penalties for those who cause them, and a call for safer vessel design (NOAA 2001). As a result, the volume of fuel spilled in the United States has decreased dramatically although the number of oil-spill incidents reported has increased (EPA 1999).

maritime ecosystems, as witnessed by the Exxon Valdez oil spill in 1982 (see Box 49). Maritime vessels also discharge solid wastes and sewage, which can also affect water quality, especially where there is a high volume of traffic (EPA 1999).

North America is also subject to a range of naturally occurring events with potentially disastrous impacts on the environment and human well-being. Earthquakes, volcanic eruptions, tornadoes, hurricanes, ice storms, droughts, dust storms, and other extreme weather events occur in different parts of the continent. North American governments have put in place many response mechanisms to prevent and alleviate the harm caused by such events. Now, it is becoming evident that some preventive actions, such as levees and wildfire suppression, have actually been part of a mix of factors—including global climate change, population growth, urbanization, and affluence—that have increased the frequency and severity of some types of natural hazards as well the economic losses they cause. Flooding and forest fires are two of the region's priority concerns.

Floods and Climate Change

Although climate change was identified as a pressing issue as early as 1972, the role of humans and their impact on natural hazards such as extreme weather events was unclear (Bruce, Burton, and Egener 1999). Today, however, there is a general consensus among a large and growing number of scientists that human activity plays a discernable role in the

Extreme Precipitation Trends in Canada and the United States, 1910-1995

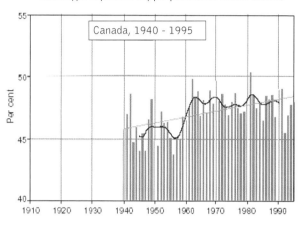

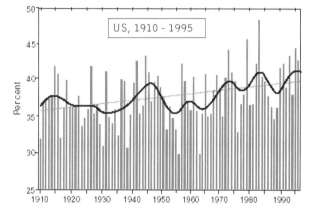

Earth's changing climate (IPCC 2001). Still, much uncertainty remains about how the shifts in climate will affect future weather-related natural hazards.

The disruption and intensification of the earth's water cycle is believed to be one of the most fundamental effects of climate change. Changes are already occurring in North America's hydrological conditions, as demonstrated by the increase in average annual precipitation over the past 30 years (see Figure 43) and in the marked increase since the 1970s of

Figure 43
Extreme precipitation trends in Canda and the United States, 1910-1995.

Source: Francis and Hengeveld 1998

intense winter storms in the Northern Hemisphere (see Figure 44) (Bruce, Burton, and Egener 1999). In the United States, the average amount of moisture in the atmosphere rose by 5 percent per decade between 1973 and 1993 (Trenberth 1999). Most of the increase derived from heavier precipitation events resulting in floods and storms (O'Meara 1997,

Frequency of Intense Winter Storms in the Northern Hemisphere, 1900-2000

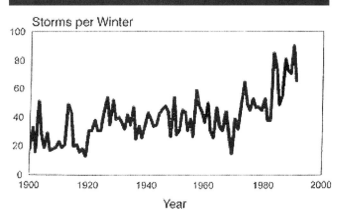

Figure 44
Frequency of intense winter storms in the northern hemisphere, 1900-2000.

Source: Bruce, Burton, and Egener 1999

Easterling, Meehl, and others 2000). During the second half of the 1900s, the relative amount of precipitation from North America's heaviest 10 percent of yearly precipitation events increased (Francis and Hengeveld 1998).

While the flooding that often follows heavy precipitation events is natural and essential to the health of watersheds, floods are also North America's most destructive and costly natural disasters. They affect large areas, cause extensive property loss and damage and are associated with large additional costs for recovery, adaptation, and prevention (Brun, Etkin, and others 1997,

USGCRP 2000). During the 1960s and 1970s, over 90 percent of the natural disasters in the United States resulted from weather or climate extremes, and many North American floods were major disasters requiring massive federal aid and costly structural mitigation measures (Changnon and Easterling 2000). In response to these events, the US National Flood Insurance Act of 1968 established the National Flood Insurance Program (NFIP). The Flood Disaster Protection Act of 1973, which offers flood insurance to those communities that adopt and enforce floodplain management ordinances, strengthened it. Many of the separate and fragmented responsibilities of parallel state and local-level disaster programs were merged in 1979 under the Federal Emergency Management Agency (FEMA 1999). The United States also maps the nation's floodplains, an effort that has helped raise public awareness of flood hazards (FEMA n.d.).

Disaster Financial Assistance Arrangements were also inaugurated in Canada in 1970 to help provinces cope with the cost of disaster recovery and in 1975, the government introduced the Flood Damage Reduction Program (FDRP). Disaster mitigation and coordination were also among the goals addressed by Canada's Emergency Preparedness Act, passed in 1988, and its related agency, Emergency Preparedness Canada (EPC). Disaster plans that had been piecemeal also were made more comprehensive and the nature of emergencies to be accommodated was broadened (McConnell 1998; EC 2000). Settlement in flood-prone areas was discouraged in Canada through mapping and the designation of over 320 flood-risk areas (EC 1998).

These programs provided better flood mitigation, preparation, response and recovery measures.

it was estimated that on average, the United States lost about US $1 billion per week to natural disasters (NSTC 1996). Despite uncertainties in the data, globally there are solid indications that over the past few decades the costs of weather-related events have grown about three times faster than those linked to earthquakes, and a similar trend is evident in North America (Bruce,

---

Box 50: Some Major Floods of the Last 30 Years

The 1993 Mississippi flood, which submerged 75 towns and killed 48 people, cost between US $10 and $20 billion, surpassing all previous US floods in terms of economic losses as well as in the area, duration, and amount of flooding (USGCRP 2000). It was the result of record-breaking spring rains in the Midwest, a larger than usual snow cover, and high soil moisture content, but also from the river's confinement to its channel by levees and dikes, which helped to increase the flood crest. In 1996, Canada experienced its most destructive and costly flood in the Saguenay River valley in Quebec. An average of nearly 126 mm of rain fell in 48 hours over an area of 100,000 km^2, resulting in 10 deaths and about US $0.8 billion in damages (EC 1998, Francis, and Hengeveld 1998; EC 2001).

In 1997, the Red River, which flows north from the United States into Canada, experienced its worst flooding in 150 years. It followed a wet autumn, a winter of unusually heavy snowfall, and the arrival of an early spring blizzard that dropped 50–70 cm more of snow or freezing rain. Altogether, the flooding generated costs of almost US $5 billion. The Red River Floodway, which diverts the Red River's spring thaw when the exit to Lake Winnipeg remains frozen, protects the 550,000 residents of city of Winnipeg from being submerged (Francis and Hengeveld 1998; IJC 2000).

Flood policies in both countries focused primarily on building structures (levees, reservoirs, and floodways), which were tested during the damaging North American floods of the1980s and '90s (see Box 50).

The costs of natural disasters are difficult to determine with accuracy. They may or may not include indirect costs related to trade losses, human health effects, and the costs of adaptation, recovery, and financial disaster assistance. In the mid-1990s,

Burton, and Egener 1999). For example, evidence shows that flood dollar damages and flood-related deaths in North America have climbed at a steep rate since the early 1970s (Etkin, Vazquez, Conde, and Kelman 1998; USGCRP 2000).

In Canada, the costs of weather-related disasters grew from about US $325 million between 1983 and 1987 to more than US $1 billion between 1993 and 1997 (EC 2001). The largest US snowstorm in more than a century occurred in 1993 along the northeast coast, and in 1998, Canada experienced a major ice storm, the result of over 100 mm of freezing rainfall over six days, accompanied by unusual weather systems. It was the country's costliest weather catastrophe ever, causing 25 deaths, leaving nearly 3 million people without heat or electricity–in some cases for a matter of weeks– and costing about US $1.3 billion in

damage (Francis and Hengeveld 1998). In the mid-1990s, weather-related disasters on the North American subcontinent caused an average of 200 deaths and cost more than US $3.5 billion in property loss and damage per year (Parfit 1998).

The world insurance industry recognizes that extreme weather events like floods are becoming more common. Although rare before 1987, 23 weather-related disasters causing billion-dollar insurance losses have occurred in the United States since then (Francis and Hengeveld 1998). More people and settlements are exposed to floods because of population increase and concentration,

while rising affluence and property values also ratchet up the costs of damage (Easterling, Meehl, and others 2000). A tendency to settle in flood-prone areas is also influenced by a perception that risk has been lowered by protective structures such as dams, dykes, and diversions and by the availability of disaster relief (Brun, Etkin, and others 1997; Bruce, Barton, and Egener 1999).

Floods can have significant environmental consequences such as washing away valuable topsoil and diminishing agricultural productivity (Francis and Hengeveld 1998). The Mississippi flood of '93 damaged much of the Midwest's fertile farm-land and altered the natural ecosystems of the region's rivers and their floodplains. Since wetlands and temporary lakes act as storage areas for excess water, their loss heightens the vulnerability of the watershed to flood. Structures that prevent rivers from flooding often provoke extremely damaging floods when water eventually overflows. For example, human modifications over the last century to make the Mississippi floodplain habitable led to the loss of over 80 percent of the river basin's wetlands and changes in riparian and in-stream habitat, thus decreasing the watershed's resilience and increasing its vulnerability to flooding (McConnell 2000-01).

Both countries have modified their approach to disaster prevention and mitigation in recent years, moving from a focus on resisting natural hazards to policies aimed at building resilience. This is particularly the case in the United States, which is subject to more frequent and severe weather events than Canada. In the 1990s, it strengthened federal mitigation legislation and initiated a new strategy to encourage non-structural

States (Barton and Nishenko 1997).

Historically, Canadian federal natural hazards action did not specifically target mitigation in a comprehensive manner (Newton 1997). The lack of coordination among disparate programs,

---

Box 51: Bilateral Agreement

Canada and the United States cooperate to deal with disasters affecting either or both countries, especially those involving floods and forest fires. The 1986 Agreement between the Government of Canada and the Government of the United States of America on Co-operation in Comprehensive Civil Emergency Planning and Management establishes 10 principles of cooperation and provides a framework for future bilateral arrangements for civil emergency planning (McConnell 1998; Government of Canada 2000).

---

approaches to flood prevention, such as resettlement projects and wetland restoration (Newton 1997; Changnon and Easterling 2000). The 1996 US Strategy for Natural Disaster Reduction advocates major policy shifts toward the goal of sustainability by anticipating and assessing risks rather than just reacting to disasters; building resilience early in the planning stage; dealing with mitigation comprehensively instead of in a piece-meal manner; and implementing warning systems that encourage human resilience. Furthermore, new strategies acknowledge the need to ensure the continued viability of both human communities and managed and natural ecosystems (NSTC 1996; FEMA 2000). FEMA's Project Impact was initiated in 1997 with the aim of reducing the risk of property loss, deaths, and the amount of federal money spent on recovery throughout the United

reductions in financial support for existing programs, and the spate of recent weather-related disasters led to the recognition of a need for more comprehensive Canadian disaster relief policies and an integrated delivery structure (Etkin, Vazquez, Conde, and Kelman 1998; White 1997; Kerry, Kelk, and others 1998). In 2001, Canada established the Office of Critical Infrastructure and Emergency Preparedness (OCIPEP) to develop and implement a more comprehensive approach to disaster prevention and to provide national leadership in protecting its critical infrastructure in both its physical and cyber dimensions (OCIPEP 2001). Canada and the United States also cooperate in emergency planning for disasters (see Box 51).

According to climate change models, the magnitude, frequency, and cost of extreme hydrological events in some regions of North

America are forecast to increase (USGCRP 2000). Among climate change's projected effects are changes in the patterns and frequency of the El Niño-Southern Oscillation (ENSO), a recurring warming and cooling pattern of surface waters in the tropical Pacific Ocean observed since the 1970s. It lasts from 12 to 18 months and occurs once every two to 10 years. El Niño's behavior has altered over the past 20 years, becoming more

frequent and persistent since the mid-1970s. El Niños are thought to be associated to some degree with the occurrence of increasingly severe and frequent weather events, especially since their recent intensification has no precedent in climate records over the past 120 years (Francis and Hengeveld 1998; Bruce, Burton, and Egener 1999). An uncommonly strong El Niño in 1997-98, for example, brought about storms, floods, droughts, and fires that killed thousands of people and displaced thousands more. It accounted for heavy floods in Florida, California, some Midwest states

and parts of New England (Trenberth 1999).

The speculation that global climate change is likely to exacerbate weather extremes is based on the expectation that increased warming will modify heat distribution and energy flows in the climate system, affecting, in turn, atmospheric and oceanic circulation patterns and altering the hydrological cycle. A warmer atmosphere can hold more moisture, which spells more precipitation (Francis and Hengeveld 1998). In addition, this more intense rainfall will likely occur over smaller areas, probably leading to greater flooding, especially in smaller catchment areas. It may also be that with longer periods between heavy rainfall events, droughts could become more severe, exacerbated by higher air temperatures and increased evaporation (Bruce, Burton, and Egener 1999).

Regional differences in hydrological processes mean that the magnitude and direction of impacts are likely to vary greatly among regions (Frederick and Schwartz 2000). Where rainstorms intensify and flooding increases, the risks to humans and the environment will be greater. Impacts include the potential for damage to low-lying settlements and dock and port facilities as well as for problems with water distribution and sewage systems that can have human health implications (EC 1999a).

Given the continental nature of climatic systems, the two countries will need to increase their cooperative efforts to address both climate change and disaster preparedness. As shown in the freshwater section, the International Joint Commission (IJC) assists both governments in managing their shared waters. A report on the 1997 Red River flooding cautioned that given impending increased flooding due to climate change, a comprehensive, integrated, binational strategy should be developed and implemented (IJC 2000).

Forest Fires

Forest fires are a natural part of North America's landscape and play an important role in maintaining and regenerating some types of forest ecosystems. The pattern or regime of fire frequency, severity, and area burned varies from place to place. In North America's boreal forests (see Box 40 in the forests section), a natural cycle of destruction and renewal occurs as robust new trees mature, quickly replacing stands burned by lightning-sparked wildfires (CCFM 2000). Fires occur in cycles ranging from 100 to 400 years, with major fires once every 50 to 100 years in Alaska's boreal forests and once every 200 years in eastern Canada (Gawthrop 1999). Such fires open spaces for new seedlings, help to increase diversity in the age and type of vegetation, clear debris, and enhance the availability of nutrients (Jardine 1994).

Since the 1970s, the annual area burned by forest fires has grown, particularly in the western United States, while the overall trend has

Total Area Burned, 1970-2000

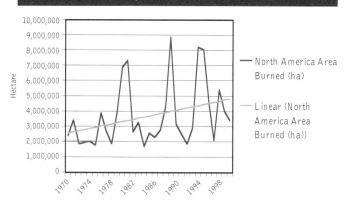

been toward decreasing numbers of fires (see Figures 45 and 46). For example, prior to 1970 only 1 million ha per year burned in Canada; it is now close to 3 million ha per year. A number of factors have sparked the increase: fuel build-up from past effective fire protection programs; aging tree stands; changes in fire policy related to prescribed burning; and expanded public access to and use of the forests. Higher temperatures and lower rainfall associated with climate change have also been implicated. The relative importance of each of these factors remains controversial.

Figure 45
Total area burned, 1970-2000.

Source: CCFM 2000, CIFFC n.d., NIFC 2000

Figure 46
Number of wildland fires, 1970-2000.

Source: CCFM 2000, CIFFC n.d., NIFC 2000

Number of Wildland Fires, 1970-2000

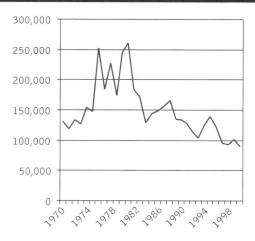

Over the past century, natural fire regimes in North America were increasingly shaped by human presence and intervention, setting the stage for fire activity in the past 30 years. In the early part of the century, extensive logging left behind an unnatural fuel load from debris, undergrowth, and smaller trees that filled gaps. As a result, when fires started, they were larger and more destructive. To save valuable timber, the United States began an aggressive policy of fire suppression and 'Smokey Bear' campaigns in the 1930s to inform the public about the dangers of igniting fires. By the 1970s, fires were kept to about 2 million ha a year in the lower 48 states compared to the 1930s, when an average of 16 million ha burned every year (H. John Heinz III Center 1999; Booth 2000).

Increasingly effective fire suppression prevented natural low-intensity fires from burning the accumulated dead trees and those that had dried during periods of drought, continuing to create excessive fuel loads. Forest structure and make-up changed as species normally eliminated by fire became dominant, with fire-resistant trees being replaced by species that burn hotter and faster than those of the past. The result was ever larger and more disastrous fires.

In the 1970s, the importance of periodic natural wildland fires began to be recognized in both Canada and the United States. Late in the decade, US policies that required suppressing all fires before they reached four ha in size by 10 am the

Box 52: The 1988 Yellowstone Fires

Yellowstone National Park in the Rocky Mountains of northwestern Wyoming is the oldest and most famous US National Park. Until the 1970s, wildfires were viewed as destructive and were suppressed. But without the natural fires, debris in the forests built up to fuel bigger fires. In recognition that wildfire is part of a natural process of change, a fire policy was launched in 1972 that allowed most fires to take their natural course. In 1988, the policy aroused controversy when parts of Yellowstone struck by lightning were allowed to burn. The fires spread quickly because of severe summer drought and high winds, and 485,623 ha burned in the Yellowstone area in eight huge fire complexes. Eventually a decision was made to suppress the fires. At the cost of US $120 million, it was the costliest fire-fighting event in US history (Robbins 1998; PBS 2000). Fire management plans were rewritten, and today policies continue to support a more natural fire regime, yet also seek to remove excess fuel loads in the forests.

The post-fire ecology of the Park has led to renewal. Usable forms of potassium and phosphorus were released from burned lodgepole pines and other vegetation, boosting production in soils, streams, and rivers. More sunlight falling on the earth also created conditions conducive to the growth of some species. By the end of the 1990s, some lodgepole pines that seeded since 1988 were already about 1.8 m tall. More than a century will be needed for Yellowstone to return to pre-fire conditions, however (Robbins 1998).

next day ended (Gorte 1996). Parks Canada and the US Forest Service and National Park Service decided not to interfere with fires in wilderness areas and parts of national parks systems unless people or neighboring lands were threatened (COTF 2000; Turner 2001). In addition, prescribed burning and 'let burn' policies to reduce built-up fuels and protect settlements and businesses were introduced. These policies call for either purposefully lighting fires or allowing lightning fires to burn. Annually, over 2 million ha are treated by prescribed fire in the United States and 7,881 ha were deliberately burned in Canada in 2000 (CIFFC n.d., Mutch 1997). This policy has not been uncontroversial, however, as illustrated by the 1988 fires in Yellowstone National Park (see Box 52). The two countries have begun to work together, along with Mexico, to learn more about wildfire at the continental level, and have engaged in several joint initiatives and field experiments though the Fire Management Study Group (FMSG) of the 1958 North American Forestry Commission (NAFC 2000).

Road building in North America's forests has opened access to both people and wildfire. US government's studies suggest that fires are almost twice as likely to occur in roaded areas of forest than in those without roads. Another view is that keeping out roads allows fuel to accumulate, prevents access of forest protection services, and increases chances for large-scale fire

damage. In 2001, a 'roadless rule' was announced in the United States that banned road building and other development on 23.7 million ha of national forests, or 2 percent of the US land base (USDA 2001).

The challenge of managing wildfire in North America has been exacerbated in recent decades by population increases in the urban-wildland interface, where settlement and other developments intermingle with flammable forests and grasslands (Hirsch 2000). The population growth rate in the US West now ranges from 2.5 to 13 percent, compared to the national annual average of about 1 percent. It is estimated that in the 1990s, wildfires damaged six times more homes than during the previous decade (Morrison, Karl and others 2000). In 1999, fire damage from all types of fire cost over US $10 billion, a 16 percent increase from the previous year (IFA 2000).

The 1988 and 1994 fire seasons were particularly severe in the United States and led to the 1995 revision in the federal wildland fire

Western Forests at Wildfire Risk, 1998

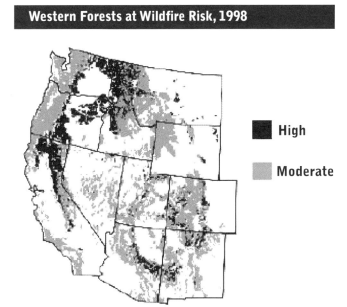

■ **High**

■ **Moderate**

Figure 47
Western forests
at wildfire risk,
1998.

*Source: WGA
2000*

policy. It underscores the important role of fire and the use of prescribed burns and thinning techniques to reduce hazardous fuel accumulations as well as the importance of further research to understand

better the ecological significance of wildfire (CEQ 2000; Chepesiuk 2001). In 2001, the Western Governors' Association agreed to a 10-year plan to prevent wildfires, which included the thinning of fuel-rich areas, a strategy that has generated some controversy (Greenwire 2001). Figure 47 shows the regions most at risk for wildfire in the Western states.

Changes in climate that bring drier conditions and more severe storms also appear to play a role in changing fire patterns in North America. In 1989, for example, record fires burned in western Canada and the areas east of James Bay. They were caused by more frequent and extreme fire-weather conditions, including high tornado activity in the Prairies and an unprecedented heat wave in the Arctic

Box 53: The 2000 Fire Season

Although not excessively high compared to the national long-term average, fire activity in 2000 was especially high and severe in some regions, such as the northern Rockies and Texas. It was one of the worst fire seasons on record in the Western states, where more than 30,000 fires burned over 2.8 million ha of forests and grasslands (WGA 2002). About 8 percent of US fires occurred in dry forests on National Forest land where previous fire exclusion policies are thought to have created a build-up of brush and small trees that led to more severe wildfires (Morrison, Karl, and others 2000). Severe, long-lasting, La Niña-related drought, accompanied by thousands of lightning strikes from a series of storms, also contributed to the severity of the 2000 fire season (USDA Forest Service 2001).

Many fires burned in areas of urban-wildland interface, causing property losses and damage and disrupting community services (USDA Forest Service 2001). Over 400 homes were destroyed in the Los Alamos area of New Mexico, for example (Ross, Lott, and Brown 2000). In many instances, fire-fighting resources were stretched to the limit (CEQ 2000). In September, a report by the secretaries of Agriculture and the Interior was released in response to the wildfires of 2000. It provided an overall framework for fire management and forest health programs that includes increased investments in reducing fire risks and requirements to work with local communities to reduce fire hazards close to settlements (USDA Forest Service 2001).

(Jardine 1994; Flannigan, Stocks, and Wotton 2000). The severity of Canada's 1995 fire season, which burned 6.6 million ha of forestland, was also due in part to extremely dry conditions (EC 1999b). Drought and frequent winds in the year 2000 also contributed to a severe fire season in the western United States when more than 2.8 million ha of public and private lands went up in flames (USDA Forest Service 2001) (see Box 53).

Apart from the threat they pose to human settlements and lives and the valuable timber they may burn, wildfires can also emit large amounts carbon that contribute to greenhouse warming and send large amounts of particulate matter into the atmosphere. They can create smoke hazards as well, and some highways, airports and recreation areas periodically have to close because of reduced visibility. In addition, smoke constitutes a health hazard because of the variety of toxic chemicals and heavy metals it contains. Contaminants in the smoke can include carbon monoxide, hydrocarbons, benzo[a]pyrene, nitrogen oxides, and volatile oxygenated organic compounds, among others. Chronic exposure can lead to a number of respiratory ailments (Chepesiuk 2001).

Fires also have a direct impact on wildlife, killing hundreds of large mammals as well as more-vulnerable amphibians, nest-bound birds, rodents, and other small animals. They alter wildlife habitat, especially in the short term. On the other

hand, many species depend on habitat that is maintained by periodic fires and suppressing fires can actually reduce the habitat available for some species (Turbak 2001). For example, the alteration of fire regimes through extensive fire suppression has contributed to the threatened status of a number of native habitats in the southern

United States (USGS 1999). The effects of wildfires also include runoff and erosion when vegetation dies and sediment and ash fall into watercourses (Chepesiuk 2001).

In the future, North America's annual fire severity rating may well grow as a result of climate change, which is predicted to augment the number of lightning strikes and the intensity and frequency of windstorms (Jardine 1994). Increasingly, research is being conducted into the potential links between climate and forest change. The Canadian Forest Service's Fire Research Network, for example, has initiated five science and technology programs (NRCan 1998).

Questions still remain about the proper roles of wildfire suppression, prescribed burning, salvage timber logging, fuel management, roadless areas, and other tools. Also part of the debate are the relative responsibilities of federal, state, and provincial governments to protect ecosystems and citizens, and those of home and landowners in the urban-wildland interface to take precautionary measures through proper home design, building materials, and property maintenance (Gorte 1996; Morrison, Karl, and others 2000).

More and more, human interference with the functioning of natural processes requires sharper scientific understanding about how the natural world functions and how humans need to adjust to live in harmony with nature. Both communities living in areas susceptible to natural hazards and the ecosystems in which they live need to maintain their resiliency in the face of naturally occurring, but potentially disastrous events that have been exacerbated by human activity.

References

Barton, Christopher , and Stuart Nishenko (1997). *Natural Disasters: Forecasting, Economic and Life Losses.* US Geological Survey, Marine and Coastal Geology Program http://marine.usgs.gov/fact-sheets/nat_disasters/. Accessed 29 January 2002

Booth, William (2000). 'Natural' Forestry Plan Fights Fires With Fire. *Washington Post,* 24 September

Bruce, James P., Ian Burton, and I. D. Mark Egener (1999). *Disaster Mitigation and Preparedness in a Changing Climate: A Synthesis Paper Prepared for Emergency Preparedness Canada, Environment Canada, and the Insurance Bureau of Canada.* Ottawa, Minister of Public Works and Government Services http://www.epc-pcc.gc.ca/research/down/DisMit_e.pdf. Accessed 13 February 2002

Brun, Soren E., David Etkin, Dionne Gesink Law, Lindsay Wallace, and Rodney White (1997). *Coping with Natural Hazards in Canada: Scientific, Government and Insurance Industry Perspectives.* A Study Written for the Round Table on Environmental Risk, Natural Hazards and the Insurance Industry by Environmental Adaptation Research Group, Environment Canada and Institute for Environmental Studies, University of Toronto http://www.utoronto.ca/env/nh/pt2ch2-3-2.htm. Accessed 29 January 2002

CCFM (2000). *National Forestry Database Program.* Canadian Council of Forest Ministers http://nfdp.ccfm.org/. Accessed 29 January 2002

CEQ (2000). *Managing the Impact of Wildfires on Communities and the Environment. A Report to the President In Response to the Wildfires of 2000, September 8.* Council on Environmental Quality, The White House http://clinton4.nara.gov/CEQ/firereport.pdf. Accessed 20 February 2002

Changnon, Stanley A., and David R. Easterling (2000). US Policies Pertaining to Weather and Climate Extremes. *Science* 289 (5487):2053-55.

Chepesiuk, Ron (2001). Wildfires Ignite Concern. *Environmental Health Perspectives* 109 (7):A364.

CIFFC (n.d.). *CIFFC Information Station.* Canadian Interagency Forest Fire Centre http://www.ciffc.ca/about.htm. Accessed 29 January 2002

COTF (2000). *Exploring the Environment: Yellowstone Fires.* Wheeling Jesuit University/NASA Classroom of the Future http://www.cotf.edu/ete/modules/yellowstone/Yffires1.html. Accessed 29 January 2002.

Easterling, David R., Gerald A. Meehl, Camille Parmesan, Stanley A. Changnon, Thomas R. Karl, and Linda O. Mearns (2000). Climate Extremes: Observations, Modeling, and Impacts. *Science* 289 (5487):2068-74.

EC (1998). *Canada and Freshwater: Experience and Practices, Monograph No. 6.* Ottawa, Environment Canada, Minister of Public Works and Government Services Canada http://www.ec.gc.ca/agenda21/98/splash.html. Accessed 29 January 2002

EC (1999a). *The Canada Country Study (CCS), Volume VIII, National Cross-Cutting Issues Volume.* Environment Canada, Adaptation and Impacts Research Group http://www.ec.gc.ca/climate/ccs/execsum8.htm. Accessed 29 January 2002

EC (1999b). *Sustaining Canada's Forests: Timber Harvesting, National Environmental Indicator Series, SOE Bulletin No. 99-4,* Environment Canada, State of the Environment Reporting Program http://www.ec.gc.ca/ind/English/Forest/default.cfm. Accessed 28 May 2002

EC (2000). *Floods (from Canada Water Book on Flooding).* Environment Canada, Freshwater Web Site http://www.ec.gc.ca/water/en/manage/floodgen/e_intro.htm. Accessed 29 January 2002

EC (2001). *Tracking Key Environmental Issues.* Ottawa, Environment Canada http://www.ec.gc.ca/tkei/main_e.cfm. Accessed 29 January 2002

EPA (1999). *Indicators of the Environmental Impacts of Transportation.* US Environmental Protection Agency http://itre.ncsu.edu/cte/Indicators.PDF. Accessed 29 January 2002

Etkin, David, Maria Theresa Vazquez Conde, and Ilan Kelman (1998). *Natural Disasters and Human Activity.* (unpublished report for the CEC Secretariat) Montreal, Commission for Environmental Cooperation of North America

EVOSTC (1999). *Legacy of an Oil Spill: Ten Years After Exxon Valdez.* Exxon Valdez Oil Spill Trustee Council http://www.oilspill.state.ak.us/index.html. Accessed 29 January 2002

FEMA (1999). *About FEMA: History of the Federal Emergency Management Agency.* Federal Emergency Management Agency http://www.fema.gov/about/history.htm. Accessed 29 January 2002

FEMA (2000). *What is Mitigation?* Federal Emergency Management Agency http://www.fema.gov/mit/whatmit.htm. Accessed 29 January 2002

FEMA (n.d.). *Report on Costs and Benefits of Natural Hazard Mitigation Land Use and Building Requirement in Floodplains: The National Flood Insurance Program.* Federal Emergency Management Agency http://www.fema.gov/mit/cb_nfip.htm. Accessed 28 January 2002

Flannigan, M.D., B.J. Stocks, and B.M. Wotton (2000). Climate Change and Forest Fires. *The Science of the Total Environment* 262:221-9.

Francis, David, and Henry Hengeveld (1998). *Extreme Weather and Climate Change.* Environment Canada http://www.msc-smc.ec.gc.ca/saib/climate/Climatechange/ccd_9801_e.pdf. Accessed 28 January 2002

Frederick, Kenneth D., and Gregory E. Schwarz (2000). *Socioeconomic Impacts of Climate Variability and Change on US Water Resources.* Resources for the Future http://www.rff.org/CFDOCS/disc_papers/abstracts/0021.htm. Accessed 29 January 2002

Gawthrop, Daniel (1999). *Vanishing Halo: Saving the Boreal Forest.* Vancouver/Toronto, Greystone Books

Gorte, Ross W. (1996). *Congressional Research Service Report for Congress: Forest Fires and Forest Health.* The Committee for the National Institute for the Environment, National Council for Science and the Environment http://cnie.org/NLE/CRS/abstract.cfm?NLEid=16443. Accessed 29 January 2002

Government of Canada (2000). *Highlights of the Canada/United States Agreement on Emergency Planning.* Public Information/Resources http://www.epc-pcc.gc.ca/publicinfo/fact_sheets/high_canada_us.html. Accessed 28 January 2002

Greenwire (2001). *Wildfires: Western Governors Reach Agreement on Land Management* http://www.eenews.net/Greenwire/Backissues/081401gw.htm#1

H. John Heinz III Center (1999). *Designing a Report on the State of the Nation's Ecosystem: Selected Measurements for Croplands, Forests, and Coasts and Oceans.* The H. John Heinz III Center for Science, Economics and the Environment http://www.us-ecosystems.org/index.html. Accessed 29 January 2002

Hirsch, Kelvin (2000). *Canada's Wildland Urban Interface: Challenges and Solutions.* Canadian Forest Service, Northern Forestry Centre http://www.nofc.forestry.ca/fire/frn/English/wui/UrbanInterface_e.htm. Accessed 29 January 2002

IFA (2000). *IFA Bulletin, July/August 2000.* Illinois Firefighters Association http://www.illinoisfirefighters.org/bulletin.shtml. Accessed 29 January 2002

IJC (2000). *International Joint Commission Cautions that Efforts Must Remain Focused on Protecting Against Flood Damages.* International Joint Commission http://www.ijc.org/news/redrelease3e.html. Accessed 20 February 2002

Jardine, Kevin (1994). *The Carbon Bomb: Climate Change and the Fate of the Northern Boreal Forest.* Greenpeace International http://www.subtleenergies.com/ormus/boreal.htm. Accessed 29 January 2002

Kerry, Mara, Greg Kelk, David Etkin, Ian Burton, and Sarah Kalhok (1999). Canada Copes with the Ice Storm of 1999. *Environment* 41 (1):6-11, 28-33.

McConnell, David (1998). *Plan for tomorrow ...TODAY! The Story of Emergency Preparedness Canada 1948-1998.* Government of Canada http://www.epc-pcc.gc.ca/publicinfo/guides_reports/plan_tomo.html. Accessed 28 January 2002

McConnell, David (2000-01). Mississippi River Flood: 1993. In *Natural Science Geology*. The University of Akron http://lists.uakron.edu/geology/natscigeo/lectures/streams/miss_flood.htm. Accessed 17 February 2002

Morrison, Peter H., Jason W. Karl, Lindsey Swope, Kirsten Harma, Teresa Allen, Pamela Becwar, and Ben Sabold (2000). *Assessment of Summer 2000 Wildfires: Landscape History, Current Condition and Ownership*. Pacific Biodiversity Institute http://www.pacificbio.org/pubs/wildfire2000.pdf. Accessed 28 January 2002

Mutch, Robert W. (1997). *Use of Fire As A Management Tool on The National Forests: Statement of Robert W. Mutch Before the Committee on Resources, United States House of Representatives Oversight Hearing*. Committee on Resources, US House of Representatives http://resourcescommittee.house.gov/105cong/fullcomm/sep30.97/mutch.htm. Accessed 28 January 2002

Newton, John (1997). *Scientific / Technical Database – Federal Legislation for Disaster Mitigation: A Comparative Assessment Between Canada and the United States, A Discussion Paper*. Evaluation and Analysis Directorate, Emergency Preparedness Canada http://www.epc-pcc.gc.ca/research/scie_tech/en_mitigat/index_e.html. Accessed 28 January 2002

NG Maps (1998). Living with Natural Hazards. *National Geographic* 194 (1):31.

NIFC (2000). National Interagency Fire Center http://www.nifc.gov/. Accessed 31 May 2002

NOAA (2001). *The Exxon Valdez Oil Spill*. Office of Response and Restoration, National Ocean Service, National Oceanic and Atmospheric Administration http://response.restoration.noaa.gov/spotlight/spotlight.html. Accessed 28 January 2002

NRCan (1998). *Global Environmental Change and Canada's Forest: Securing Our Future*. Natural Resources Canada, Canadian Forest Service http://www.nrcan.gc.ca/cfs/proj/sci-tech/strategic/global2.html. Accessed 8 February 2002

NSTC (1996). *Natural Disaster Reduction: A Plan for the Nation*. National Science and Technology Council, Committee on the Environment and Natural Resources, Subcommittee on Natural Disaster Reduction http://www.usgs.gov/sndr/report/. Accessed 28 January 2002

O'Meara, Molly (1997). The Risks of Disrupting Climate. *World Watch* 10 (6):10-24

OCIPEP (2001). *The Office of Critical Infrastructure Protection and Emergency Preparedness*. Home Page http://www.epc-pcc.gc.ca/home/index_e.html. Accessed 28 January 2002

Parfit, Michael (1998). Living with Natural Hazards. *National Geographic* 194 (1):2-39

PBS (2000). *Yellowstone: America's Sacred Wilderness*. PBS Online http://www.pbs.org/edens/yellowstone/shaped.html. Accessed 29 January 2002

Robbins, Jim (1998). Yellowstone Reborn. *Audubon* 100 (4):64-9

Ross, Tom , Neal Lott, and William Brown (2000). *Significant U|S Weather and Climate Events for 2000*. National Climatic Data Center http://lwf.ncdc.noaa.gov/oa/climate/research/2000/ann/usevents2000.PDF. Accessed 29 January 2002

Trenberth, Kevin E. (1999). The Extreme Weather Events of 1997 and 1998. *Consequences: The Nature and Implication of Environmental Change* 5 (1) http://www.gcrio.org/CONSEQUENCES/vol5no1/toc.html. Accessed 8 February 2002

Turbak, Gary (2001). Wildlife Under Fire: Charred Land in Yellowstone Became a Symbol of Renewal. *Wildlife Conservation* 104 (4):37-43

Turner, Carla (2001). *Fighting Fires: Blazing a Trail*. CBC News http://cbc.ca/news/indepth/fightingfires/blazing.html. Accessed 29 January 2002

USDA (2001). *Roadless Area Conservation: Rulemaking Facts*. US Department of Agriculture, Roadless Area Conservation http://www.roadless.fs.fed.us/documents/rule/zRULE_Facts_1-5-01.htm. Accessed 20 February 2002

USDA Forest Service (2001). Urban Wildland Interface Communities Within the Vicinity of Federal Lands That Are at High Risk From Wildfire. *Federal Register* 66 (3):751-77. (From the Federal Register Online via GPO Access: wais.access.gpo.gov; DOCID:fr04ja01-26) Accessed 29 January 2002

USGCRP (2000). *Climate Change Impacts on the United States: The Potential Consequences of Climate Variability and Change.* US Global Change Research Program, National Assessment Synthesis Team http://www.usgcrp.gov/usgcrp/Library/nationalassessment/overview.htm. Accessed 29 January 2002

USGS (1999). *USGS Fire Research in the Southeast.* US Department of the Interior, US Geological Survey http://www.usgs.gov/public/press/public_affairs/press_releases/pr1025m.html. Accessed 29 January 2002

WGA (2000). *The Catastrophic Wildfires of 2000: Collaborative Effort Key to Prevention and Improved Ecosystem Health.* Western Governors' Association http://www.westgov.org/wga/testim/Forest_policy.pdf. Accessed 20 February 2002

White, Rodney (1997). Executive Summary. In *Coping with Natural Hazards in Canada: Scientific, Government and Insurance Industry Perspectives.* A Study Written for the Round Table on Environmental Risk, Natural Hazards and the Insurance Industry by Environmental Adaptation Research Group, Environment Canada and Institute for Environmental Studies, University of Toronto, http://www.utoronto.ca/env/nh/execsum.htm. Accessed 29 January 2002

Human Health and the Environment

Human Health and the Environment

Environmental conditions are relatively safe for North Americans: for the most part, the air is relatively safe to breathe, potable water is supplied to most of the population, and ample food of good quality is available. Many human-made chemicals used in agriculture, industry, and medicine have improved health and environmental quality. But the same beneficial substances may become pollutants when found in the wrong place, at the wrong time, and in the wrong quantity. Two opposite approaches have guided efforts to identify individual pollutants: one promoting the assumption that a substance is not harmful until evidence proves otherwise, and the other espousing precautionary consideration of a substance as potentially harmful until found otherwise (UN 1972).

In the past, the more obvious environmental health threats, such as asbestos, benzene, and formaldehyde, were investigated and their links to the environment understood. The fact that hundreds of children are poisoned each year by

accidentally ingesting toxic household products was clear and therefore many substances were removed from use (Grier 2001). Early decision-making in North America banned some very hazardous substances—witness the EPA ban on the manufacture of polychlorinated biphenyls (PCBs) in 1977 (Kaplan and Morris 2000). By the late 1970s, risk assessment, which enabled continued use of toxic chemicals at scientifically 'acceptable' levels, was the generally recognized regulatory tool (Cooper, Vanderlinden, and others 2000).

More than 35,000 substances are currently in commercial use in Canada and over 62,000 in the United States. Some 1,500 new chemicals are introduced each year in the United States alone, but complete data on the health and environmental effects are only available for 7 percent of those produced in high volume (EC 1998a, Cooper, Vanderlinden, and others 2000). Many of these chemicals become pollutants when they are released to the air, water, and land,

and North Americans are exposed to countless kinds of them in their immediate environments.

Although the linkages between health and the environment are often difficult to determine, knowledge of the more subtle human health effects of environmental pollution is now coming to light. For example, as a result of risk assessments for many chemicals for a range of subpopulations over the years, it has become clear that children and other vulnerable populations are more susceptible than the average adult to the harmful health effects of most pollutants. (See Box 54). Children's environmental health is an issue of high priority in North America.

Air pollution is emerging as a key contributor to some respiratory and cardiovascular diseases that are impairing health and killing vulner-able people. About 80 million US citizens are exposed to levels of air pollution that can impair health, and more than 2 percent of all deaths annually in that country can be attributed to air pollution (WRI, UNEP, UNDP, and World Bank 1998). Air pollution is also linked to an alarming rise over the past two decades in the prevalence of asthma among children and young adults worldwide, mostly in affluent countries such as Canada and the United States. Ozone, a principal component of smog, is thought to exacerbate asthma symptoms. There is also clear evidence that acidic air pollutants affect the health of sensitive individuals, especially the young, the elderly, and those with respiratory ailments.

Another priority issue is the recent emergence or resurgence of some vector-borne disease. It is

Box 54: Children's Special Vulnerablility

Children are more susceptible than adults to the harmful health effects of most pollutants because of their developmental, physiological and behavioral characteristics. For instance, in some circumstances, children cannot excrete toxins as well as adults, and so are more vulnerable to them. The ratio of skin surface area to body weight is also higher in children than in adults, which makes it possible for an excessive portion of toxins to enter their bodies. And because their airways are narrower, children breathe more rapidly and inhale more air per kg of body weight. Children also drink more fluids and eat more food per unit of body weight compared to adults. In addition, crawling and a tendency to put their hands in their mouths provides more opportunities for chemical or heavy metal residues in dust, soil, and heavy vapors to be ingested or to contact the skin (EPA 1997; PMRA 2002; CEHN n.d.).

Children (like all people and animals) may be exposed to toxic or hazardous chemicals through chemically treated building materials, furnishings, appliances, cleaning products, lawn and farm chemicals, and other materials as well as some foods—such as fruits and vegetables—that may have minute residues of pesticides. Children may also consume chemical residues in breast milk and formula (CEC 2000a; Kaplan and Morris 2000; PMRA 2002). Pollutants in the air indoors and out—cigarette smoke and vehicle exhaust, for example—and the sun's damaging rays can also affect children more than adults.

believed that climate change and human-induced land use change are important factors in the emergence of diseases new to North America and the resurgence of some organisms that have heretofore been held in check by public health controls.

Children's Health and Environmental Contamination

Recent estimates suggest that one in every 200 US children suffer developmental or neurological deficits due to exposure to known toxic substances (NET, PSR, and NDAA 2000). Scientific understanding of the trend is still limited, especially since genetic, social, economic, and cultural factors affect the risk determinant and the statistics. For example, data bias can be related to better detection, inherited susceptibility, improved access to health care, medications, and the presence of allergies, among other factors. Economic and social elements are also significant variables. Poor and aboriginal children are more often at greater risk of environment-related health problems for a number of reasons (Alpert 1999; Cooper, Vanderlinden, and others 2000). With better understanding of children's environmental health, it has become clear that children are not just 'little adults' in terms of their susceptibility to the health effects of exposure to environmental contaminants (see Box 54). The story of lead illustrates how exposures and standards that were once thought to be safe require continued revision to protect children's health (see Box 55).

Exposure to a wide range of chemicals during pregnancy or after birth may also be implicated in neurodevelopmental effects in children. Exposure to PCBs has been tied to lack of coordination, diminished IQ, and poor memory in some children. It is estimated that problems such as autism, aggression, dyslexia, and attention deficit hyperactivity disorder affect one out of every six children in the United States, and increasing evidence suggests that environmental contaminants and nutrition are primary causative factors (CEC 2000a; Kaplan and Morris 2000).

Mounting evidence implicates exposure to pesticides in adverse health effects, including cancer, birth defects, reproductive harm, neurological and developmental toxicity, immunotoxicity, and disruption of the endocrine system (NRDC 1997; Cooper, Vanderlinden, and

Box 55: The Phase-out of Lead

In the 1970s, lead in gasoline, paints, solders, and cans was recognized as causing grave neurobehavioral health risks to children. Attention deficits, lower IQ scores, hyperactivity, and juvenile delinquency are among these potential effects (Cooper, Vanderlinden, and others 2000; CEHN n.d.). In response, mandatory childhood blood-lead testing was instituted in the late 1980s and early 1990s in the United States. A 1981 survey found that one in every 25 US preschool children and one of every five inner-city black preschool children had dangerous lead levels in their blood (Miller Jr. 1985). Lack of definitive proof of the harmful nature of lead in gasoline, abetted by commercial interests in the additive, sparked a lengthy debate while environmental contamination and the threats to children's health continued. But thanks to a strong lobby of health and children's advocates, lead additives to gasoline were banned in the late 1980s in the United States and in 1990 in Canada. The situation improved dramatically as lead emissions declined (see Figure 48), and as acceptable blood lead levels were revised downward in the early 1990s (EC 1996; Cooper, Vanderlinden, and others 2000; Cooper 2002). Today, the average gasoline lead content in North America is among the lowest in the world and the average blood lead level in North American children has declined steadily (UNEP, UNICEF, and UNITAR 1998).

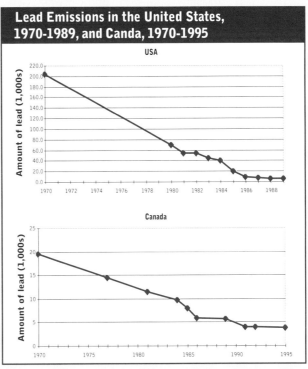

Figure 48 *Source: EC 1996*

Despite all this progress, mid-1990 estimates indicated that some 1.6 million North American children still had blood-lead levels in the range known to have health effects (GBPSR 1999; Cooper, Vanderlinden, and others 2000). Lead in paint is now considered to be the most common high-dose source of lead exposure for pre-school children in the United States. Children are more likely to ingest lead-containing paint chips and dust and so are particularly vulnerable to lead poisoning. Paint with levels higher than 600 parts per million (ppm) was banned in the United States in 1978, while the same low limit on lead-based exterior paint was introduced in Canada by voluntary agreement in 1991 (LDAC 2000). Thus, many older homes in North America still contain paint with levels of lead that are dangerous to children's health. Poor children are at greater risk since a larger percentage of low-income families live in older homes. It is now thought that there is likely no acceptable threshold for health effects in children from lead exposure (UNEP, UNICEF, and UNITAR 1998).

More recently, there is evidence that children are exposed to new and unexpected sources of lead, like that found in some cheap jewellery, candles with lead wicks and PVC (polyvinyl chloride) mini-blinds. So the risk assessment for this toxic metal remains crucial (Cooper 2002). From the lessons learned with lead, the North American governments are now supporting more rigorous research into childhood risks from environmental contaminants, are issuing warnings and advisories, and implementing stronger standards.

others 2000). Pesticides are used on the farm and elsewhere to control indoor and yard pests where children are present. When pesticides run off fields into waterways or groundwater or become airborne, drinking water can be contaminated. Pesticides can be ingested in food, and most fruit and fruit juices, as well as breast milk.(NRDC 1997; NRDC 1998).

Another environmental risk to children is air pollution, both outdoor and indoor, which is among the most significant triggers for asthma symptoms. Childhood asthma is on the rise, affecting over 5 and a half million children in North America and accounting for more than 60 percent of all their hospital visits (PSR 1997; Health Canada 1998). In Canada, childhood asthma increased fourfold between 1978-79 and 1994-95, with environmental change a possible contributor to the increase (Kidder, Stein, and Fraser 2000). Asthma is now the number one childhood illness in the United States (PEHC 2000). Scientific understanding of the trend is still limited and must account for the influence of hereditary characteristics, social and cultural variables, and the fact that medications for treating the illness have greatly improved (Alpert 1999).

The links between air pollution and human health in general also require more study. On average, air quality has improved in North America, although it remains true that more than half the US

population lives in areas that exceed federal standards for many pollutants. These include those associated with asthma such as ozone, sulphur dioxide, and particulates (PSR 1997). Almost every major Canadian city exceeded the nation's stringent ozone guidelines at least once between 1984 and 1991. Researchers now conclude that even ozone levels below federal standards (see the atmosphere section) cause ill effects that contribute to asthma (PSR 1997). There is also clear evidence that acidic air pollutants affect children's cardio-respiratory health (Burnett, Dales, and others 1995).

With the increase in asthma prevalence and concerns over the links to environmental pollutants, more research money is being dedicated to studying children's health, particularly to what is being called a childhood asthma epidemic (PEHC 2000).

In recent years, there has been a dramatic surge in the recognition of children's environmental health issues, and as a result stricter regulations have been introduced that take children's vulnerabilities into account. In the mid-1980s, the EPA began to consider developmental risks in its assessment protocol (Cooper, Vanderlinden, and others 2000). A key event was a 1993 National Academy of Science study showing that pesticide regulation did not allow for the special risks faced by children. It prompted the 1996 US Food Quality Protection Act (FQPA) to apply a 10-fold child-protective safety factor as well as requirements to aggregate chemical exposures and to assess groups of chemicals with common mechanisms of toxicity. It also stipulated the review of some 9,000 pesticides to determine whether they pose a health risk for children. The FQPA sets standards for exposure to hazardous substances through risk assessment, a practice that has evolved over the years from focusing disproportionately on adult cancer, to considering developmental risks, including those that affect children (EPA 1999; Cooper 2002).

In Canada, the Pest Management Regulatory Agency's (PMRA) consideration of the increased sensitivity to a pesticide experienced by the young and other vulnerable populations, as well as the exposure of infants, children, and pregnant women, is consistent with FQPA practice. Also in keeping with the EPA, it uses a case-specific determination regarding the size of the additional safety factor where reliable scientific data are available. Canada's Food and Drugs Act now also takes into account the dietary patterns and special needs of children (PMRA 2002).

Both federal governments recently initiated special bodies or actions to deal with the issue of children's health. In 1996, the EPA adopted a National Agenda to Protect Children's Health From Environmental Threats. In 1997, the Office of Children's Health Protection (OCHP) and the President's Task Force on Environmental Health Risks and Safety Risks in Children

were formed to identify, assess, and address children's disproportionate environmental health and safety risks. In April 1998, the Task Force identified childhood asthma, accidental injury, developmental disorders, and childhood cancer as priority areas for immediate attention (EPA 2001). Beginning in 1997, Health Canada strove to strengthen departmental and interdepartmental linkages among legislation, policies, and programs aimed at children and contributed to the 1997 National Children's Agenda, which includes the need for safe and secure environments and communities for healthy childhood development (Health Canada 1999).

Canada and the United States are party to the 1989 UN Convention on the Rights of the Child and also support Agenda 21, which acknowledges the dangers and risks of environmental pollution to children. Agenda 21 urges governments to develop programs to protect children from the effects of environmental and occupational toxic compounds. In addition, the Declaration of the Environment Leaders of the Eight on Children's Environmental Health (G7 countries plus Russia 1997) acknowledges that current levels of protection may not provide children with adequate protection and provides a framework for national, bilateral, and international efforts to improve the protection of children's health from environmental threats such as pesticides (CEC 2000a). And at the Health and Environment Ministers

Box 56: Bilateral Cooperation

Canada and the United States, together with Mexico, are working cooperatively in the field of children's environmental health. In 2000, the Commission for Environmental Cooperation for North America's (CEC) Council of Ministers resolved to apply the perspective of children's health to their work, including increasing information exchange and public awareness and education about environmental threats to children's health and how to prevent them. Building on the outcomes of its 2000 Symposium on Children's Health and the Environment in North America, the CEC Council called for cooperative efforts to address asthma and other respiratory diseases, and the effects of lead and other toxic substances as a matter of priority. With the involvement of health and environment officials from the three countries, an Expert Advisory Board and members of the public, the CEC has developed a Cooperative Agenda for Children's Health and the Environment in North America which will serve as the blueprint for trilateral action on issues of common concern (CEC 2000a; CEC 2000b).

The Canadian PMRA and the US EPA also work cooperatively under the umbrella of the NAFTA Technical Working Group on Pesticides to provide expert guidance to other scientists generating data to refine residential exposure estimates for infants and children (PMRA 2002). In addition, 10 US Pediatric Environmental Health Specialty Units, forming a network joined by one Canadian counterpart, now receive US public funding. US researchers are currently initiating a pilot Longitudinal Cohort Study to track environmental exposures and health effects on children (Cooper 2002).

of the Americas meeting in 2002, it was agreed to develop a set of indicators for children's health and the environment (EC 2002). The two countries also work together on a number of joint projects (see Box 56).

At the grassroots, people are invoking 'The Right to Know' and local initiatives are being taken to protect children's health in many communities. In both countries, a strong preventive and precautionary approach to risk assessment is slow to emerge, however. People still tend to require positive evidence of health and exposure risks before taking action (Cooper 2002). Governments are under increasing pressure from scientists, pediatricians, academics, and parents for more rigorous tests for neurotoxic effects, prenatal and early postnatal exposures, and cumulative health effects from exposure to environmental contaminants, as well as regulations for shifting onus from the public to the chemical manufacturers by requiring the latter to prove that their products are safe instead of leaving it to governments to report on their toxicity (Cooper, Vanderlinden, and others 2000; Kaplan and Morris 2000).

Emergence/Resurgence of Vector–borne Diseases

Vector-borne diseases—those that can infect humans through transmission by insects or ticks, or by direct contact with host animals or their body excretions (see Box 57)—were once common in the southern United States. By 1972, public health policies and the effective use of pesticides had significantly reduced the threat of diseases like malaria and dengue fever. In the last 20 years, however, new vector-borne infectious diseases are emerging and some old ones resurging (Gubler 1998a; Gubler 1998b).

Natural or human-caused environmental change affecting any segment of the vector's natural cycle might lead to the emergence or re-emergence of infectious diseases. This can take place when other species introduce existing pathogens into human populations or pathogens are further disseminated from smaller to larger populations. Ecological or environmental changes; population movements; changes in industrial processes, economic development, land use, and international travel and commerce as well as breakdowns in public health measures can create conditions that encourage the process. Natural environmental events, such as weather changes, can especially affect vector-borne diseases. Local

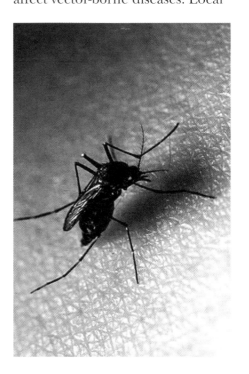

Box 57: Vector-borne Disease

A vector is an organism that spreads an infectious disease by amplifying and transmitting it, often without becoming ill itself. Anthropods such as mosquitoes and ticks, or mollusks such as freshwater snails typically harbor the infectious agents at some part of their life cycle. Hundreds of viruses, bacteria, protozoa, and helminths (parasitic worms) rely on such blood-sucking arthropods to be transmitted between vertebrate hosts. Yellow Fever, Dengue Fever, Lyme disease, Arboviral encephalitis, and West Nile Virus are examples of vector-borne infectious diseases (Gubler 1998a; NIAID 2001).

bio-geographical conditions, immunological history, and genetic change in pathogens are yet other factors that can influence infectious disease emergence (Epstein 1998; CDC 2000a; NIAID 2001).

Some scientists suggest that certain vectors may be expanding their geographic ranges into previously inhospitable areas in response to climate change. The International Panel on Climate Change (IPCC) reports that "changing climate conditions may lead to the northward spread of vector-borne infectious diseases and potentially enhanced transmission dynamics as a result of warmer ambient temperatures" (Watson, Zinyowara, and others 1997).

Climate change and human-induced land use change may also change predator-prey relationships, increasing the numbers of disease-carrying pests and human contact with them (EC 1998b). For example, there appears to be a relationship between the expansion of suburbs and reforestation, the abundance of deer and deer ticks, and a rise in the numbers of reported tick bites and infections of Lyme disease in the eastern United States (CDC 2001; NIAID 2001) (see Box 58).

Climate limits the distribution of vector-borne diseases, while the timing and intensity of outbreaks are affected by weather. With increases in average temperatures, studies indicate the potential for mosquito-borne encephalitis to move into northern United States and Canada (EC 1998b; Epstein, Diaz, and others 1998). Indeed, since 1990, the beginning of the hottest decade in historical record, locally transmitted malaria outbreaks—although limited to only a few cases—have occurred in numerous states during hot spells (Gubler 1998a). Warmer weather may also have influenced the occurrence of West Nile Virus in North America (see Box 59).

Climate variability is only part of a complex mix of factors that explain the emergence/resurgence of vector-borne diseases, and transmission depends on factors that are unique for each pathogen. Increased international trade can lead to the introduction of a pathogen to new populations or to an expansion in the range of vectors. The tiger mosquito *(Aedes albopictus)*, for example, was introduced to the United States in 1986 in used tires imported from Asia. It is capable of

Box 58: Lyme Disease

Lyme disease is a bacterial tick-borne infection. The *Ixodes dammini* tick, found in grassy, brushy, shrubby, and wooded areas of the northeastern United States, is responsible for most of the cases of Lyme disease. The ticks feed on a variety of warm-blooded animals including humans and domestic animals. The tick's life cycle has three stages, each of which requires separate hosts. During the nymphal stage, the tick prefers the white-footed mouse, the main reservoir of the Lyme disease bacteria, while the adult ticks prefer to feed on white-tailed deer (Miller n.d.).

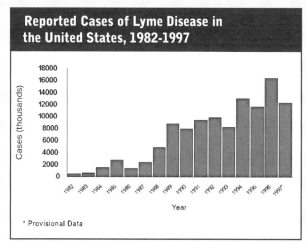

Reported Cases of Lyme Disease in the United States, 1982-1997

* Provisional Data

Lyme disease is the leading cause of vector-borne infectious illness in the United States, with about 15,000 cases annually, although many are unreported (CDC 2001). It occurs mostly in the northeastern United States, the upper Midwest, and northern California but may also extend northward as far as Canada with climate change (EC 1998b).

Figure 49 *Source: Gubler 1998a*

National surveillance for Lyme disease started in 1982 and since then, incidence of the disease has increased (see Figure 49) as has its geographic distribution (Gubler 1998a). Managing deer populations where Lyme disease occurs may reduce tick abundance (CDC 2001).

Box 59: West Nile Virus

The unanticipated first-time appearance of the West Nile Virus (WNV) in New York State in 1999 aroused concern over the potential for new viruses to penetrate prosperous northern climes. Mosquitoes that have fed on the blood of infected birds transmit the virus. Most people who contract the virus show no symptoms or only mild flu-like symptoms, but in rare cases the virus can cause meningitis or encephalitis, usually affecting vulnerable people such as young children, the elderly, and those with suppressed immune systems (Health Canada 2001). Of the 62 human cases of clinical illness resulting from infection with WNV in the United States in 1999, seven were fatal. Where extensive mosquito controls and risk-reduction campaigns were undertaken, no new cases occurred among humans (CDC 2000b). Its reappearance in four northeastern states in 2000, however, was evidence that it had over-wintered and transmission had increased (Brown 2000). In 2000, there were 21 human cases and two deaths (USDA 2000). When the temperature falls below 13°C, the mosquitoes become dormant and the virus stops spreading. But it can spread once more in the spring when the mosquitoes are active and birds are migrating (Simao 2001).

WNV was first isolated in Uganda in 1937 and outbreaks have occurred in several countries outside North America, but it is not yet known how it was introduced into the United States (Health Canada 2001). It is thought that a sequence of warm winters, followed by hot, dry summers—a pattern predicted by climate change models for some regions—favors the transmission of this type of virus. To counteract increases in this and other vector-borne diseases, improved disease surveillance and prevention strategies at state and local levels will be needed as well as more research into climate-health relationships (Epstein 2000; USGCRP 2000).

transmitting viruses responsible for dengue fever and several forms of encephalitis (NIAID 2001).

Since the 1970s and the near elimination in North America of malaria and other diseases that infect humans through host carriers of pathogens, the public health infrastructure required to deal with them and prevention, surveillance, control, and training programs were discontinued or merged with other programs as less need for them was perceived (Gubler 1998a). Now, however, the need to reinvest in these measures has become evident. With the resurgence of Hantavirus pulmonary syndrome in 1993, for example (see Box 60, next page), control measures were stepped up,

and although climate conditions were subsequently ripe for more outbreaks, episodes have been limited. Early-warning systems increased public awareness and prompted people to rodent-proof homes, set traps, and avoid the rodents' droppings (Bonn 1998; Epstein 2000).

The level of socioeconomic development is another significant factor in preventing vector-borne diseases. Between 1980 and 1996, for example, 43 cases of dengue fever, a mosquito-borne virus, were reported in Texas, versus 50,333 in the three adjacent Mexican states, providing clear evidence that where people prosper, they are able to take preventive measures—in this case, air conditioning and window screens were key factors—and to devote resources to public health and surveillance measures (Manning 2000; USGCRP 2000).

Better control and surveillance strategies alone may be able to counteract potential increases in vector-borne pathogens in North

tion of water and food (see the land section). Increasing insect resistance is also compromising the efficacy of pesticides (Epstein, Diaz, and others 1998). Thus, more research on environmentally safe insecticides, vaccines, and alternative approaches to vector control are also crucial (Gubler 1998a). At the same time,

---

Box 60: Hantavirus Pulmonary Syndrome

The example of the resurgence of Hantavirus pulmonary syndrome (HPS) in the United States illustrates the effect of 1990s climatic variability in the outbreak of vector-borne disease. Rodent species bearing HPS live throughout the United States and cases of the syndrome have occurred nation-wide. It is carried primarily by the deer mouse and can be transmitted to humans when they inhale infected air from the rodents' saliva or excreta (CDC 1999). HPS is a viral disease characterized by severe pulmonary illness, with a case fatality rate of about 50 percent (WHO 1996). In the early 1990s, the population of white-footed mice in the southwest United States increased 10-fold. A combination of prolonged drought that killed its predators and subsequent heavy rains, which expanded the rodent's food supply, conspired to spur population increase and allowed the inactive or restricted virus to explode (WHO 1996; Epstein 2000). Only 191 cases have been reported since its first reappearance in 1993, but the virus is considered by some to be an important public health concern (Bonn 1998).

America (Gubler 1998a). Control strategies, however, often involve the use of pesticides, which have been called a 'double-edged sword' in view of human health problems attributed to pesticide contamina-

given that climate change may have a significant and increasing role in this trend, it is also important to find solutions to the human causes of recent and future changes in climate.

References

Alpert, Mark (1999). *The Invisible Epidemic.* Scientific American.com http://www.scientificamerican.com/1999/1199issue/1199infocus.html. Accessed 15 February 2002

Bonn, Dorothy (1998). Hantaviruses: An Emerging Threat to Human Health? *The Lancet* 352 (9131):886

Brown, David (2000). West Nile Virus May be Here to Stay, Official Says. *Washington Post*, 11 August

Burnett, R.T., R. Dales, D. Krewski, R. Vincent, T. Dann, and J.R. Brook (1995). Associations Between Ambient Particulate Sulfate and Admissions to Ontario Hospitals for Cardiac and Respiratory Diseases. *American Journal of Epidemiology* 142 (1):15-22

CDC (1999). Update: Hantavirus Pulmonary Syndrome–United States, 1999. *Morbidity and Mortality Weekly Report* 48 (24):521-525

CDC (2000a). *Emerging Infectious Diseases: A Public Health Response.* National Center for Infectious Diseases, Centers for Disease Control and Prevention http://www.cdc.gov/ncidod/emergplan/summary/index.htm. Accessed 25 February 2002

CDC (2000b). West Nile Virus Activity – New York and New Jersey, 2000. *Morbidity and Mortality Weekly Report* 49 (28):640

CDC (2001). *CDC Lyme Disease Home Page.* Centers for Disease Control and Prevention, National Center for Infectious Diseases, Division of Vector-Borne Infectious Diseases http://www.cdc.gov/ncidod/dvbid/lyme/index.htm. Accessed 16 February 2002

CEC (2000a). *Background Paper prepared for the Symposium on North American Children's Health and the Environment,* Toronto, 10 May. Montreal, Commission for Environmental Cooperation of North America

CEC (2000b). *Council Resolution 00-10: Children's Health and the Environment.* Montreal, Commission for Environmental Cooperation of North America http://www.cec.org/who_we_are/council/resolutions/disp_res.cfm?varlan=english&documentID=121. Accessed 15 February 2002

CEHN (n.d.). *An Introduction to Children's Environmental Health.* Children's Environmental Health Network http://www.cehn.org/cehn/WhatisPEH.html. Accessed 15 February 2002

Cooper, Kathleen, Loren Vanderlinden, Theresa McClenaghan, Karyn Keenan, Kapil Khatter, Paul Muldoon, and Alan Abelsohn (2000). *Environmental Standard Setting and Children's Health.* Toronto, Canadian Environmental Law Association and the Ontario College of Family Physicians Environmental Health Committee

Cooper, Kathleen (2002). Experimenting on Children. *Alternatives* 28 (1):16-21

EC (1996). *The State of Canada's Environment – 1996.* Environment Canada http://www.ec.gc.ca/soer-ree/English/1996Report/Doc/1-1.cfm. Accessed 28 May 2002

EC (1998a). *Toxic Contaminants in the Environment: Persistent Organochlorines, National Environmental Indicator Series, SOE Bulletin No. 98-1.* Ottawa, Environment Canada, State of the Environment Reporting Program: http://www.ec.gc.ca/Ind/english/Toxic/default.cfm. Accessed 5 February 2002

EC (2002). Meeting of Health and Environment Ministers of The Americas: Ministerial Communiqué. *International Relations.* http://www.ec.gc.ca/international/regorgs/docs/english/hema_Comm_e.htm. Accessed 28 May 2002

EC (1998b). *The Canada Country Study: Climate Impacts and Adaptation, Volume VII: National Sectoral Volume.* Environment Canada, The Green Lane

EPA (1997). Children's Exposure to Pesticides. *Star Report* 1 (1):1

EPA (1999). *Summary of FQPA Amendments to FIFRA and FFDCA.* US Environmental Protection Agency, Office of Pesticide Programs http://www.epa.gov/oppfead1/fqpa/fqpa-iss.htm#consumer. Accessed 15 February 2002

EPA (2001). *President's Task Force on Environmental Health Risks and Safety Risks to Children.* US Environmental Protection Agency, Office of Children's Health Protection http://www.epa.gov/ children/whatwe/fedtask.htm. Accessed 14 February 2002

Epstein, Paul (1998). Global Warming and Vector-borne Disease. In *Letters to the Editor, The Lancet.* JunkScience.com http://www.junkscience.com/news2/reiter.htm. Accessed 15 February 2002

Epstein, Paul R., Henry F. Diaz, Scott Elias, and Georg Grabherr (1998). Biological and Physical Signs of Climate Change: Focus on Mosquito-borne Diseases. *Bulletin of the American Meteorological Society* 79 (3):409-417

Epstein, Paul (2000). Is Global Warming Harmful to Health? *Scientific American* 283 (2):50-7

GBPSR (1999). *In Harm's Way: Toxic Threats to Child Development, Executive Summary.* Cambridge, MA, Greater Boston Physicians for Social Responsibility http://home.earthlink.net/ ~gmarch1723/execsumm.pdf. Accessed 16 February 2002

Grier, Ruth (2001). Making the North American Environment Safe for our Children. *Trio.* Commission for Environmental Cooperation of North America http://www.cec.org/trio/ stories/index.cfm?varlan=english&ed=3&id=21. Accessed 25 February 2002

Gubler, Duane J. (1998a). *Resurgent Vector-Borne Diseases as a Global Health Problem.* National Center for Infectious Diseases, Centers for Disease Control and Prevention http://www.cdc.gov/ ncidod/eid/vol4no3/gubler.htm. Accessed 15 February 2002

Gubler, Duane J. (1998b). Vector-Borne Infectious Diseases. Paper read at the International Conference on Emerging Infectious Diseases, 8-11 March, at Atlanta, Georgia

Health Canada (1998). *Childhood Asthma in Sentinel Health Units: Findings of the Student Lung Health Survey 1995-1996.* Health Canada, Health Protection Branch–Laboratory Centre for Disease Control http://www.hc-sc.gc.ca/hpb/lcdc/publicat/asthma/. Accessed 15 February 2002

Health Canada (1999). *Health Canada's Sustainable Development Strategy : Report on Progress for 1998-1999.* Health Canada, Office of Sustainable Development http://www.hc-sc.gc.ca/susdevdur/ progress_report98-99.pdf. Accessed 14 February 2002

Health Canada (2001). *West Nile Virus – The Facts.* Health Canada, Population and Public Health Branch http://www.hc-sc.gc.ca/pphb-dgspsp/publicat/info/wnv_e.html. Accessed 15 February 2002

Kaplan, Sheila, and Jim Morris (2000). Kids at Risk. *US News and World Report* 128 (24):47-53

Kidder, Karen, Jonathan Stein, and Jeannine Fraser (2000). *The Health of Canada's Children: A CICH Profile.* 3 ed. Ottawa, Canadian Institute of Child Health

LDAC (2000). *Watch Out For Lead.* Learning Disabilities Association of Canada http://www.ldac-taac.ca/briefs/watchoutlead.htm. Accessed 15 February 2002

Manning, Anita (2000). Climate Control isn't a Cure-all: Poverty Overwhelms Global Warming as a Public Health Threat. *USA Today,* 18 July

Miller, Lloyd E. (n.d.). *Lyme Disease – General Information and FAQ* http://www-2.cs.cmu.edu/afs/ cs.cmu.edu/user/jake/mosaic/lyme.html. Accessed 16 February 2002

Miller Jr., G. Tyler (1985). *Living in the Environment: An Introduction to Environmental Science.* Vol. 4. Belmont, CA, Wadsworth Publishing Company

NET, PSR, and LDAA (2000). *Polluting Our Future: Chemical Pollution in the US that Affects Child Development and Learning.* Washington, DC, The National Environmental Trust, Physicians for Social Responsibility and The Learning Disabilities Association of America

NIAID (2001). *The NIAID Research Agenda for Emerging Infectious Diseases.* National Institute of Allergy and Infectious Diseases, National Institute of Health http://www.niaid.nih.gov/ publications/execsum/contents.htm. Accessed 15 February 2002

NRDC (1997). *Our Children at Risk: The 5 Worst Environmental Threats to Their Health.* New York, Natural Resources Defense Council. http://www.nrdc.org/health/kids/ocar/ocarinx.asp. Accessed 16 February 2002

NRDC (1998). *Trouble on the Farm: Growing Up with Pesticides in Agricultural Communities.* New York, Natural Resources Defense Council http://www.nrdc.org/health/kids/farm/farminx.asp. Accessed 16 February 2002

PEHC (2000). *Attack Asthma: Why America Needs a Public Health Defense System to Battle Environmental Threats.* The Pew Environmental Health Commission at the John Hopkins School of Public Health http://pewenvirohealth.jhsph.edu/html/reports/PEHCAsthmaReport.pdf. Acccssed 15 Fcbruary 2002

PMRA (2002). *Children's Health Priorities within the Pest Management Regulatory Agency. Science Policy Notice.* Submission Coordination and Documentation Division, Pest Management Regulatory Agency, Health Canada http://www.hc-sc.gc.ca/pmra-arla/english/pdf/spn/spn2002-01-e.pdf. Accessed 14 February 2002

PSR (1997). *Asthma and the Role of Air Pollution.* Physicians for Social Responsibility http://www.psr.org/docupsr.htm. Accessed 15 February 2002

Simao, Paul (2001). *Update: Deadly West Nile Virus Spreading in US – CDC.* Reuters News Service http://www.planetark.org/dailynewsstory.cfm?newsid=11800. Accessed 16 February 2002

UN (1972). *United Nations Conference on the Human Environment. A/CONF.48/8. Identification and Control of Pollutants of Broad International Significance. (Subject Area III),* United Nations

UNEP, UNICEF, and UNITAR (1998). *Global Opportunities for Reducing the Use of Leaded Gasoline.* United Nations Environment Programme, United Nations Children's Fund, United Nations Institute for Training and Research, Inter-Organization Programme for the Sound Management of Chemicals (IOMC)

USDA (2000). *West Nile Virus in the United States, 2000.* US Department of Agriculture, Animal and Plant Health Inspection Service http://www.aphis.usda.gov/oa/wnv/summary2000.html. Accessed 16 February 2002

USGCRP (2000). *Climate Change Impacts on the United States: The Potential Consequences of Climate Variability and Change.* Washington DC, National Assessment Synthesis Team, US Global Change Research Program. http://sedac.ciesin.org/NationalAssessment/. Accessed 13 February 2002

Watson, Robert T., Marufu C. Zinyowara, Richard H. Moss, and David J. Dokken eds. (1997). *The Regional Impacts of Climate Change: An Assessment of Vulnerability.* http://www.usgcrp.gov/ipcc/SRs/regional/index.htm, Intergovernmental Panel on Climate Change. Accessed 15 February 2002

WHO (1996). *World Health Report 1996: Fighting Disease, Fostering Development.* World Health Organization http://www.who.int/whr/1996/exsume.htm. Accessed 15 February 2002

WRI, UNEP, UNDP, and World Bank (1998). *World Resources 1998-99, A Guide to the Global Environment: Environmental Change and Human Health,* Oxford University Press, New York, United States, and Oxford, United Kingdom

Urban Areas

10

Urban Areas

Northern America is a highly urbanized region. In the past 30 years, North America's urban population increased from 72 to 77.2 percent (see Figure 50) (UNCHS 2001). The actual increase in urban populations over the period is even higher and more significant. By the year 2020, some 300 million people will be living in the region's urban or metropolitan areas (see Box 61).

Urbanization is related to many of the environmental issues highlighted in this report, including the loss of agricultural land, wildlife habitat and biodiversity loss and degradation, regional air pollution, global climate change, coastal degradation, an expanded urban-wildlife interface, and polluting inputs to fresh and marine waters.

Suburban sprawl, a key characteristic of North American settlement patterns, has an important impact on the environment and is a high-priority issue in the region. A house in the suburbs is often a component of what has been called the 'American Dream'. In general, a large percentage of North Americans have enjoyed a high quality of life since the 1950s, and during this time, ever-larger proportions of the population could aspire to possess a single-family home with garage and yard, removed from the downtown core. But as the social, economic, and environmental consequences of sprawling suburbs come to light, more and more municipalities are encouraging denser settlement patterns confined to urban boundaries.

While dense settlement patterns have the potential to reduce environmental impact if planned for sustainability, at present,

Figure 50
Trend in urban population, 1980-2020

Source: WRI, UNEP, UNDP, and World Bank 1998

Trend in Urban Population, 1980-2020

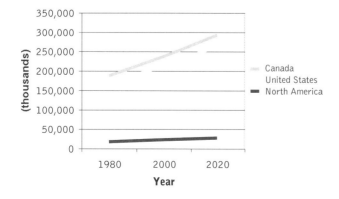

Box 61: Definition of Urban Areas

The US Census Bureau defines an urbanized area as all territory, population, and clusters of housing units with at least 387.59 people per km². It includes the surrounding census blocks with an overall density of at least 193 people per km² (US Census Bureau 2000). Statistics Canada defines a census metropolitan area (CMA) as an urban core population of at least 100,000, together with urban and rural fringes possessing a high degree of social and economic integration with the urban core (Statistics Canada 2001a). Canadian census authorities are now using a definition of 400 persons per km², which is close to the US definition (Wendell Cox Consultancy 2000a).

North American urban populations use high levels of energy and other resources and dispose of large amounts of waste. The concentration of people and industry has implications for the production, removal, and treatment of solid waste generated as a by-product of regular consumption, as well as hazardous wastes produced by industry. Canadian and US citizens are some of the highest per capita producers of municipal waste in the world, putting out, respectively, an annual average of 630 and 720 kg per person in the mid-1990s. These amounts represent respective increases of 24 percent and 19 percent since 1980 (CEC 2000). Quantities of waste and pollution generated by North America's urban-industrial complex are part of the make-up of

the region's ecological footprint, which is an aggregated measure of human impact on the global environment. Because of their significant contribution to both regional and global pollution and to declines in the earth's natural resources, North American cities have large ecological footprints. The implications of the region's global impact is a high-priority issue for the North American environment as well as the global one.

Sprawl

By the 1970s, North America's postwar exodus from central cities had led to a settlement pattern characterized by low-density suburbs surrounding city cores, commonly referred to as sprawl (see Box 62). In the United States, a cycle of

Box 62: Sprawl

Sprawl may be defined as low-density, non-contiguous, automobile-dependent residential development (Dowling 2000). It is equated with intrusion into rural or undeveloped land on the periphery of a central city or town, beyond the edge of service and employment areas (Chen 2000). Sprawl's dominant characteristic is that each of its components—clusters of housing, shopping centers, offices, civic institutions, and roadways—is strictly segregated from the others (Duany, Plater-Zyberk, and Speck 2000). Abetted by a vocal grassroots movement, federal, regional, and municipal governments are increasingly recognizing the environmental and social impacts of sprawl and attempting to address them.

Figure 51
US per capita private and public transport use, 1972-1999.

Source: compiled from EC 1998b; Wendell Cox 2000; and United Nations Population Division 2001

transit declines, rising car use, and commuting longer distances took place over the 1970s and '80s and was mirrored by Canada during the 1990s. These changes were fueled after World War II by a number of polices that encouraged the settlement dispersal. In the United States, loan programs provided low-cost mortgages for new, single-family suburban construction. At the same time the government launched a 65,983 km interstate highway program and provided subsides for road improvement, helping to make commuting by car affordable and convenient for the average citizen (Duany, Plater-Zyberk, and Speck 2000). Local single-use zoning and

subdivision ordinances also encouraged the pattern of isolated residential, retail, and workspaces characteristic of sprawl (ULI 1999). In addition, governments funded the extension of sewers and water lines to sprawling developments, paid for emergency services to them, built new schools, and helped suburban developers in other ways (Sierra Club 2000a).

State-level powers over programs and services devolved to local governments, undermining the potential for coordinated regional land use and transportation policies (Raad and Kenworthy 1998). While government infrastructure subsidies, middle-income families, and tax bases left for the suburbs, city centers encountered rising service costs. US cities came to be impoverished city cores surrounded by car-dependent suburbs serviced by malls.

Until recently, sprawl has been relatively more controlled in Canada. A strong tradition of land use planning and higher transit usage created urban areas that are more integrated with their surrounding suburbs. In response to suburban growth, municipalities initially amalgamated or created upper-tier agencies to coordinate regional services and infrastructure and reconcile the needs of suburbs with those of the central city (Raad and Kenworthy 1998). During the 1970s and 1980s, large-scale government subsidies helped transit systems to expand, curbing low-density sprawl. Across the country, public transport

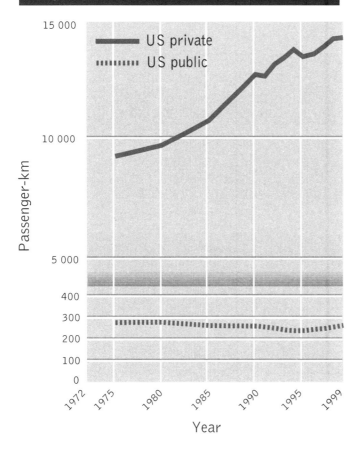

US Per Capita Private and Public Transport Use, 1972-1999

was usually a coordinated, high-quality, and relatively profitable service that helped maintain thriving central cities (Pucher 1998).

During the 1990s, however, low-density suburban sprawl expanded significantly in Canada while continuing apace in the United States. A growing population in Canada increasingly spilled over into areas outside regional government control. Mirroring fragmented municipal governance in the United States, responsibility for social services including transit began devolving to municipalities, depriving regional governments of the tools to contain sprawl (Pucher 1998; Raad and Kenworthy 1998). Large fare increases and service cutbacks, stagnating subsidy levels, and escalating operating and capital costs contributed to declining transit use, and a cycle of car use increases, sprawling suburbs, longer commuting distances, and further transit decreases began. Between 1981 and 1991, the number of car kilometers traveled by Canadian and US citizens grew by 23 and 33.7 percent, respectively, while the distances traveled by public transport shrank (see Figures 51 and 52) (EC 1998; Raad and Kenworthy 1998). Although US cities have higher car use and lower transit use, the rate of growth in the number of car kilometers traveled in Canada began to resemble the United States, rising 20 percent and 23 percent respectively between 1981 and 1991 (Raad and Kenworthy 1998).

The 1990s saw new road building in the United States, which

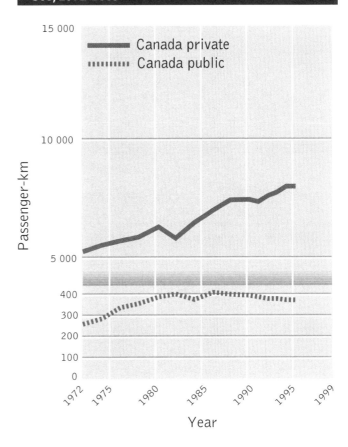

Canadian Per Capita Private and Public Transport Use, 1972-1995

continued to encourage driving and fed into the cycle of sprawl and car dependency. At the same time, the high costs of roads deprived public transit services and other transportation options of potential funding. Between 1996 and 1997, new road construction in 21 US states consumed over half of transportation dollars at the expense of transit (Pope 1999). One report reveals that today, about 85 percent of US federal transportation money encourages sprawl (Dowling 2000). Artificially low gas prices in North America also benefit the suburban commuter rather than the urban transit user (Baker 2000).

Figure 52
Canadian per capita private and public transport use, 1972-1995.

Source: compiled from EC 1998b; Wendell Cox 2000; and United Nations Population Division 2001

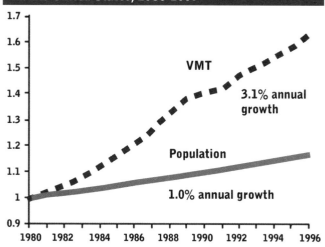

Increase in Vehicle Miles of Travel and Population in the United States, 1980-1997

VMT

3.1% annual growth

Population

1.0% annual growth

Scale: 1980 value = 1.0

Figure 53
Increase in vehicle miles of travel and population in the United States, 1980-1997.

Source: EPA 2001

Contributing to recent suburbanization trends in both countries is the substantial loss of central-city jobs (Pucher 1998). High-tech employment, for example, is growing 30 percent faster in US suburbs than in cities, helping

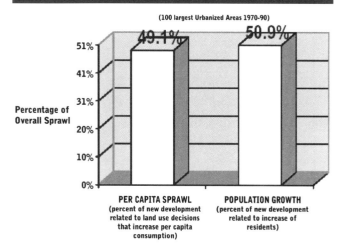

Urban Sources of Sprawl in the United States, 1970-1990

(100 largest Urbanized Areas 1970-90)

49.1%   50.9%

Percentage of Overall Sprawl

51%
41%
31%
20%
10%
0%

PER CAPITA SPRAWL
(percent of new development related to land use decisions that increase per capita consumption)

POPULATION GROWTH
(percent of new development related to increase of residents)

Figure 54
Urban sources of sprawl in the United States, 1970-1990.

Source: Kolankiewicz and Beck 2001

to drive residential and business development to fringe settlements (HUD 2000). While the close proximity of jobs and housing can promote more sustainable urban

settlement patterns, the question of whether employment centers in suburban areas are part of a sustainable solution to sprawl is still being debated.

Demographic trends are also fueling sprawl. For example, the percentage of the population between the ages of 25 and 64—the segment most likely to own households and cars and to commute to work—is growing (Pucher 1998; NAHB 1999). But population growth does not entirely explain the increases in travel miles. For example, between 1980 and 1996, the increase in the number of vehicle miles traveled in the United States exceeded an annual growth rate of 3 percent while annual population growth was only 1.0 percent (see Figure 53).

The growth of ex-urban housing also reflects the ability of an increasingly affluent segment of society to afford a 'dream house' in a country setting. Indeed, in both nations, sprawl is as much an effect of the preference for house type and locations as it is of population growth. As the overall US population grows, suburbs are growing faster than central cities: suburban population grew by 11.9 percent between 1990 and 1998, compared to 4.7 percent for central cities (Pope 1999; Baker 2000; HUD 2000). Only one-half of US sprawl appears to be related to population increase, with the other half attributable to land use and consumption choices that increase the amount of urban land occupied per resident (Kolankiewicz and Beck 2001) (see Figure 54). Similarly, the growth of suburbs in Canada is reflected by a steady decline in population densities—from an average of 1,030 persons per km² in 1971 to 796 per km² in 1996. The accelerated expansion of urban areas was influenced by preferences in housing location and type of homes, resulting in more land per urban dwelling. Almost 60 percent of all dwellings in Canada are single detached houses (Statistics Canada 2001b).

The North American suburban lifestyle has many benefits that are coveted by other, less developed regions of the world. But some North Americans increasingly recognize the multiple negative effects of unbridled growth in low-density suburban development (Chen 2000). The environmental consequences of sprawl begin with land conversion. The total amount of land dedicated to urban uses in the United States expanded by more than 7.7 million ha between 1970 and 1990 (Sierra Club 1998). The American Farmland Trust estimates that between 1982 and 1992, an average of 1,620 km² a year of prime farmland in the United States was developed (Sorensen, Greene, and Russ 1997). During the following decade, this loss rate doubled as almost 65,000 km² of private forest, agricultural land and open spaces were claimed by development so that by the end of the 1990s, some 4,050 km² continued to be lost each year, a substantial portion of which was devoted to suburban homes on lots of half a hectare

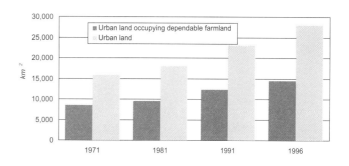

Urban Land Occupying Dependable Farmland in Canada, 1971-1996

(Dowling 2000; HUD 2000). In Canada, the amount of urban land occupying 'dependable' land (suitable for long-term crop production) increased from about 9,000 km² in 1971 to 14,000 km² in 1996 (see Figure 55). During this period, some 12,250 km² of land, half of which was dependable agricultural land, were converted to urban uses (Statistics Canada 2000b).

Apart from agricultural land, other natural landscape features are also lost to urban and suburban development, such as wetlands, forests, and wilderness areas, as well as the services they provide, such as wildlife habitat, flood and runoff control, and soil productivity (Parfrey 1999). Sprawl is a serious threat to wildlife and plants as it destroys and degrades the habitat on which these species depend for their survival. Habitat conversion to urban, suburban, or agricultural development accounts for 2 to 20 percent of species loss in the lower 48 states (The Biodiversity Project 2000). In the 10 years between 1982 and 1992, fully 2,085,945 ha of forestland, 1,525,314 ha of cultivated cropland, 943,598 ha of

Figure 55
Urban land use occupying dependable farmland in Canada, 1971-1996.

Source: Statistics Canada 2000c

Box 63: Smart Growth

In the past 10 years, a 'smart growth' movement has emerged in North America to combat sprawl. Smart growth is promoted by a broad coalition including environmental NGOs, social justice activists, local government officials, urban planners, affordable-housing advocates, and most recently, among some developers and others in the real estate industry (Katz and Liu 2000). The movement—including sustainable city initiatives (see Box 64) and the new urbanism approach, which advocates redesigning conventional suburban developments as small towns—promotes high-density neighborhoods characterized by a balance of mixed residential, office, and retail land uses in close proximity, with civic buildings clustered in a town center; the shrinking of travel distances, which encourages walking and cycling and privileges public transit; the preservation of open green spaces and farmland; the involvement of residents in city planning processes; and respect for the area's history and architecture (Parfrey 1999;

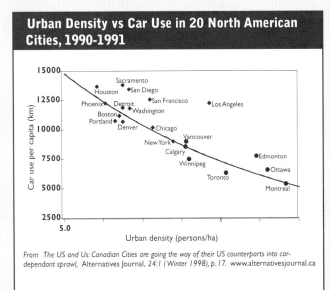

Urban Density vs Car Use in 20 North American Cities, 1990-1991

From The US and Us: Canadian Cities are going the way of their US counterparts into car-dependant sprawl, Alternatives Journal, 24:1 (Winter 1998), p. 17. www.alternativesjournal.ca

Figure 56 *Source: Raad and Kenworthy 1998*

Baker 2000; Duany 2000; Sierra Club 2000b). This agenda emphasizes 'smart' growth, rather than 'no' growth, and seeks to reform codes and ordinances to permit the development of smart growth characteristics and create urban growth boundaries (ULI 1999). Figure 56 shows that where urban density is highest, car use per capita is lowest, and illustrates the fact that Canadian cities are much less affected by sprawl than their US neighbors. Public transportation use is three times higher and population densities 1.8 times greater than in US metropolitan areas (Raad and Kenworthy 1998).

Compact development techniques advocated by smart growth include building within an already urbanized area, redeveloping on cleaned-up contaminated sites or 'brownfields', and cluster development on reduced-size lots. Such development encourages smart growth attributes by using up less land area and helping to reduce travel distances; encouraging walking and cycling; privileging public transit; preserving open green spaces, wildlife habitat, and farmland; and reducing impervious surface areas in order to improve drainage and water quality (EPA 2001).

pastureland, and 774,029 ha of rangeland were converted to urban uses in the United States (WRI, UNEP, UNDP, and World Bank 1996).

The spread of paved areas accompanying urban and suburban sprawl increases the risk of floods as rain flows into gutters instead of seeping into the ground to replenish groundwater supplies. Urban runoff is also a significant source of pollutants such as oil and heavy metals that are washed into water courses (WRI,

UNEP, UNDP, and World Bank 1996). With accumulated sediments, habitat disturbance, and declining water quality, many US urban water-sheds are suffering changes to the natural hydrological cycle (Samuelsohn 2001).

Sprawl also has social and eco-nomic consequences, including traffic congestion and related costs for petrol burned and time lost, deteriorating inner cities that are often fragmented along class and racial lines, and suburban problems of isolation and lack of sense of community (Raad and Kenworthy 1998; Dowling 2000). Sprawl-exacer-bated congestion costs an estimated US $72 to 78 billion a year for lost time and fuel in the United States, representing an estimated 4.5 billion hours of extra travel time and 25.7 billion liters of fuel wasted during traffic jams. The average annual

delay per person rose from 11 hours in 1982 to 36 hours in 1999 (Dowling 2000; TTI 2001). Studies also reveal that low-density, non-contiguous settlement requires more money for municipal services and infrastructure than compact development does (Chen 2000).

Car-centered development can exacerbate disparities between the rich and poor and worsen the plight of the underprivileged. For ex-ample, although the automobile is the only practicable means of transport in some US cities, one-third of the nation's population is too young, too old, or too poor to drive a car (O'Meara Sheehan 2001). Inner cities and their resi-dents also bear the costs of sprawl. Once-thriving downtown businesses in some places close as urban tax bases lose funding. Furthermore, most US federal housing subsidies

Box 64: Sustainable Cities

Sustainable city and community approaches, which address economic, environmental, and social issues through public participation, have also been applied to urban sprawl, and inner-city and brownfield development to build healthy communities with the features characteristic of smart growth (Lachman 1997).

Seattle, Washington, was one of the first US cities to explicitly incorporate sustainability into its community development plans. One of the city's policies, the Seattle Comprehensive Plan, aimed to increase the density of jobs, housing, and amenities; reduce urban sprawl and traffic congestion; and create an 'urban village' of distinct neighborhoods (Lachman 1997). Seattle also developed a set of sustainability indicators to measure the quality of economic, ecological, social, and cultural health in its communities, and its 'Sustainable Seattle' reports have won international awards and inspired other communities in North America and around the world to monitor their own progress toward a more sustainable future (SCN 1998).

A number of 'urban villages' throughout Canada display some of the features of sustainable neighborhoods: Kitsilano in Vancouver, Fort Rouge in Winnipeg, the Beaches in Toronto, Plateau Mont-Royal in Montreal and Spring Garden in Halifax (CMHC 2001). North America is home to 44 of the some 350-member governments of the International Council for Local Environmental Initiatives (ICLEI), which commits them to develop sustainability plans (ICLEI 2000).

go to well-off suburban homeowners, not to inner-city residents. While there has been a recent trend toward resurgence in many US downtowns, such as Philadelphia, Chicago, New York, Denver, and Houston, it has generally benefited better-off residents. Also, there is evidence that gentrification of inner cities can raise housing costs and slow employment growth (Jud 2001), pushing out low-income families. A 2001 United Nations report warns that despite North America's general prosperity com-

pared to other world regions, problems of residential segregation, discrimination in housing markets, and affordability persist, particularly in its larger cities (UNCHS 2001).

As highlighted in the atmosphere section, the increased reliance on automobiles that is both a cause and consequence of sprawl has created air quality problems and related human health impacts from car emissions. Cleaner, more efficient vehicles and more stringent emissions regulations have generally improved air quality in many North

American cities since the 1970s. These gains are being eroded, however, due in some degree to decentralized development. Although today's cars are 90 percent cleaner than those of the 1970s, US citizens now drive on average more than twice as many kilometers as they did in the 1970s (see Figures 51 and 52) (Dowling 2000; HUD 2000). Furthermore, as underscored in the atmosphere section, transportation is a leading contributor to greenhouse gases, and the consequences of climate change due to human activity are a cause of increasing concern. Health can be affected in other ways, too. For example, the sedentary lifestyle that often comes with reliance on cars contributes to obesity problems in adults and children (Chen 2000).

Increasingly, state and local governments are implementing smart growth and sustainable city plans to address sprawl (see Boxes 63 and 64, previous page). Successful 'infill' projects in which decaying properties or vacant lots are developed to help cities rebound are now more common. On the other hand, in many places it is still less expensive in the short term for developers to buy and build on land outside city zones (Chen 2000).

The smart growth movement in the United States has enjoyed a broad base of popular support over the past decade. In 1998, voters passed 70 percent of 240 smart growth ballot initiatives focused on preserving green space (Dowling 2000). Although most activity has been directed at the planning levels of government, the agenda has more recently gained acceptance by national and municipal leaders across the country (Nelson 2000). At the federal level, smart growth has been endorsed through a number of new initiatives. In 1996, the US Environmental Protection Agency joined with several non-profit and government organizations to form the Smart Growth Network (SGN) to encourage sustainable urban development (Arigoni 2001).

The US 1998 Transportation Equity Act (TEA-21) reduces the share of funding dedicated to new highways and provides some additional funding for transit and paths for pedestrians and cyclists (ULI 1999). But critics point out that TEA-21 dedicates more than four times more money to highways than to public transit (Sierra Club 2000a). The Livable Communities Initiative budget also gives money to mass transit, invests in local initiatives to ease congestion, and acts as a clearinghouse to help voluntary grassroots initiatives find resources to combat sprawl (FTA 2000). The 2000 budget included a large one-time investment for land protection through the Land Legacy Initiative (Baker 2000). And another federal initiative, the New Markets urban revitalization plan, is intended to stimulate business investment in poor communities and reverse or curb gentrification that pushes poor families out (HUD 2000). Business initiatives are also appearing: in 1999, the National Association of

Home Builders published its policy on smart growth, which includes the promotion of building to higher densities, revitalizing cities and older suburbs, and preserving meaningful open space and protecting environmentally sensitive areas (NAHB 1999).

The anti-sprawl movement is not as strong in Canada, largely because sprawl and its impacts are less evident. However, most of Canada's major urban regions are instituting long-range transportation plans aimed at reducing car dependency and adopting strategies for higher-density, mixed-use urban development (Raad and Kenworthy 1998). The province of Ontario's initiative involves developing a vision and overall goals for smart growth, growth plans for 5 zones through stakeholder consultation, and a 10-year US $5.9 billion Transit Investment Plan (Government of Ontario 2001). The Transportation Association of Canada (TAC) provided national leadership for sustainable urban transportation through its 1993 long-term generic vision for multi-use urban development, compact communities, and viable transport options that include pedestrian, cycling, and transit infrastructure. Many local governments across the country have adopted the TAC's New Urban Vision key objectives and principles (Stephens 2000). Reflecting this trend is the rise in the popularity of public transit since 1996, with a major surge in ridership in 1999 and 2000 (EC 2001).

Canada and the United States share a common airshed, common watersheds and common routes for migratory species in the transboundary Georgia Basin/Puget Sound region of the west coast. Through the Joint Statement of Cooperation for the Georgia Basin/Puget Sound Ecosystem, Environment Canada and the US EPA agreed to develop and identify forums and mechanisms for residents and decision-makers to share information on Smart Growth/Sustainable Development issues. Two such forums in 2001 gave multi-stakeholder participants a chance to share their experience and knowledge on best practices in smarter urban design and sustainable growth. The two countries are also developing a suite of coordinated transboundary sustainability indicators (EC 2002)

As part of its action plan on climate change, in 2000 Canada established the Green Municipal Fund to stimulate investment in innovative municipal infrastructure projects and environmental practices to help municipalities reduce greenhouse gas emissions, address air, water, and soil pollution, and promote renewable resources (FCM 2001). The Canada Mortgage and Housing Corporation also recently began promoting housing in sustainable neighborhoods that feature smart growth attributes (CMHC 2001). Canada and the United States also joined forces to tackle sprawl in the ecosystems they share in the Georgia Basin (see box 65).

There are still many hurdles on the path to smart growth and sustainable cities: powers to address sprawl are generally fractured among federal, state/provincial, and local governments and their proper roles are still undefined (Stoel Jr. 1999; Dowling 2000); adequate funding and effective compliance regimes to ensure policy implementation are lacking (Raad and Kenworthy 1998); policy solutions fail to reflect the many forces driving development patterns and to make the link between affordable housing and smart growth; and transportation strategies are short of funding and clear thinking. To some, smart growth implies the loss of individual freedom and property rights, and this fear fuels an anti-smart growth lobby (Stoel Jr. 1999; Katz and Liu 2000). Vested interests of the car manufacturing industry are so powerful and suburban sprawl is so entrenched in the North American landscape, infrastructure, and psyche that reversing the trend is a formidable challenge.

Ecological Footprint
North America's urban and suburban pattern of growth is one of the principal forces driving the global increase in energy demand, even though the region has only 5 percent of the world's population (WRI, UNEP, UNDP, and World Bank 1996). North American cities, with three-quarters of the region's population, are major consumers of the world's natural resources and major producers of its wastes. As a result, their impact on the global environment is larger than that of any other region.

Urbanization has a profound effect on the amount and kind of energy consumed, and, along with population growth, economic development, industrialization, and low-priced energy, it is one of the principal forces driving the global increase in energy demand (WRI, UNEP, UNDP, and World Bank 1996). Per capita consumption rose steadily over the past three decades: on average, in industrialized countries such as Canada and the United States, it grew at 2.3 percent per year over the past 25 years. Like all urban areas, North American cities need to import their basic requirements of food, fuel, and water from a distance. Globalization has been an important driving force in changing consumption and production patterns as the accelerated movement of goods, information, and people provides consumers with an

Box 66: The Ecological Footprint

The impact of a region, a nation, a city, or an individual on the global environment is increasingly referred to as the ecological footprint. This term expresses the impact of a given population as the amount of productive land and water needed to produce the resources it consumes and to assimilate its

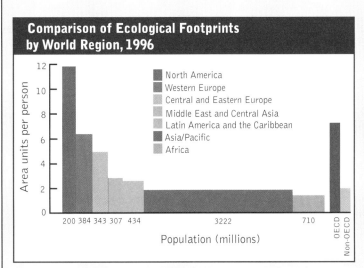

Figure 57 *Source: WWF 2000*

wastes, using prevailing technology (Wackernagel 1999). Thus, it is not simply a measure of the amount of land consumed by an average city resident or by an entire city within its national borders, but rather includes all the land or land equivalent in other parts of the world required by that individual or city to function. The ecological footprint is measured in 'area units' with one unit representing one ha of biologically productive space. Although the approach is still evolving, it is a useful tool to aggregate human impact on the earth into one number. It vividly expresses the notion that the larger the footprint of an individual, a city, or a nation, the more of the world's global resources it consumes and the more it uses the planet's available waste sinks. According to *The Living Planet Report 2000*, in 1996, North America's total ecological footprint was about four times larger than the world average (WWF 2000) (see Figure 57). Compared to the amount of land the average US citizen uses to support his or her current lifestyle, however, the average Canadian lives on a footprint that is 30 percent smaller (Redefining Progress 2002).

A person's ecological footprint can be calculated by dividing the regional or national total consumption by its population size. Using this method, the City of Toronto needs about 7.6 ha of productive ecosystem per capita to satisfy primary consumption of food, wood products, fuel, and waste-processing capacity, which means that the city, newly amalgamated to include its suburban neighborhoods, impacts an area over 280 times its actual size (Onisto, Krause, and Wackernagel 1998).

increased variety of choices (UN 2001). Wealthy cities and the wealthier groups within cities tend to appropriate more materials, food, and energy as well as waste assimila-

Comparison of CO_2 Footprints by World Region, 1996

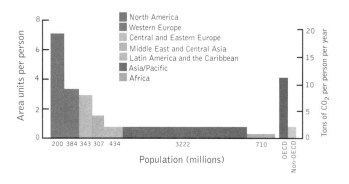

Figure 58

Comparison of CO_2 footprints by world region, 1996.

Source: WWF 2000

tion capacity from other regions. Thus, wealthy cities, or neighborhoods in cities, of which there are many in North America, contribute disproportionately to global environmental and social problems (WRI, UNEP, UNDP, and World Bank 1996; Onisto, Krause, and Wackernagel 1998). This is especially the case when the materials consumed originate in countries where environmental, public health, and worker protection laws are inadequate (US IWG 1999).

One of the most significant aspects of North America's large impact or its ecological footprint (see Box 66, previous page) is its large and growing energy use and related CO_2 emissions from fossil fuels (see also the atmosphere section). Total energy use in North America grew by 31 percent between 1972 and 1997 (UNEP 2001). Although the efficiency with which it

uses energy has improved over the past few decades, in per capita terms, efficiency gains have been much slower, reflecting an overall increase in energy use (OECD 1998). In 1996, North America's energy consumption represented 25 percent of total world primary energy consumption (UNEP 2001).

Between 1972 and 1996, the region's CO_2 emissions increased from 1.3 to 1.6 billion tons of carbon equivalent (Marland, Bowden, and Andres 1999). As shown in the atmosphere section, the United States is the leading producer of greenhouse gas emissions; by comparison, per person, they generate about 20 times the per capita emissions of India (Sandalow and Bowles 2001). Although Canada produces only 2.5 percent of global greenhouse gases, Canadians are the world's second-largest per capita energy consumers. Cities are not responsible *per se* for increased greenhouse gas emissions, but presently urban lifestyles, especially of the wealthy, are linked to higher consumption and energy use patterns. An estimated 40 percent of total North American carbon dioxide emissions come from 50 metropolitan areas (UNDP, UNEP, World Bank, and WRI 2000). In 1996, North America's CO_2 footprint was almost five times that of the world average (WWF 2000) (see Figure 58).

In terms of fuel, North America's per capita annual gasoline consumption for motor vehicles was 1,637 litres per person in 1997, or nine times the world average (UNDP,

UNEP, World Bank, and WRI 2000; UN 2001). In addition to fossil fuels, the region consumes more per capita of many other raw and processed resources than any other region in the world. There is, however, a modest trend toward decoupling economic growth and natural resource use (WRI 2000). Per capita consumption is relatively stable, except for plastic and paper, but population growth means that total resource consumption is still increasing. In 1990, the United States used almost seven times the per capita world average in plastic and petroleum feed stocks (PCSD 1996a).

The nation also consumes nearly a quarter of the world's industrial round wood, of which about 40 percent is used for construction. Most of this wood goes to building homes. Three times as many homes were built in the past 30 years as in the preceding three decades and although the average US family size dropped by 16 percent, the size of newly built single-family homes expanded by 48 percent (Abramovitz and Mattoon 1999; Bartuska 2000). Wood is used more efficiently, however, as old-growth forests decline and economic and social pressures spur improvements in forest practices and in new harvesting, processing, and recycling technologies (Abramovitz and Mattoon 1999). Paper consumption is also large and growing despite the growth of paper recycling. Average per capita paper consumption in North America in 1998 was six times

the world average (UNDP, UNEP, World Bank, and WRI 2000). According to *The Living Planet Report 2000*, in 1996, North America's 'forest footprint' was 4.4 times that of the world average (WWF 2000).

North America also produces more municipal solid waste per person than any other region. Municipal solid waste generated in the United States continues to grow, but at a much slower rate than before 1970, as waste recovery increases and discards to land fills decrease (see Figure 59). Light-

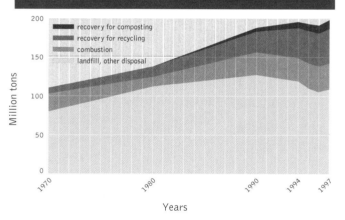

Solid Waste Disposal in the United States, 1970-1997

weight but high-volume materials such as paper and plastic are replacing dense and heavy materials in the waste stream, however, increasing waste volumes (PCSD 1996a). The continued use of older technologies coupled with a consumer lifestyle based on the desire for mobility, convenience, and product disposability has limited the further advancement of resource efficiency and waste reduction (UN 2001).

The impacts of waste, experienced both locally and at great

Figure 59
Solid waste disposal in the United States, 1970-1997.

Source: Franklin Associates 1999

distances from cities themselves, are a product both of urbanization (wastes concentrated in one place) and economic growth and industrialization. The wealthier the city, the more waste it produces. In addition, waste composition changes from

primarily biodegradable organic materials to plastics and other synthetic materials that take much longer to decompose (WRI, UNEP, UNDP, and World Bank 1996).

Clearly, North America's urban industrial society has an inequitable and unsustainable impact on the global environment. Agenda 21 identified unsustainable consumption and production, especially by industrialized countries, as the major cause of global environmental deterioration (UN 2001).

Since 1993, the issue of sustainable patterns of consumption and production has entered policy debate. Both federal governments promote ecoefficiency through a number of their programs. The US President's Council on Sustainable Development (PCSD) has recommended national goals for natural resources stewardship, population planning, and sustainable consumption (PCSD 1996a; PCSD 1996b). The US EPA has a number of programs to increase energy efficiency, including the Energy Star Building Program, the Green Lights Program and the Design for the Environment Program. Resource reduction efforts have led to the tripling of the proportion of waste recovered between 1970 and 1993 (UN 1997). In Canada waste minimization is also part of a variety of federal and provincial initiatives to promote more sustainable production and consumption. A 1992 target set by the National Packaging Protocol of reducing the amount of packaging sent for disposal by 20 percent was exceeded. And the federal government has developed energy efficiency programs, including greening its motor vehicle fleet and conducting research into bio-diesel fuels. Its Environmental Choice Program is designed to support the reduction of energy and materials consumption (UN 1997).

Industry is increasingly restructuring its processes and re-sourcing raw materials to reduce their environmental impact. Some are turning to the environmental goods and services sector to make the savings that often come with investing in eco-efficient operations. In 1995, the United States accounted for 40 percent of the current market in the pollution control industry and in Canada, business sales in environmental goods and services rose 11 percent in 1997 from the previous year (Statistics Canada 1999). There is also a perceptible rise in the number of 'green' or socially and environmentally conscious consumers (Coop America 2000).

North America's urban industrial society simultaneously provides a quality of life envied by many of the world's developing countries and levels a disproportionate environmental impact on the planet. As shown above, dense settlement patterns that are planned to be compact and efficient can reduce pressures on the environment. Compared to dispersed settlement patterns, cities can provide environmental and economic savings from economies of scale—recycling initiatives and per capita energy use for heating, cooling, and mass transit, for example, all benefit from high population densities. High-density development can also reduce pressures to convert agricultural and wilderness areas to urban uses (WRI, UNEP, UNDP, and World Bank 1996). While North America's smart growth and sustainable city programs have the potential to help reduce its ecological footprint, more resources and political support are needed to make them a reality.

References

Abramovitz, Janet N., and Ashley T. Mattoon (1999). Reorienting the Forest Products Economy. In *State of the World 1999: A Worldwatch Institute Report on Progress Toward a Sustainable Society*, edited by L. Starke. New York, W.W. Norton and Company

Arigoni, Danielle (2001). *Affordable Housing and Smart Growth: Making the Connection.* Smart Growth Network and the National Neighborhood Coalition, US Environmental Protection Agency, Development, Community, and Environment Division http://www.smartgrowth.org/pdf/epa_ah-sg.pdf. Accessed 8 February 2002

Baker, Linda (2000). Growing Pains/Malling America: The Fast-Moving Fight to Stop Urban Sprawl. *Emagazine.com*, (10) 3: http://www.emagazine.com/may-june_2000/0500feat1.html. Accessed 8 February 2002

Bartuska, Ann (2000). *Statement of Ann Bartuska Director of Forest Management Forest Service, United States Department of Agriculture, before the Subcommittee on Forests and Forest Health, Committee on Resources United States House of Representatives, July 25, 2000 Concerning The Future of National Forest Timber Sales.* Committee on Resources, Subcommittee on Forests & Forest Health http://resourcescommittee.house.gov/106cong/forests/00jul25/bartuska.htm. Accessed 8 February 2002

CEC (2000). *Booming Economies, Silencing Environments, and the Paths to Our Future: Background Note by the Commission for Environmental Cooperation on Critical and Emerging Environmental Trends.* Montreal, Commission for Environmental Cooperation of North America http://www.cec.org/pubs_docs/documents/index.cfm?varlan=english&ID=66. Accessed 26 February 2002

Chen, Donald, D.T. (2000). The Science of Smart Growth. *Scientific American* 283 (6):84-91

CMHC (2001). *Your Next Move: Choosing a Neighbourhood with Sustainable Features.* Ottawa, Canada Mortgage and Housing Corporation

Coop America (2000). *Forty-four Million Americans Can't be Wrong.* Coop America http://www.coopamerica.org/business/B44million.htm. Accessed 8 February 2002

Dowling, Timothy J. (2000). Reflections on Urban Sprawl, Smart Growth, and the Fifth Amendment. *University of Pennsylvania Law Review* 148 (3):873

Duany, Andres (2000). A New Theory of Urbanism (Box in The Science of Smart Growth, by Donald D.T. Chen). *Scientific American* 283 (6):90

Duany, Andres, Elizabeth Plater-Zyberk, and Jeff Speck (2000). *Suburban Nation: The Rise of Sprawl and the Decline of the American Dream.* New York, Farrar, Straus and Giroux

EC (1998). *Canadian Passenger Transportation, National Environmental Indicator Series, SOE Bulletin No. 98-5.* Ottawa, Environment Canada, State of the Environment Reporting Program http://www.ec.gc.ca/ind/English/Transpo/default.cfm. Accessed 28 May 2002

EC (2001). *Sustainable Transportation: The Canadian Context. Monograph No. 15.* Environment Canada. A Canadian Contribution to the Dialogue at the Ninth Session of the United Nations Commission on Sustainable Development, April 16 to 27, 2001 http://www.ec.gc.ca/agenda21/2001/pdfs/transport.pdf. Accessed 14 February 2002

EPA (2001). *Our Built and Natural Environments: A Technical Review of the Interactions between Land Use, Transportation, and Environmental Quality.* Vol. EPA 231-R-01-022. Washington DC, US Environmental Protection Agency, Development Community and Environment Division, http://www.smartgrowth.org/pdf/built_environment/chapter3.pdf. Accessed 8 February 2002

FCM (2001). Green Municipal Funds Investments Worth $4.5 Million Will Improve Municipal Infrastructure and the Environment. In *News Release.* Federation of Canadian Municipalities, Government of Canada http://www.fcm.ca/english/. Accessed 26 February 2002

Franklin Associates (1999). *Characterization of Municipal Solid Waste in the United States: 1998 Pudate.* US Environmental Protection Agency http://www.epa.gov/epaoswer/non-hw/muncpl/pubs/98charac.pdf. Accessed 31 May 2002

FTA (2000). *Livable Communities*. Federal Transit Administration http://www.fta.dot.gov/library/policy/IFT/iftb.htm. Accessed 8 February 2002

HUD (2000). *The State of the Cities 2000: Megaforces Shaping the Future of the Nation's Cities*. US Department of Housing and Urban Development, Andrew Cuomo, Secretary http://www.hud.gov/pressrel/socrpt.pdf. Accessed 8 February 2002

ICLEI (2000). *About ICLEI*. The International Council for Local Environmental Initiatives http://www.iclei.org/about.htm. Accessed 8 February 2002

Jud, Donald (2001). *Growth Can be 'Smart', But Also Costly*. The Business Journal http://triangle.bcentral.com/triangle/stories/2001/09/03/editorial1.html. Accessed 7 February 2002

Katz, Bruce, and Amy Liu (2000). Moving Beyond Sprawl: Toward a Broader Metropolitan Agenda. *Brookings Review* 18 (2): 31-4

Kolankiewicz, Leon, and Roy Beck (2001). *Weighing Sprawl Factors In Large US Cities: A Report on the Nearly Equal Roles Played by Population Growth and Land Use Choices in the Loss of Farmland and Natural Habitat to Urbanization*. Sprawl City http://www.sprawlcity.org/studyUSA/. Accessed 6 February 2002

Lachman, Beth E. (1997). *Linking Sustainable Community Activities to Pollution Prevention: A Sourcebook*. RAND http://www.rand.org/publications/MR/MR855/. Accessed 7 February 2002

Marland, G., T.A. Boden, and A.L. R.J. Andres (2001). *Global, Regional, and National Fossil Fuel Emissions*. US Department of Energy, Carbon Dioxide Information Analysis Center http://cdiac.esd.ornl.gov/trends/emis/tre_afr.htm. Accessed 8 February 2002

NAHB (1999). *Smart Growth: Building Better Place to Live, Work and Play*. National Association of Home Builders http://www.smartgrowth.org/pdf/smart.pdf. Accessed 26 February 2002

Nelson, Arthur C. (2000). Smart Growth: Urban Containment and Housing Prices. *Journal of Housing and Community Development* 57 (5):45-9

O'Meara Sheehan, Molly (2001). *City Limits: Putting the Brakes on Sprawl*. Washington DC, Worldwatch Institute

OECD (1998). *Toward Sustainable Development: Environmental Indicators*. Paris, Organization for Economic Co-operation and Development

Onisto, Lawrence J., Eric Krause, and Mathis Wackernagel (1998). *How Big is Toronto's Ecological Footprint? Using the Concept of Appropriated Carrying Capacity for Measuring Sustainability*. Centre for Sustainable Studies and the City of Toronto http://www.city.toronto.on.ca/eia/efreport.pdf. Accessed 7 February 2002

Parfrey, Eric (1999). *Stop Sprawl: What is "Smart Growth"?* Sierra Club http://www.sierraclub.org/sprawl/community/smartgrowth.asp. Accessed 8 February 2002

PCSD (1996a). *Population and Consumption: Task Force Report*. Washington DC, The President's Council on Sustainable Development

PCSD (1996b). *Eco-Efficiency: Task Force Report*. Washington DC, The President's Council on Sustainable Development

Pope, Carl (1999). *Solving Sprawl: The Sierra Club Rates the States*. Sierra Club: 1999 Sierra Club Sprawl Report http://www.sierraclub.org/sprawl/report99/. Accessed 8 February 2002

Pucher, John (1998). Back on Track: Eight Steps to Rejuvenate Public Transport in Canada. *Alternatives* 24 (1):26-34

Raad, Tamim, and Jeff Kenworthy (1998). The US and Us: Canadian Cities are Going the Way of their US Counterparts into Car-Dependent Sprawl. *Alternatives* 24 (1):14-22

Redefining Progress (2002). *Sustainability Program: Ecological Footprint Accounts* http://www.rprogress.org/programs/sustainability/ef/. Accessed 29 May 2002

Samuelsohn, Darren (2001). *Watershed Studies Find Big Challenges for Urban Areas*. Greenwire, 14 August http://www.eenews.net/Greenwire/Backissues/081401gw.htm#6. Accessed 26 September 2001.

Sandalow, David B., and Ian A. Bowles (2001). Fundamentals of Treaty-Making on Climate Change. *Science* 292 (5523):1839-40

SCN (1998). *Sustainable Seattle Indicators 1998*. Seattle Community Network http://www.scn.org/sustainable/indicat.htm. Accessed 7 February 2002

Sierra Club (1998). *The Dark Side of the American Dream: The Costs and Consequences of Suburban Sprawl*. 1998 Sierra Club Sprawl Report http://www.sierraclub.org/sprawl/report98/. Accessed 8 February 2002

Sierra Club (2000a). *Sprawl Costs Us All: How Your Taxes Fuel Suburban Sprawl*. 2000 Sierra Club Sprawl Report http://www.sierraclub.org/sprawl/report00/sprawl.pdf. Accessed 8 February 2002

Sierra Club (2000b). *Smart Choices or Sprawling Growth: A 50-State Survey of Development*. The Sierra Club Report on Sprawl http://www.sierraclub.org/sprawl/50statesurvey/. Accessed 8 February 2002

Sorensen, A. Ann, Richard P. Greene, and Karen Russ (1997). *Farming on the Edge*. DeKalb, Ill., American Farmland Trust, Center for Agriculture in the Environment, Northern Illinois University

Statistics Canada (1999). Environment Industry. *The Daily: Statistics Canada* Thursday, March 4

Statistics Canada (2000c). *Human Activity and the Environment*. http://estat.statcan.ca/HAE/english/modules/module-5/mod-5b.htm Statistics Canada. Accessed 6 February 2002

Statistics Canada (2001a). *Concept: Geography*. Statistics Canada http://www.statcan.ca/english/concepts/definitions/geography.htm. Accessed 6 February 2002

Statistics Canada (2001b). Urban Consumption of Agricultural Land. *Rural and Small Town Canada: Analysis Bulletin* 3 (2)

Stephens, Don (2000). *Measuring Progress: Toward the New Vision for Urban Transportation*. Transportation Association of Canada http://www.tac-atc.ca/products/briefing/indicators.pdf. Accessed 8 February 2002

Stoel Jr., Thomas B. (1999). Reining in Urban Sprawl. *Environment* 41 (4):6-11, 29-33

The Biodiversity Project (2000). *Getting on Message: Making the Biodiversity-Sprawl Connection*. The Biodiversity Project http://www.biodiversityproject.org/messagekit.htm#fact%20sheets. Accessed 8 February 2002

TTI (2001). *2001 Urban Mobility Study*. Texas Transportation Institute http://mobility.tamu.edu/ums/. Accessed 7 February 2002

ULI (1999). *Smart Growth: Myth and Fact*. Urban Land Institute http://www.uli.org/Pub/Media/A_issues/A_SmL4_Myth.pdf. Accessed 8 February 2002

UN (1997). *Earth Summit + 5: Special Session of the General Assembly to Review and Appraise the Implementation of Agenda 21*. United Nations Department of Economic and Social Affairs http://www.un.org/esa/earthsummit/. Accessed 8 February 2002

UN (2001). *Commission on Sustainable Development Acting as the Preparatory Committee for the World Summit on Sustainable Development Organizational Session: Report of the Secretary-General*, Advance Unedited Copy: E/CN.17/2001/-: United Nations Economic and Social Council

UNCHS (2001). *Costs, Benefits of Globalization Unevenly Distributed In Cities, Says UN Report*. United Nations Centre for Human Settlements (Habitat) http://www.un.org/News/Press/docs/2001/hab173.doc.htm. Accessed 7 February 2002

UNDP, UNEP, World Bank, and WRI (2000). *World Resources 2000-2001: People and Ecosystems, the Fraying Web of Life*. Washington DC, World Resources Institute

UNEP (2001). *UNEP Data Portal (Data derived from WRI sources)* United Nations Environment Programme

United Nations Population Division (2001). *World Urbanization Prospects: The 1999 Revision: Key Findings*. United Nations Population Division http://www.un.org/esa/population/pubsarchive/urbanization/urbanization.pdf. Accessed 31 May 2002

US Census Bureau (2000). *Urban and Rural Classification: Urban and Rural Criteria*. US Census Bureau, United States Census 2000 http://www.census.gov/geo/www/ua/ua_2k.html. Accessed 6 February 2002

US IWG (1999). *Materials*, US Interagency Working Group on Industrial Ecology, Material and Energy Flows

Wackernagel, Mathis (1999). *What We Use and What We Have: Ecological Footprint and Ecological Capacity*. San Francisco, Redefining Progress

Wendell Cox Consultancy (2000a). *Urban & Government Area Geographical Concepts*. Demographia, Wendell Cox Consultancy http://www.demographia.com/db-ua.htm. Accessed 6 February 2002

Wendell Cox (2000b). *US Urban Personal Vehicle & Public Transport Market Share from 1945*. The Public Purpose, Urban Transport Fact Book http://www.publicpurpose.com/ut-usptshare45.htm. Accessed 8 February 2002

WRI, UNEP, UNDP, and World Bank (1996). *World Resources 1996–97, A Guide to the Global Environment: The Urban Environment*, Oxford University Press, New York, United States, and Oxford, United Kingdom

WRI, UNEP, UNDP, and World Bank (1998). *World Resources 1998-99, A Guide to the Global Environment: Environmental Change and Human Health*, Oxford University Press, New York, United States, and Oxford, United Kingdom

WRI (2000). *Resource and Materials Use*. World Resources Institute http://www.wri.org/materials/. Accessed 8 February 2002

WWF (2000). *The Living Planet Report 2000*. World Wildlife Fund, UNEP, WCMC, The Centre for Sustainability Studies and Redefining Progress http://www.panda.org/livingplanet/lpr00/download.cfm. Accessed 7 February 2002

Analysis and Policy Options

11

The 30-Year Legacy

Signs of Progress

This survey of priority environmental issues in North America shows that the region has made notable progress in addressing a number of its most evident and serious environmental problems in the past 30 years:

- since the early 1970s, point sources of nitrogen and phosphorous, principally from the discharge of municipal sewage and industrial wastes, declined significantly;
- in many places, ambient air quality improved, industrial effluents declined, hazardous waste threats were reduced, and community recycling initiatives began;
- increasingly, protected areas were set aside for conservation and recreation;
- a new awareness of the regional and global nature of some environmental issues was aroused during the 1980s as the two countries joined forces to stop producing substances that deplete stratospheric ozone and control acid rain, and to tackle the grave pollution problems in the Great Lakes;
- during the 1990s, technological change in some sectors of the economy helped to curb a number of environmental pressures through less intensive focus on material production and moderate efficiency gains.

Significant Challenges Remain

While these are encouraging signs of progress, it is clear that significant challenges remain before North America is on a sustainable path. In many instances, the gains made in arresting environmental pollution and degradation have more recently been eroded by choices related to consumption increases and population growth. For example:

- progress in fuel efficiency has been offset by increases in the number of automobiles and the total number of kilometers traveled, and by a trend since 1984 toward heavier and less fuel-efficient passenger vehicles; and

- a consumer lifestyle based on the desire for mobility, convenience, and product disposability has undercut the further advancement of resource efficiency and waste reduction.

In addition, some problems persist despite notable progress. For example:

- soil and wetland losses still outpace gains;
- although withdrawal rates have declined, many aquifers are still being depleted; and
- even with large sulphur reductions, some regions still experience acid rain's long-term effects.

In other areas, new problems are emerging as scientific research reveals that some standards once thought adequate to protect human and environmental health are actually insufficient. For example:

- research in the last decade has demonstrated that ozone (O_3) and fine particulates impose far greater burdens on human health than previously thought;
- children are especially vulnerable to even trace amounts of environmental contaminants; and
- the potential for exposure to persistent toxic substances to cause reproductive and hormonal disruption is of growing concern.

Furthermore, new problems have emerged. For example, the movement of contaminants throughout ecosystems, water- and airsheds is increasingly recognized as an environmental and health issue:

- we know now that much water pollution is caused by pollutants from the air and that many are carried far from their sources to contaminate areas that appear pristine—some US National Parks and Arctic ecosystems and peoples, for instance; and
- diffuse pollution from non-point sources travels extensively through water courses. Nitrogen runoff into surface waters eventually reaches sensitive coastal ecosystems, contributing to 'dead zones', as in the Gulf of Mexico, and probably to red tides. It also seeps into groundwater and aquifers, where it is difficult to detect and to treat.

In addition, resource conservation has been less successful than local pollution abatement. Non-renewable resources, including water, have been intensively exploited:

- the collapse of the Atlantic cod fishery, increased concern over the fate of Pacific salmon, and international attention to the harvest of old-growth forest in the Pacific Northwest highlight the difficulty in reconciling conservation and economic goals and in persuading people of their inextricable linkage.

Finally, North America's ecological footprint exceeds that of any other region, extending beyond its borders to affect the global climate in particular. The region's energy use and vehicle use are among the pressures implicated in anthropogenic climate change, one of the world's most pressing environmental challenges.

Major Messages

The Environment Matters

Environment, the basis of existence
The environment is the foundation of human health, well-being, and security. Only with a healthy environment can we meet our physiological needs for air and water; obtain raw materials for food, clothing, shelter, tools, and recreation; and, less obviously, take advantage of the essential, unseen services that fully functioning ecosystems provide, like cleansing water, building soil, and regulating climate. In industrial urbanized societies like North America's, the link between the products we use and their original earthly sources becomes obscured. Failing to see the ecological—not to mention the cultural and spiritual—benefits we derive from nature, we too often take the biosphere's functions for granted, assuming its services to be free, and trusting that it will serve us in perpetuity.

Despite policy commitments to sustainable development and greater recognition of the connectedness of environmental and economic objectives, economic development is still the primary driver in North America. All too often, the environment is still treated as separate from human existence and relatively inessential.

Environment has economic value
Yet the fact remains, environmental goods and services have high international, national, and local value, and their misuse incurs economic and social costs. In recent years, researchers have conducted studies to determine the economic costs of environmental damage. Warning signs of degradation of our ecosystems are increasingly being felt by the economy—this report notes several examples:

- there is a strong correlation, for instance, between episodic, high ground-level ozone and hospitalization and worker absenteeism. The hidden costs of health care and labor losses, and reduced agricultural productivity are borne by society as a whole;
- damage from ozone is also to blame for more than US $500 million in annual reductions of agricultural and commercial forest yields in the United States;
- damage caused by bioinvasions in North America is also extremely costly to the agricultural industry, as well as to other industries, in terms of human health and outlays for pest control: about a quarter of the annual US agricultural GNP was lost to invasive species in 1998 in direct damage and control costs;
- there are also hidden costs related to the expansion of harmful algal blooms (HABs), which have been linked to excess nitrogen from land-based activities: over the past 20 years, HABs

in the United States led to losses of about US $100 million per year in medical-related expenses and impacts on the fishing and tourism industries, among others; and

- the collapse of the North Atlantic cod fishery had direct costs including the loss of enormous revenues from this once lucrative industry, considerable hardship inflicted on local communities, and costs to taxpayers through job creation and retraining programs in the Atlantic provinces, not to mention possibly irreparable harm to the marine ecosystem of which the species was a part.

Reforms Are Possible

In view of the world economy's dependence on the environment, respect for its limited carrying and assimilative capacities should be the foundation of sustainable development decision-making.

Need for indicators and environmental accounting

- indicators measuring the use and availability of resources are increasingly being developed in some economic sectors, and there has been progress as well in asset valuation and in developing various approaches to measuring sustainability. Better measures of the economic value of the environment and of the environmental impacts of economic activity are still needed, however.

- in addition to the need for novel indicators of progress, we also need to learn how to use them properly. Setting measurable policy goals and targets that are clearly linked to sustainability is one of the new frontiers. Although many of the natural environmental benefits we enjoy are beyond measure, putting a price on environmental goods and services by integrating environmental accounting within all sectors of the economy and at the company level as well can help heighten our understanding of the environment's crucial importance to human well-being and security.

Underpricing, or implicit subsidization, has stimulated North America's intensive exploitation of non-renewable resources, including energy and water. For example, cheap parking and other hidden subsidies, such as funds for highway development and low fuel prices, continue to promote car dependency and feed into a 'vicious cycle' of urban sprawl and declining transit use.

Need for reformed subsidies, incentives, and taxation

- without energy subsidies, energy prices would rise encouraging the adoption of more efficient vehicles and industrial equipment and reducing pollutant emissions. And without the incentives that road transport subsidies provide to drivers, traffic congestion, urban air pollution, and carbon-dioxide emissions might well be significantly lowered. Thus, reforming unnecessary subsidies could reduce government expenditures. Another way to reduce the hidden costs of environmental damage is through taxing pollution, resource depletion, or ecosystem degradation.

- energy price increases during the oil shocks, for example, had the effect of reducing energy intensity. Taxation should include pricing the (mostly free) environmental media such as clean air and clean water (such as water pricing). And a means of identifying situations in which environmental protection has contributed to economic development needs to be developed and effective processes disseminated. Green accounting also needs to be integrated into industries and businesses, as well as into local decision-making.

Costs to the environment should also be assessed through environmental assessments, which should continue to be promoted in all development processes, including trade agreements and international protocols.

Policy Performance

Sustainable development is part of government strategies
The establishment of environmental departments in national and state/provincial governments and regional and local agendas, along with new environmental laws and policies such as Clean Air and Clean Water acts, were instrumental in improving North America's environment early in the last 30 years. And following the 1987 Brundtland Report, sustainable development terminology entered environmental policies, although neither country adopted clear and measurable sustainability goals. In 1995, the Government of Canada required that federal departments prepare sustainable development strategies and report systematically on progress, and in 1992, the United States began to craft a national sustainability strategy. Most recently, policies have also taken a more integrated, holistic approach, as reflected in the shift in policy focus in resource-based industries from sustaining yields to environmentally and socially sound stewardship. As shown in this report, wetlands, forests, fish, and fire are increasingly valued over the longer term for the roles they play as parts of larger ecosystems and for the natural services they provide.

Command-and-control has been successful
Command-and-control measures, aided by some successful market instruments, have been successful in addressing issues with clear cause-

and-effect relationships such as stratospheric ozone depletion at the global level and local point-source pollution. The key regulatory tool established early in the 30-year period was controlling the amount of pollution tolerable for human safety. Most of the challenges North America now faces are more diffuse, pervasive, subtle, and complex than those confronted in the past, and are hence more difficult to deal with.

Need for more preventive approaches
As the region continues to address familiar environmental issues, these new problems pose more difficult challenges, and traditional centralized command and control regulations, which focused on controlling and mitigating pollution, and single-issue or sectoral approaches, no longer suffice. Halting POPs to prevent pullution is an example of the shift to more sustainable solutions. Included in the Stockholm 2001 POPs treaty both countries signed are commitments to the precautionary approach that move chemical regulation and management from a 'regulate-and-reduce' approach to a preventive one. A lack of scientific certainty regarding potential harm is no longer regarded as a barrier to taking preventive action. There is a need to continue to embrace this preventive approach to chemical regulation and environmental protection and entrench it into policies and decision-making.

Need for policy linkages
In the past decade, progress has been made in shifting away from studying physical impacts on the environment and the physical vulnerability of different ecosystems, to a more integrated understanding of the linkages between environmental change, and social, and economic strategies for coping with them. As we become more aware of the complex nature of environmental issues and ecosystem functions, and as new environmental challenges emerge, we need to introduce more integrated management policies and tools. Policies must continue to integrate social-economic-environmental approaches and move from environmental protection to the broader concept of resource management—witness the approach recently agreed upon for the management of old-growth forests in the Pacific Northwest.

Need to support municipal governments
Recent efforts to overcome environmental and social problems related to sprawl also provide lessons in how to address issues that require broader, more inclusive decision-making and land use planning. Local environmental governing bodies, especially where community- and city-level cooperation are integral aspects of decision-making, can help to steer and prioritize not only local action, but also international and national action. Since strengthening the voice of cities and municipal regions in decision-making creates capacity for successful policy, more emphasis should be placed on local and regional levels of environmental policy development and strengthening regional

initiatives, institutes, and alliances. Governments at all levels need to invest more in public transportation and to promote a move away from the use of personal vehicles, especially for commuting and short trips. Overcoming investments already made in present-day energy and transportation infrastructure to allow the adoption of renewable energy and alternative fuels, and moving toward new technologies while avoiding major disruptions remains a significant challenge.

Shared Ecosystems and Bilateral Cooperation

Long-standing history of cooperation
Canada and the United States have one of the longest common borders in the world and share ecosystems, air, and watersheds, wildlife and fishery resources. The two countries enjoy a long history of cooperation in managing their shared environment through numerous bilateral treaties, agreements, and other accords. The International Joint Commission (IJC) was instrumental in the cleanup of the Great Lakes over the past 30 years, and the Canada–US Air Quality Agreement has achieved notable success in regulating the pollutants that cause acid rain. Transboundary air pollution has more recently emerged as a problem requiring even greater cooperation between the two countries and they have strengthened these measures, agreeing to more aggressive NOx emission controls under the Ozone Annex to the Agreement, for example. The 1972

Great Lakes Water Quality Agreement (GLWQA) is another long-standing effort that committed the two countries to work together for a common cause.

International organizations help manage shared environments
During the 1990s, North American free trade strengthened the economic ties between the countries, and the movement of goods, services, capital, and ideas accelerated. At the same time, regional environmental degradation evoked heightened recognition of the interdependent nature of cross-border ecosystems. Since 1994, the Commission for Environmental Cooperation of North America (CEC) has created opportunities and forums for the two countries, together with Mexico, to soundly manage chemicals, assess and reduce the impacts of trade on the environment, and prioritize ways to conserve biodiversity, among other actions. The IJC and the CEC continue to be effective international organizations for managing transboundary resources, serving as models for similar challenges in the rest of the world.

Cross border management and research increasing
Government departments such as Forestry Canada and the US Forest Service, disaster prevention agencies, and fisheries departments also work hand in hand across the border. To better monitor and manage their shared agendas, the two countries have reconciled standards, such as those related to corporate average

fuel consumption and policies for greater road transportation energy efficiency and alternative fuels. They also conduct research together, including their international work on bioinvasions and bilateral research on children's health.

Need for ongoing environmental cooperation
In addition, Canada and the United States are party to many international accords in which they work with other countries to address global environmental problems. All these successful cooperative efforts between the two countries reveal the importance of bilateral action for both transboundary pollution and shared ecosystems and biodiversity. More than any other step, cooperative action helped to stem acid rain and to protect wetlands, for example. And even in transboundary issues of conflict the need for cooperation prevailed, as in the case of the Pacific Salmon Treaty.

Ongoing environmental cooperation is in the mutual interest of both countries. They need to continue to support bilateral institutions through stable funding arrangements, ensuring full transparency, the participation of all stakeholders, and the collaboration of the scientific community. Given the continental nature of climatic systems, it is vital that the two countries intensify their cooperative efforts to address both climate change and disaster preparedness by planning and implementing a comprehensive, integrated, binational strategy.

Public Participation and Stakeholder Involvement

NGOs influential
The birth of the modern environmental movement in North America early in the 1970s and continued pressure from NGOs have contributed significantly to the region's success in addressing environmental problems. Since the 1980s and the adoption of national and international goals for sustainable development, civil society has gained more opportunities for participation in environmental decision-making. Through NGOs and other voluntary organizations, working with corporate and financial interests and consumers, civil society has won a louder voice in influencing decisions and assumed a larger role in ensuring that environmental problems are addressed. NGOs were influential in helping to clean up the Great Lakes, for example.

Indigenous peoples gaining a voice
More recently, indigenous communities, which had been overlooked in decisions about resources that affect their livelihoods and cultures, have participated in land agreements and settlements and gained new rights and responsibilities over their environments. Examples highlighted in this report include the establishment of new forms of resource management based on shared responsibility by the James Bay Cree in Quebec and the Nuu-chah-nulth First Nation in BC, Canada. The integration of civil society, including indigenous

peoples, into the policy process in North America is also underscored earlier by the combined efforts of multiple parties to support a comprehensive plan to restore and preserve the Florida Everglades and the multi-stakeholder work to address habitat restoration and other concerns to help salmon recovery.

Need to increase public participation
Nongovernmental organizations and increased scientific understanding of ecosystems have both been instrumental in moving toward more holistic management systems and their adoption by governments and industry. Implementing these sustainability goals remains a challenge, and NGO observation will likely continue to play a role in helping to turn the concept of sustainable development into reality. It is critical that we continue to acknowledge the importance of local peoples' rights, improve the participation of all stakeholders, increase transparency, and invite more cooperative resource management in developing and implementing sustainable development programs. Indigenous knowledge systems (IKS), particularly those that reinforce sustainable development, should be more thoroughly researched and documented. Consultative processes to ensure that they are enshrined adequately in laws are a precondition for instituting such principles and rights. Legal and regulatory measures should also define community property rights and provide institutional legitimacy to community-based resource management practices by making communities part of the national legal and regulatory framework.

Need to increase industry ecoefficiency
While for the most part the environment is either ignored or still a peripheral consideration to economic interests in industry, some firms are trying to build it into their core strategies, as illustrated by the changes taking place in some logging companies in the Pacific Northwest highlighted in this report. Policy changes may still be required, however, to encourage the more holistic changes needed for industries to adopt ecoefficiency, especially if market incentives prove inadequate (CEC 2001).

Affluence and the Environment

Consumption offsetting environmental gains
The ability to address pollution and other problems that became apparent over the 30-year period was influenced not only by the institution of environmental governance and pressure from an informed and active civil society, but also by economic growth and general prosperity. On the other hand, it is ever more apparent that affluence stimulates consumption and energy use, which have offset advances in environmental efficiency. Fueled by economic prosperity, low energy prices, and population growth, per capita consumption has increased steadily since 1972. Rising per capita incomes and accompanying lifestyle changes are closely tied to many

environmentally significant consumption patterns. By 1996, North America's ecological footprint was four times greater than the world average, its forest footprint was 4.4 times larger, and its CO_2 footprint almost five times the world average. Per capita annual gasoline consumption for motor vehicles was nine times the world average. Thus, transportation in North America strongly affects worldwide CO_2 emissions. In 1997, the US transport sector accounted for more than one-third of total world transportation energy use and about 5 percent of CO_2 emitted worldwide as a result of human activity. Reliance on private automobiles for transport is a significant factor in North America's greenhouse gas emissions.

Climate change will have important impacts
Unsustainable patterns of consumption and production in North America are a major cause of global environmental deterioration. Clearly, North America has an inequitable and unsustainable impact on the global environment in particular, and contributes to a disproportionate degree to the changing global climate. Climate change will inevitably cause damage, especially to low-lying islands, coastal systems, and arid and semi-arid ecosystems, affecting millions of inhabitants of these regions, rich and poor. It may also contribute to a rise in the scale and intensity of natural weather hazards. Developing countries, particularly small-island developing states, are least able to cope with or

adapt to these changes and events, raising difficult questions of equity between the North and the South in terms of the emissions that cause human-induced climate change.

Global climate change will also have important impacts on North America. It is likely to increase the risks associated with invasive species and certain vectors may already be expanding their geographic ranges. The magnitude, frequency, and cost of extreme hydrological events in some regions of North America are forecast to increase, while higher temperatures could lead to an increase in insect populations and outbreaks of fire and human health threats. Water levels in inland lakes and streams may decline with consequences for both irrigation and human water consumption.

Urgent need to address climate change
Many of the environmental changes that will occur over the next 30 years have already been determined by past and current actions. Land degradation, natural resource use, biodiversity loss, freshwater scarcity, and impacts from a changing climate are shaping up as the most difficult issues to address. Even if the United States and Canada were to meet the Kyoto targets, it would have a marginal effect on the concentration of greenhouse gases in the atmosphere, and even with their stabilization in the long term, warming will continue for several decades. Given its large share of the planet's CO_2 emissions, which are directly proportional to fuel use, the region will need a substantial

change in its automobile use, more fuel-efficient technologies, and changes in municipal planning and urban development strategies, including investment in public transport. None of this will happen without understanding the role of policy drivers and having the political will to introduce improvements.

Need for more appropriate models
Many of North America's environmental policies underscored in this report provide blueprints for other regions. With globalization, however, there is the danger that inefficient and wasteful consumption patterns will spread. To prevent this, North America along with other developed countries need to accept more responsibility for environmental change. To date, lacking guaranteed protection of economic interests and the individual capacity to connect climate to individual behavior, North America has not achieved committed cuts to greenhouse gas emissions and the United States has declined to support the Kyoto Accord, a step with uncertain impacts on Canada-US relations and their cooperation toward environmental goals.

To achieve sustainable development and equal shares in a world with limited resources and capacities for renewal, producers and consumers—especially in high-income nations such as Canada and the United States—will need to adopt development approaches that limit material growth. The use or waste of nonrenewable resources must be minimized. Appropriate national

and regional development policies should provide a viable alternative to inappropriate and unsustainable levels of consumption and point the way to move from material-intensive development to material-minimal development.

A strategic policy framework built on a vision of human well-being based on quality and values rather than quantity and materials is required. Reduction of resource use, energy, and waste must be encouraged through policies aimed at changing behavior to curb conspicuous consumption and adopt new, appropriate production and consumption patterns.

Need to move towards dematerialization and ecoefficiency
Various measures and tools need to be promoted, as suggested above, such as incorporating environmental costs, environmental taxes, and the removal of perverse subsidies. Adapting infrastructure and logistics that encourage the commercialization of 'sustainable', 'fairly traded', and 'environmental' products and other products with special 'green' connotations will facilitate the move toward dematerialization and ecoefficiency amongst producers. The use of economic instruments focusing especially on industrial ecology and cleaner production practices can provide incentives for ecoefficient production. Active financing of sustainable production and consumption should be encouraged. By all these means, revenue can be generated to finance sustainable development and send

signals to the market that help to change patterns.

Need to support ENGOs

The work of community groups and environmental NGOs in promoting a greater sense of belonging to local environments in North American cities and taking personal responsibility for them should be supported with a view both to educating civil society about their impacts on the global environment and to promoting community and individual action to decrease environmental footprints of the wealthy. Such groups promote a variety of initiatives such as smart growth planning, community gardening or community-supported agriculture projects, transport alternatives like cycling and bike paths, green belt projects, energy-saving measures, and organic food cooperatives; among others.

Need to understand human impact

Efforts should be made to obtain and exchange better data that will provide needed information about how to effect production and consumption changes at the consumer, business, and corporate levels. Information should be generated, for example, on the impacts of corporate actions at the level of local communities and the environment; on ways to promote corporate responsibility and accountability; on ways to create consumer ethics and responsibilities for environmental and social impacts; and on the impacts of environmental scarcity and over consumption on the health of vulnerable human groups. Re-

search should be targeted through pilot projects and monitoring of alternative approaches at the local level, including material recycling. More support is needed for research and promotion of fuel alternatives and energy-saving vehicles.

Information and Education

Need for better information

Expanding human interference with natural processes and the complexity of new and emerging environmental issues in North America point to the need for better scientific understanding about how the natural world functions and how humans can adjust to live in harmony with nature. At present, we lack adequate information about ecosystem health, resilience, and carrying capacities; the more subtle, long-term, diffuse, cumulative, complex, and cross-cutting environmental problems; links between trade and environment; impacts of environmental change on vulnerable sectors of society; and links between environmental issues in developed and developing countries, and especially the link between affluent lifestyles and global climate change. Without reliable, credible, comprehensive, and accessible data and information, it is not possible to assess the state, condition, and trends of ecosystem components; the effectiveness of policy; or the links between our actions, environmental conditions, and economic costs. Yet government cutbacks have weakened or eliminated many of the basic monitoring systems that provide baseline data. There is a need to rethink what is essential data, and to make sure that resources are in place to produce it. This is a precondition for having meaningful and reliable sustainability indicators.

Need for more environmental education
Environmental education offers an excellent and relatively untapped opportunity to impart environmental values and lay out the costs of overexploitation to society. Improved knowledge about, and valuing of, ecosystem functions can stimulate better policy and management approaches to minimize or halt adverse trends where ecosystems and the provision of environmental goods and services are threatened by environmental change and degradation. Education should play a larger role in helping to instruct societies about the importance of a healthy environment, the links to personal behavior, and the reasons for modifying consumption patterns. The role of the mass media and advertising in influencing our decisions needs to be better appreciated. Consumers can be influenced by the use of socially and environmentally conscious marketing that highlights consumption as a key motor of environmental degradation. Consumers need to be able to make informed choices and to understand how their buying can influence the market for environmental and social gains.

Education and awareness raising is needed for policymakers, citizens, and media alike. It should be used forcefully to help change unsustainable lifestyles and consumerist behavior. Environmental education should therefore be integrated and comprehensively covered in academic, business, and economic curricula. Environmental study also needs to become an integral part of economic theory and practice and should be taught in all university economics courses. Ministries of Environment and Education should be encouraged to integrate environmental education in all academic curricula, at all levels, and in all subjects, including those in professional, economics, and business schools.

The Next 30 Years

On the eve of the World Summit on Sustainable Development, it has become evident that protecting the environment and human security is a more challenging task than it may have seemed 30 years ago, or even 10 years ago. We live with the decisions of the past just as future generations must live with our decisions. The sustainable development vision needs a long time horizon but immediate action. Achieving, within the next 30 years, the social and environmental vision laid out in the 1990s, will require drastic steps. To begin with, there is an ever more urgent need to recognize that human security depends on the abundance and health of environmental assets, goods, and services. We must find ways to ensure that their benefits are delivered in a sustainable and equitable way for current and future generations. At the same time, we must develop environmental and human resilience to cope with the environmental and climatic changes that are inevitable.

Suggested Readings

Bass, Stephen, and Barry Dalal-Clayton (2002). Strategies For Sustainable Development: Meeting The Challenge. *Opinion: World Summit on Sustainable Development* May

CEC (2001). *The North American Mosaic: A State of the Environment Report.* Montreal, Commission for Environmental Cooperation of North America

DFAIT (2000). *Current Issues in Canada – US. Relations.* Department of Foreign Affairs and International Trade, Embassy of Canada, Washington DC http://www.canadianembassy.org/foreignpolicy/report.asp. Accessed 15 March 2002

Huq, Saleemul, Youba Sokona, and Adil Najam (2002). Climate Change and Sustainable Development Beyond Kyoto. *Opinion: World Summit on Sustainable Development*

IIED (2001). *International Institute for Environment and Development: Marking 30 Years in Environment & Development.* International Institute of Environment and Development http://www.iied.org/

IIED (2001). *The Future is Now: Equity for a Small Planet.* Vol. 2, November, International Institute for Environment and Development

IIED (2001). *The Future is Now: For the UN Summit on Sustainable Development.* Vol. 1, April, International Institute for Environment and Development

IIED, UNDP, and UK DFID (2002). National Strategies for Sustainable Development: New Thinking and Time for Action. *Opinion: World Summit on Sustainable Development*

IJC (2000). *Tenth Biennial Report on Great Lakes Water Quality.* International Joint Commission http://www.ijc.org/comm/10br/en/indexen.html. Accessed 4 February 2002

MacNeill, Jim, Pieter Winsemikus, and Taizo Yakushiji (1991). *Beyond Interdependence: The Meshing of the World's Economy and the Earth's Ecology.* New York, Oxford University Press

OECD (2001). *OECD Environmental Outlook.* Paris, Organisation for Economic Co-Operation and Development

RONA (2002). *About the Region.* United Nations Environment Programme, Regional Office for North America http://www.rona.unep.org/region/region.php3. Accessed 15 March 2002

Shutkin, William A. (2001). *The Land the Could Be: Environmentalism and Democracy in the Twenty-First Century.* Cambridge MA, The MIT Press

UNEP (1999). *Global Environment Outlook 2000.* Nairobi, United Nations Environment Programme

Acknowledgments

Sarah Albertini, Bureau of Transportation Statistics, United States Department of Transportation, United States; Paul Allen, Environment Canada, Canada; Stephen O. Andersen, Atmospheric Pollution Prevention Division, United States Environmental Protection Agency, United States; Geoffrey Anderson, Office of Policy Economics and Innovation, United States Environmental Protection Agency, United States; Ray C. Anderson, Interface Inc., United States; Bruce Angle, Meteorological Service, Environment Canada, Canada; Gérald Aubry, Canadian Environmental Assessment Agency, Environment Canada, Canada; Richard D. Ballhorn, International Environmental Affairs Bureau, Canadian Foreign Affairs, Canada; Sabrina Barker, International Policy and Cooperation Branch, Environment Canada, Canada; David Bassett, United States Department of Energy, United States; David Berry, Department of the Interior, Council on Environmental Quality, United States; Leonard Berry, Florida Center for Environmental Studies, Florida Atlantic University, United States; John Michael Bewers, Bedford Institute of Oceanography, Canada; Roger L. Blair, National Health and Environmental Effects Research Laboratory, United States Environmental Protection Agency, United States; Greg Block, Commission for Environmental Cooperation, Canada; Harvey Bootsma, Great Lakes Water Institute, University of Wisconsin, United States; Ian Bowles, Council on Environmental Quality, United States; Thomas J. Brennan, Bureau of International Organizations Affairs, United States Department of State, United States; Keith W. Brickley, Department of Fisheries and Oceans, Canada; Terry Bronson, American Public Transportation Policy Project, United States; Lillith Brook, Canada; Thomas M. Brooks, Center for Applied Biodiversity Science, Conservation International, United States; Ronald J. Brown, Canada Center for Remote Sensing, Canada; Ian Burton, Canada; Eric Bush, Centers for Epidemiology and Animal Health, United States; Laurence Campbell, United States Department of Commerce, United States; Danielle Cantin, Boreal and Temperate Forests Programme, IUCN - The World Conservation Union, Canada; Jeff Carmichael, Sustainable Development Research Institute, University of British Columbia, Canada; Chantal-Line Carpentier, North American Commission for Environmental Cooperation, Canada; Jennifer Castleden, International Institute for Sustainable Development, Canada; Julie Charbonneau, Environment Canada, Canada; Alain Chung, Pollution Data Branch, Environment Canada, Canada; William Clark, The John F. Kennedy School of Government at Harvard, United States; Cynthia Cluck, National Mapping Division, United States Geological Survey, United States; Richard Connor, World Water Council, Canada; Ted Cooke, Fisheries and Oceans Canada, Canada; Tom Cooney, United States Department of State, United States; Philippe Crabbé, Institute for Research on Environment and Economy, University of Ottawa, Canada; Rudy D'Alessandro, United States Department of the Interior, United States; Edward C. De Fabo, Medical Centre, School of Medicine, The George Washington University, United States; Patricia V. Dickerson, Bureau of Census, United States; Robert A. Duce, Department of Oceanography and Atmospheric Sciences, Texas A&M University, United States; Jennifer Duggan, International Institute for Sustainable Development, Canada; Linda Dunn, Industry Canada-Trade Team, Canada; Paul R. Epstein, Center for Health and the Global Environment, Harvard Medical School, United States; Hari Eswaran, United States Department of Agriculture, The Natural Resources Conservation Service, United States; Dan Fantozzi, Bureau of Oceans and International Environmental and Scientific Affairs, United States Department of State, United States; Camilla Feibelman, Sierra Student Coalition, United States; Lowell Feld, Energy Information Administration, United States Department of Energy, United States; Angus Ferguson, Environment Canada, Canada; Karen Fisher, Department of Fisheries and Oceans, Canada; Amy Fraenkel, Senate Committee on Commerce, Science and Transportation, United States; Karen Freedman, Energy Information Administration, United States Department of Energy, United States; Peter Frenzen, Mount St. Helens National Volcanic Monument, United

States; David Frost, Geography Department, Concordia University, Canada; Tom Furmanczyk, Environment Canada, Canada; Nouria Gagné, Consultant Jacques Gagnon, Natural Resources Canada, Canada; Michelle Garland, Surface Transportation Policy Project, United States; Mark Gillis, Natural Resources Canada, Canada; Andy Gilman, Office of Sustainable Development, Health Canada, Canada; Dagny Gingrich, Biodiversity Convention Office, Environment Canada, Canada; Peter H. Gleick, Environment and Security, Pacific Institute for Studies in Development, United States; Stephen Gray, Landscape Management, Natural Resources Canada, Canada; Michael Grillot, United States Department of Energy, United States; Pablo Gutman, United States; Brian Haddon, National Forestry Database Programme, Natural Resources Canada Statistics, Canada; Andrew Hamilton, Resource Futures International, Canada; Allen Hammond, World Resources Institute, United States; Arthur J. Hanson, International Institute for Sustainable Development, Canada; Peter Hardi, International Institute for Sustainable Development, Canada; Asit Hazra, Environment Canada, Canada; Alan D. Hecht, Office of International Activities, United States Environmental Protection Agency, United States; David Henry, Canadian Heritage, Environment Canada, Canada; John Herity, Environment Canada, Canada; George Herrfuth, United States Department of State, United States; Christine T. Hogan, International Affairs Directorate, Environment Canada, Canada; Mark Hovorka, Environment Canada, Canada; Tom Iavari, Natural Resources Conservation Service, United States; Gary Ironside, Environment Canada, Canada; Heather James, Pacific Operations, Fisheries and Oceans, Canada; Yvan Jobin, Foreign Affairs and International Trade, Canada; Margaret Kain, Forest Service, United States Department of Agriculture, United States; John Karau, Fisheries and Oceans Canada, Canada; Margaret Kenny, Environment Canada, Canada; Mara Kerry, Canadian Nature Federation, Canada; Frederick W. Kutz, United States Environmental Protection Agency, United States; Jim LaBau, Forest Service, United States Department of Agriculture, United States; Keith Laughlin*, Council on Environmental Quality, United States; Jay Lawimore, National Oceanic and Atmospheric Agency, United States; Douglas J. Lawrence, Natural Resources Conservation Service, United States Department of Agriculture United States; Rick Lee, University of Victoria, Canada; Annick LeHenaff, Environment Canada, Canada; Perry Lindstrom, United States Department of Energy, United States; Amory Lovins, Rocky Mountain Institute, United States; H. Gyde Lund, Forest Information Services, United States; Mary Ann Lyle, Federal Emergency Management Agency, United States; Late Elisabeth Mann Borgese, International Ocean Institute, Dalhousie University, Canada; Alex Manson, Environment Canada, Canada; Ian Marshall, Environment Canada, Canada; Tim Marta, Agriculture and Agri-Food Canada, Canada; Gordon McBean, University of Western Ontario,

Canada; Jessica McCann, Community Transportation Association of America, United States; Beverly D. McIntyre, Office of Global Change, United States Department of State, United States; Elizabeth McLanahan, National Oceanic and Atmospheric Agency, United States; Mary Lou McQuaide, Solid Waste Association of North America, United States; Terry McRae, Agriculture and Agri-Food Canada, Canada; Richard Meganck, Unit for Sustainable Development and Environment, Organization of American States, United States; Valdis E. Mezainis, International Programs, United States Forest Service, United States; Craig Miller, Environment Canada, Canada; Paul Miller, North American Commission for Environmental Cooperation, Canada; Rebecca Milo, Environment Canada, Canada; Charles E. Morrison, East-West Center, United States; Gloria Mundo, United States Census Bureau, United States; Pumulo Muyatwa, International Institute for Sustainable Development, Canada; Tony Myers, Health Canada, Canada; Adil Najam, Department of International Relations, Center for Energy and Environmental Studies, Boston University, United States; Brenda O'Conner, Environment Canada, Canada; Edward Ohanion, Office of Water, United States Environmental Protection Agency, United States; Robin O'Malley, The H. John Heinz III Center for Science, Economics and the Environment, United States; Jim Osborne, Environment Canada, Canada; Gail Osherenko, Dartmouth College, United States; Christine Padoch, The New York Botanical Garden, United States; Jeanne Pagnan, Twin Dolphins Consultants, Canada; Dennis Peacock, United States National Science Foundation, United States; Phil Perkins, Yellowstone National Park, United States; Erica Phipps, North American Commission for Environmental Cooperation, Canada; Cindy Pollack-Shea, Florida Sustainable Communities Center, United States; Sharon Powers, National Agricultural Statistics Service, United States; Don Pryor, National Oceanic and Atmospheric Agency, United States; Thomas Pyle, Office of Polar Programs, United States National Science Foundation, United States; David J. Rapport, The University of Western Ontario, Canada; Walter Rast, Great Lakes Water Quality Board, International Joint Commission, Canada; David Redford, United States Environmental Protection Agency, United States; Dieter Riedel, Health Canada, Canada; Richard Robarts, Environment Canada, Canada; Brian Roberts, Indian and Northern Affairs, Canada; Guy Rochon, Environment Canada, Canada; Jane M. Rohling, United States Department of Agriculture, United States; David Roodman, World Watch Institute, United States; Carol Rosen, World Resources Institute, United States; Denyse Rousseau, Foreign Affairs and International Trade, Canada; Clay Rubec, Environment Canada, Canada; David Runnalls, International Institute for Sustainable Development, Canada; Kathleen Sullivan Sealey,

Department of Biology, University of Miami, United States; Stephen Seidel, United States Environmental Protection Agency, United States; Parvina A. Shamsieva-Cohen*, Global Resource Information Database, Sioux Falls, United States; Victor Shantora, Commission for Environmental Cooperation, United States; Cameron Siles, Environment Canada, Canada; Brad Smith, Forest Service, United States Department of Agriculture, United States; Bryan Smith, Environment Canada, Canada; Sharon Lee Smith, Environment Canada, Canada; Susan Solomon, National Ocean and Atmospheric Administration, United States; Jim Steele, Commercial Services, Environment Canada, Canada; Janet Stephenson, Natural Resources Canada, Canada; John W. B. Stewart, University of Saskatchewan, Canada; Anita Street, Office of Planning, Analysis and Accountability, United States Environmental Protection Agency, United States; Nick Sundt, United States Global Change Research Program, United States; David Sutherland, National Ocean and Atmospheric Administration, United States; James Tansey, University of British Columbia, Canada; Charles Tarnocai, Agriculture and Agri-Food, Canada Research Branch, Canada; Jeffrey A. Thornton, International Environmental Management Services Ltd., United States; Kelly Torck,

Environment Canada, Canada; John R. Townshend, University of Maryland, United States; Suzanne Tremblay, Statistics Canada, Statistical Reference Centre, Canada; Jacques Trencia, Canadian Forest Service-Science Branch, Natural Resources Canada, Canada; Daniel Tunstall, World Resources Institute, United States; David G. Victor, Science and Technology Council on Foreign Relations, United States; Jean-Louis Wallace, Environmental Relations Division, Foreign Affairs and International Trade, Canada; Frank Wania, University of Toronto at Scarborough Canada; R. Douglas Wells, Forestry Transportation Operations Branch, Transportation and Works Department, Canada; Thomas E. Werkema, Atofina Chemicals Inc., United States; Denis White, United States Environmental Protection Agency, United States; Gilbert F. White, University of Colorado, United States; Keith Wiebe, United States Department of Agriculture, United States; Tara Wilkinson, Commission for Environmental Cooperation, Canada; Heather Wood, Environment Canada, Canada; Oran R. Young, Dartmouth College, United States; John Zacharias, Urban Studies Programme, Department of Geography, Concordia University, Canada.

Note: *Since moved or retired

Acronyms and Abbreviations

AOC   Areas of Concern

ARNEWS   Acid Rain National Early Warning System

BC   British Columbia

BFW   Boreal Forest Watch

CAS   College of Agricultural Sciences

CBC   Community-Based Conservation

CBD   Convention on Biological Diversity

CCD   Convention to Combat Desertification

CCFM   Canadian Council of Forest Ministers

CD-ROM   Compact disk–read only memory

CEC   Commission for Environmental Cooperation

CEHN   Children's Environmental Health Network

CFC   Chlorofluorocarbon

CGIAR   Consultative Group on International Agricultural Research

CH_4 Methane

CIAT   International Centre for Tropical Agriculture

CICH   Canadian Institute of Child Health

CIDA   Canadian International Development Agency

cm   Centimeter

CNG   Compressed Natural Gas

CNW   Canadian News Wire

CO   Carbon Monoxide

CO_2 Carbon Dioxide

DDT   Dichlorodiphenyltrichloroethane

DFAIT   Department of Foreign Affairs and International Trade

DPSIR   Driving force-Pressure-State-Impact-Response

EC   European Community

ECOHAB   Ecology and Oceanography of Harmful Algal Blooms

EIA   Environmental Impact Assessment

ENGO   Environmental Non-Governmental Organization

ENS   Environment News Service

ENSO   El Niño Southern Oscillation

EPA   Environmental Protection Agency

EPC   Emergency Preparedness Canada

EPCA   Energy Policy and Conservation Act

EPCRA   Emergency Planning and Community Right-to-Know Act

ERS   Economic Research Service

ESA   Endangered Species Act (United States)

EU   European Union

FAO   Food and Agriculture Organization of the United Nations

FSC   Forest Stewardship Council

FDRP   Flood Damage Reduction Program

FEMA   Federal Emergency Management Agency

FICMNEW   Federal Interagency Committee for the Management of Noxious and Exotic Weeds

FSC   Forest Stewardship Council

G7   Group of Seven: Canada, France, Germany, Italy, Japan, United Kingdom, United States

GDP   Gross Domestic Product

GEO   Global Environment Outlook

GFW   Global Forest Watch

GLWQA   Great Lakes Waters Quality Agreement

GMO   Genetically Modified Organism

GNP   Gross National Product

GRID   Global Resource Information Database

HABs   Harmful Algal Blooms

HDI   Human Development Index

HMIS   Hazardous Materials Incidents System

IABIN   Inter-American Biodiversity Information Network

ICLEI   International Council for Local Environmental Initiatives

IEA   International Energy Agency

IIED   International Institute of Environment and Development

IISD   International Institute for Sustainable Development

IJC   International Joint Commission

IPCC	Intergovernmental Panel on Climate Change		PSIR	Pressure-State-Impact-Response
IPM	Integrated Pest Management		PSR	pressure-state-response
JISAO	Joint Institute for the Study of the Atmosphere and Ocean		PSR	Physicians for Social Responsibility
			RAP	Remedial Action Plan
LDAC	Learning Disabilities Association of Canada		SARA	Species At Risk Act (Canada)
			SO_2	Sulphur Dioxide
MASS	Montane Alternative Silvicultural Systems		SOE	State Of the Environment
MSRM	Ministry of Sustainable Resource Management		SUV	Sport Utility Vehicles
			TEA	Transportation Equity Act
NAACO	National Ambient Air Quality Objectives (Canada)		TU	Trout Unlimited
			UK	United Kingdom
NAFTA	North American Free Trade Agreement		UN	United Nations
NASS	National Agricultural Statistics Service		ULI	Urban Land Institute
NESCAUM	Northeast States for Coordinated Air Use Management		UNCCD	United Nations Secretariat of the Convention to Combat Desertification
NFDP	National Forestry Database Program		UNCED	United Nations Conference on Environment and Development
NG	National Geographic			
NGO	Non-Governmental Organization		UNCHS	United Nations Centre for Human Settlements
NIAID	National Institute of Allergy and Infectious Diseases		UNCOD	United Nations Conference on Desertification
NMFS	National Marine Fisheries Service		UNCTAD	United Nations Conference on Trade and Development
NOx	Nitrous Oxides			
NOAA	National Oceanic and Atmospheric Administration		UNDP	United Nations Development Programme
NRCan	Natural Resources Canada		UNEP	United Nations Environment Programme
NRDC	Natural Resources Defense Council		UNEP-WCMC	United Nations Environment Programme-World Conservation Monitoring Centre
NRTEE	National Round Table on the Environment and the Economy			
NSWCP	National Soil and Water Conservation Program		UNESCAP	United Nations Economic and Social Commission for Asia and the Pacific
O_3	Ozone		UNESCO	United Nations Educational, Scientific and Cultural Organization
OCIPEP	Office of Critical Infrastructure and Emergency Preparedness			
ODS	Ozone-Depleting Substance		UNFCCC	United Nations Framework Convention on Climate Change
OECD	Organization for Economic Cooperation and Development		US	United States
			USDA	US Department of Agriculture
OCIPEP	Office of Critical Infrastructure and Emergency Preparedness		US EPA	United States Environmental Protection Agency
OMA	Ontario Medical Association		USGCRP	US Global Change Research Program
PCB	Polychlorinated Biphenyls		USGS	United States Geological Survey
PCP	Permanent Cover Program (Canada)		US IWG	US Interagency Working Group
PDO	Pacific Decadal Oscillation		VOC	Volatile Organic Compound
PEHC	Pew Environmental Health Commission		WHO	World Health Organization
PFRA	Prairie Farm Rehabilitation Administration		WRI	World Resources Institute
			WWF	World Wide Fund for Nature
$PM_{2.5}$	Particulate matter with a diameter of 2.5 microns or less		WRM	World Rainforest Movement
			YCELP	Yale Center for Environmental Law and Policy
PMRA	Pest Management Regulatory Agency			
POPs	Persistent Organic Pollutants			
PSC	Pacific Salmon Commission			